DIFFICULT SUBJECTS

DIFFICULT SUBJECTS

Insights and Strategies for Teaching
About Race, Sexuality, and Gender

Edited by

Badia Ahad-Legardy and OiYan A. Poon

Foreword by Lori Patton Davis

STERLING, VIRGINIA

Published by Stylus Publishing, LLC 22883 Quicksilver Drive
Sterling, Virginia 20166-2102

Library of Congress Cataloging-in-Publication-Data
Names: Ahad-Legardy, Badia, editor. | Poon, OiYan, editor.
Title: Difficult subjects : insights and strategies for teaching about race,
sexuality and gender / edited by Badia Ahad-Legardy and OiYan Poon.
Description: First edition. |
Sterling, Virginia : Stylus Publishing, LLC., [2018] |
Includes bibliographical references and index.
Identifiers: LCCN 2017047161 (print) |
LCCN 2018001896 (ebook) |
ISBN 9781620367933 (uPDF) |
ISBN 9781620367940 (mobi, ePUB) |
ISBN 9781620367919 (cloth : acid free paper) |
ISBN 9781620367926 (paperback : acid free paper) |
ISBN 9781620367933 (library networkable e-edition) |
ISBN 9781620367940 (consumer e-edition)
Subjects: LCSH: Race--Study and teaching. |
Gender identity--Study and teaching.
Classification: LCC HT1506 (ebook) |
LCC HT1506 .D54 2018 (print) |
DDC 305.80071--dc23
LC record available at https://lccn.loc.gov/2017047161

13-digit ISBN: 978-1-62036-791-9 (cloth)
13-digit ISBN: 978-1-62036-792-6 (paperback)
13-digit ISBN: 978-1-62036-793-3 (library networkable e-edition)
13-digit ISBN: 978-1-62036-794-0 (consumer e-edition)

Bulk Purchases
Quantity discounts are available for use in workshops
and for staff development.
Call 1-800-232-0223

First Edition, 2018

OiYan
For Te Te

Badia
For Ma

CONTENTS

FOREWORD

Teaching is hard. Anyone who disagrees with this statement is simply clueless about the challenges associated with teaching. The act of teaching subjects such as race, gender and sexuality, and doing so with a level of critical consciousness, thoughtfulness, and care presents even greater difficulty. When I reflect on my journey to the professoriate and the training I received to be an effective teacher, I can recall a few memories that served as learning moments to help me grapple with difficult dialogues that would ultimately emerge in the classroom. Furthermore, my exposure to resources that would guide me along this journey were limited. Often, I was mentored on the mechanics of teaching and skills associated with teaching, but NEVER was I deeply engaged in conversations regarding difficult and controversial topics and how I as a teacher should show up in those moments.

Badia Ahad-Legardy and OiYan A. Poon have produced an important and necessary edited volume to serve as a resource for teachers who are committed to tackling difficult conversations in the classroom and delving deeper into issues surrounding race, gender and sexuality. *Difficult Subjects: Insights and Strategies for Teaching About Race, Sexuality, and Gender* is timely and long overdue. As a consultant for various institutions, I have had opportunities to connect with faculty and listen to the challenges they face in their classrooms. For some faculty, issues of race, sexuality, and gender are too personally difficult to grasp, thus limiting their capacity as instructors to grapple with such topics in the classrooms. With other faculty, especially within the areas of science, technology, engineering, and mathematics, topics regarding race, sexuality, and gender are treated as separate and disconnected from course content, making them less likely to be incorporated in the classroom. Then there are those with a keen awareness that deep dialogues about these topics are important for enhancing students' learning, yet these same instructors do not know how to broach the subjects nor do they know how to incorporate such perspectives into their syllabus; class assignments; in-class activities; and more importantly, classroom dialogue and engagement. Finally, there are faculty (particularly those with minoritized identities) who regularly engage such topics in the classroom, but know all too well that such efforts are rarely rewarded in cases of tenure and promotion, especially when teaching evaluations are less than positive. Herein lies the value of *Difficult Subjects*. This book addresses the needs of faculty in each of these categories. Whether a faculty member with limited experience regarding these topics or one with significant experience, this book provides a roadmap to assist teachers in navigating the tumultuous terrain of difficult classroom dialogues.

There are at least three major considerations related to difficult dialogues that the contributors illuminate for readers. First, there is no such thing as a difficult dialogue without feelings of fragility that prompt individuals to retreat from confrontation in hopes of maintaining comfort. Fragility and discomfort are also fueled in classroom spaces where learners (especially those with privileged identities) attempt to manage discomfort by attempting to dictate the depth of conversations about race and racism. Moreover, difficult dialogues are often cloaked in neutrality, providing White people the benefit of being perceived as critically conscious despite their unchecked biases. And while fragility in classrooms is quite challenging and daunting, there are instructors committed to unpacking race, sexuality, and gender through intersectional lenses and courageous questioning of self, students, and oppressive structures.

Second, effectiveness in difficult dialogues must be connected to an embodied praxis that is grounded in individuals' stories, identities, and emotions. This requires the understanding that how teachers and learners "show up" can be read in multiple ways in the classroom. Every actor and action is promulgated by the self they bring into the learning space and the extent to which that self is subjected to opportunities to be both vulnerable and valued. The contributors to *Difficult Subjects* share critical and thought-provoking stories of their own experiences as teachers, noting that embodied praxis, much like the act of teaching, is extremely difficult, but overwhelmingly necessary.

Third, difficult dialogues about race, sexuality, and gender should not be relegated to the humanities. Indeed, they should be occurring in every space on campus in which the designated goal is to learn. A more expansive view of difficult dialogues allows them to transverse particular subjects and fields and inhabit learning spaces throughout a given campus setting.

Difficult Subjects is a stellar contribution for faculty at any level, as well as those aspiring to the professoriate. Each chapter in this book reveals the realities associated with difficult dialogues and provides an avenue through which readers gain a more comprehensive understanding of the teaching process. Moreover, the various authors make clear that teaching is particularly challenging for those committed to educating for social justice through engagement in difficult classroom dialogues about race, sexuality, and gender. The authors expound on these challenges through thoughtful narratives that highlight questions regarding positionality, the need for educators to disrupt the status quo in the curriculum, how different identities and bodies are read in the classroom, and relevant strategies for dealing with challenges as they emerge.

Through rich narratives and thoughtful strategies, the contributors have provided a much-needed framework for grappling with race, sexuality, and gender through multiple lenses.

Teaching is hard. . . . Nonetheless, Badia Ahad-Legardy and OiYan A. Poon should be commended for realizing the need for this book and assembling an amazing cast of scholars to write about the challenges plaguing postsecondary classrooms, as well as strategies for disrupting the status quo in teaching and learning. Yes, teaching is hard, but this book, if nothing else, fills a gap in the literature, while validating people and challenging oppressive structures and their manifestation within teaching.

Lori Patton Davis
Professor
Higher Education and Student Affairs
Indiana University School of Education

ACKNOWLEDGMENTS

Every manuscript is tactile evidence of the well-worn saying "it takes a village." This book would not have been possible without the village that is the South Loop/Pilsen Write-on-Site group (Elizabeth Todd Breland, Lorena Garcia, Marisha Humphries, Gregory Larnell, Twyla Blackmond Larnell, Danny Martinez, Elizabeth Montaño, and Chavella Pittman). It is the space where we (OiYan and Badia) first met and where we engaged in the weekly ritual of communal writing, sharing strategies for navigating "difficult subjects" in our classrooms and at our institutions, and fellowshipping over countless bagels and coffees.

We would also like to thank all of the scholars/writers who contributed to this manuscript. Reading through each of your essays for the first time was an act of inspiration, so much so that we text messaged one another throughout the process to exclaim how moved we were. We have learned so much from each of you about the value of bringing your full self to the classroom and the transformative possibilities of affective pedagogies.

An editor that believes in the project from day one is every author's aspiration. We could not have been more fortunate to have David Brightman as an editor for this collection. His insights and enthusiasm have made this volume more than we thought it could be.

To our Loyola University Chicago students and supportive colleagues, thank you for challenging us and helping us strengthen our own pedagogical approaches over the years.

We would like to thank our husbands, Nathan and Todd, for being self-less and supportive of our endeavors, and our children, Clemente, Lauren, and Nathan Jr., for inspiring us to do our work with a renewed commitment.

INTRODUCTION

When the Shit Hits the Fan, Do We Throw Out the Lesson Plan?

OiYan A. Poon and Badia Ahad-Legardy

July 13, 2013: Acquittal of George Zimmerman, who killed Trayvon Martin in Miami Gardens, Florida.

August 9, 2014 and November 22, 2014: Police murders of 18-year-old Mike Brown in Ferguson, Missouri, and 12-year-old Tamir Rice in Cleveland, Ohio.

December 3, 2014: No indictment of the police officers involved in the killing of Eric Garner in Staten Island, New York.

April 2015: Death of Freddie Gray and subsequent mass uprising in Baltimore, Maryland.

June 17, 2015: Cynthia Hurd, Susie Jackson, Ethel Lee Lance, Depayne Middleton-Doctor, Clementa Pinckney, Tywanza Sanders, Daniel Simmons, Sharonda Coleman-Singleton, and Myra Thompson are gunned down at a bible study gathering in a historic Black church in Charleston, South Carolina, by Dylann Roof.

October 2015: Concerned Student 1950 launches a campaign for racial justice at the University of Missouri and inspires a renewal of student activism nationally.

November 2015 to March 2016: Dashcam video of the police killing of 17-year-old Laquan McDonald released, followed by sustained protests in Chicago, Illinois.

June 12, 2016: 49 murdered and 53 injured in a mass shooting during Latin Night at Pulse, an LGBT nightclub in Orlando, Florida.

June 20, 2016: The United Nations High Commissioner for Refugees reports that the number of people displaced from the Syrian civil war, half of whom are children, is higher than during World War II.

July 5, 2016 and July 6, 2016: Fatal police shootings of Alton Sterling in Baton Rouge, Louisiana, and Philando Castile in a suburb of St. Paul, Minnesota.

July 7, 2016: A sniper fires on a peaceful protest against police brutality, killing five police officers in Dallas, Texas.

November 2016: Presidential election of Donald Trump and an aftermath of hate crimes, harassment, intimidation, and fear.

These are just a handful of events between 2013 and 2016 that have prompted intense national discussion and debate, especially over racial conflict and polarization; inequalities; and systemic racism, sexism, and violence. There have been many more events in the United States and around the world that deserve public attention and dialogue about an endless number of interconnected problems of human suffering and conflict. However, there are moments and events, like the ones listed earlier, that punctuate and spotlight the pressing nature of specific issues. They can capture the emotional attention, energy, and time of the general public. These events have caused both of us, the coauthors of this introduction and coeditors of this volume, to stop our daily routines and contemplate their implications for our own lives and for our families, friends, and communities, as well as our moral and professional commitments as college educators. As we engage in our own emotionally laden processes of reflection and analysis, we must know that our students are likely going through their own processes of meaning-making that deserve acknowledgement, support, and encouragement.

In these moments, when the proverbial shit hits the fan, and events in the world take our breath away, what is our educational responsibility? Do we engage with our students in a collective process of contemplation and learning from these instances? According to revolutionary educational philosopher Paulo Freire (1985):

> Political events are educational and vice versa. Because education is politicity, it is never neutral. When we try to be neutral, like Pilate, we support the dominant ideology. Not being neutral, education must be either liberating or domesticating. (Yet I also recognize that we probably never experience it as purely one or the other but rather a mixture of both.) . . . It does not mean that we have the right to impose on students our political choice. But we do have the duty not to hide our choice. Students have the right to know what our political dream is. They are then free to accept it, reject it, or modify it. Our task is not to impose our dreams on them, but to challenge them to have their own dreams, to define their choices, not just to uncritically assume them. (pp. 17–18)

Some have argued that teaching should be ideologically neutral, essentially free from the influences of the world. In other words, teachers should be prevented from expressing their own perspectives. For instance, shortly after the contentious 2016 U.S. presidential election, a conservative organization launched an online professor watchlist to identify, and essentially intimidate, faculty whose teachings and scholarship question or challenge conservative political ideologies (Flaherty, 2016). Though not the first of its kind, this 2016 version of projects seeking to publicly expose professors with left-leaning ideologies seeks to advance a mythical notion of political neutrality in higher education. In threatening academic freedom, the esteemed value for an open exchange of ideas and discourse in higher education, these efforts take aim at fundamental principles of an inclusive democracy.

Moreover, the professor watchlist and its predecessors' work to silence educators are an attack on teaching and learning as human experiences and relationships. Through these efforts and in an increasingly corporatized culture of higher education, which values budget efficiency and economies of scale, teaching and learning are reduced to automated transfers of information between teacher and student. Efforts to sanitize higher education of the complex processes of teaching and learning can greatly hinder the development of skills in critical thinking, leadership, cross-cultural interpersonal communication, innovation, and creativity. These skills are all hallmarks of vibrant discourse and exchanges of ideas and information in healthy and inclusive democratic societies.

High-quality teaching and learning requires a resistance to dehumanization, standardization, and corporatization (Berg & Seeber, 2016; hooks, 2003). At the same time, however, confronting racism, sexism, classism, homophobia, and transphobia, among other forms of human subjugation, in the classroom requires an uncomfortable recognition of unequal privileges that counter national narratives of life, liberty, happiness, and equal opportunity for achieving the "American dream." Engaging in a process of questioning one's accepted worldviews, which have been cultivated by family and community, can be challenging, overwhelming, and even blasphemous for some. Humanity is messy and complicated. Nonetheless, Paulo Freire (2000) deliberately encourages us as teachers to embrace our humanity, and to encourage our students to do the same in developing their own perspectives through a process of reflection and self-examination to counter dehumanizing and oppressive forces. For these reasons, when unspeakable events in the world shock us and disrupt daily routines in our lives, it is important that we consider whether and how we might break down the border between our classrooms and the world to teach in socially engaged ways.

However, teaching in ways that confront such difficult subjects presents even more challenges for college educators, especially those of us with marginalized identities or professionally vulnerable positions such as contingent faculty or pretenure faculty. Notably, women and faculty of color are disproportionately represented among contingent faculty (Finley, 2009). In the market-focused university, contract faculty job continuation is heavily reliant on student evaluations of courses, which are unreliable measures of "class success," to retain their jobs. Women and faculty of color also tend to score far lower on these evaluations, due to implicit and explicit biases against minoritized faculty (Lazos, 2012). The increased primacy placed on teaching and job retention for contingent faculty members is especially frustrating as they are also often unable to make full use of university-designed peda-gogical resources, like centers for teaching and learning, for example. The dilemma between employment security and professional ethics is real in the increasingly corporatized university, especially for minoritized faculty who seek to challenge students in considering and examining systems and cultures of oppression.

Certainly, discussions of race, gender, and sexuality are always hot-button issues in the college classroom, whether they emerge in response to a national event or tragedy, or constitute the content of the class over a semester-long term. Even seasoned professors who specialize in these areas find it difficult to talk about identity politics in a room full of students. And many professors for whom issues of racial or sexual identity is not a primary concern in pedagogical practice or scholarship find it even more challenging, and even intimidating, to raise these issues with students choosing instead to ignore them. Regardless of the context, the topics of race, gender, and sexu-ality invite a host of dilemmas: How should we address the event in a way that doesn't alienate or marginalize students? Do we pretend as though we are unaffected or lack a perspective? Do we allow ourselves to be vulnerable? Especially for pretenure- or nontenure-track faculty, would addressing world events that might not be clearly connected to the syllabus invite harsh criti-cism from students, colleagues, and even the public? (Flaherty, 2016). When contemporary crises arise, should we pretend as though nothing happened and stay the course as planned in the syllabus? When the shit hits the fan, do we throw out the lesson plan?

The answers to these central questions guiding this chapter, and underly-ing this edited volume, depend on one's response to the following question: What is the purpose of teaching and learning in higher education? If the fundamental goals of higher education include the cultivation of a capacity for critical thinking and problem-solving, deep self-reflection, the develop-ment of interpersonal and cross-cultural communication skills, and increased engagement in civil discourse and dialogue for an inclusive, healthy, and par-ticipatory democratic society able to confront and reconcile conflict and dif-ferences, then it would seem imperative to encourage students to reflect on and analyze significant world events. If we view higher education as merely a place for information transfer, where students are tasked with completing coursework toward certification for narrow personal economic gains, then world events may be seen as a distraction from a process of professional accreditation. Put another way, a teacher's choice to integrate world events into the process of teaching and learning in any given subject may be guided by how the teacher, and their employing institution, define *education*—as a public good or a private commodity.

Offering contemplations and practical guidance to encourage faculty across disciplines to boldly teach difficult subjects, our introduction ends with an overview of this book. It is imperative for educators, who are committed to contributing toward vibrant democratic societies, to engage in thoughtful and intentional actions congruent with their pedagogical philosophies. Therefore, this introduction and the edited volume as a whole accounts for a range of challenges facing such college educators who are increasingly faced with dilemmas of the corporatized academy, and encourages us to teach with courage and conviction, especially when it feels as though the world around us is crashing down upon our students and ourselves.

When world events stop me in my tracks, what do I do in class?

Following many of the events listed at the start of this chapter, we observed faculty on social media wondering whether and how they should discuss the events in their classes. They were moments when we were challenged in wondering what to do in our classrooms, knowing that we, and some of our students, were distressed and distracted from our course plans. We have each found ourselves confronted with the question: What do I do in light of this event?

OiYan

After the election of Donald Trump, I had five days before my next class meeting. During this time, I cried over the increased imminent danger the election presented to communities of color, especially those under threat of deportation, vulnerable to hate crimes, and endangered by police surveillance and violence. I had five days to gather myself, process my emotions, and make meaning of the moment for my professional and personal commitments. I wondered what would happen to my students, friends, and family who are Muslim and those who are immigrants, both with and without legal documentation. I felt relieved that my one-year-old daughter was too young to understand many words, but worried how I would raise her to be a strong and intelligent Asian American girl in a nation that elected a man who has bragged about sexually assaulting women with impunity, and where it was becoming crystal clear that "American" meant White.

During this catastrophic time, I wanted to be home with my family, but instead I was in the odd situation of being at an academic conference, where many seemed to feel similarly, but we all seemed to be expected to maintain a level of academic decorum and professionalism that seemed quite removed from what was happening in the world. At the same time, the small bubble of our academic conference could not operate fully removed from the world. For example, during the conference, a Chinese American friend and colleague was racially assaulted and told to "go back to where you came from." In the day after the election, I sat at lunch with a Filipina colleague and two Latinx colleagues, when a White middle-aged-appearing man walked up to us and silently waved a small U.S. flag dangerously close to our faces. No words were exchanged, and he simply smirked at us. It struck me that as a Chinese American woman who was born in Boston, the U.S. flag had suddenly become a threatening symbol to my racialized existence in that moment. Reports began to emerge of college instructors across the country being "exposed" for discussing the Trump election and conservative political ideologies in a negative light. Several of us in attendance at the annual meeting of the Association for the Study of Higher Education (ASHE) discussed whether and how we would discuss the election in our classes. Most, if not all, of my colleagues with whom I spoke had already decided to engage in this difficult dialogue, specifically to help students discuss the implications of Trump's proposed policies for higher education.

With five days between the election and my next classes, I had decided to cancel the student presentations scheduled for my student affairs profession class and forgo the lecture and discussion about college affordability in my higher education policy class. Instead, I offered my students a lecture on Jeff Duncan-Andrade's (2009) notion of critical hope, discussed in contrast to false hope, which is often presented to anaesthetize the development of critical consciousness and analysis. Critical hope is needed to initiate mindful collective study, reflection, and analysis to cultivate and sustain transformative change for more just futures, especially when confronted by overwhelmingly oppressive realities. Through a framework of critical hope, my students, who are all enrolled in a higher education MEd or PhD program, and I reflected on what it means to be a college educator when so many of us and our students feel threatened by a disturbing increase of hate crimes connected to Trump's rhetoric and proposed policies. We took the time to make meaning of the moment, allowing a space to embrace a range of emotions, worries, and anxieties. We knew we would soon return to focusing on the predetermined topics for the course, but that the new reality also required us to contemplate, investigate, and articulate what a Trump presidency would mean for ourselves and for our professional endeavors. As a result of intentionally reflecting on the moment, new transformative pedagogical opportunities opened for us as we began to consider and apply the assigned readings in new and innovative ways.

Badia

The day after the election, I visited the office of a good friend and colleague. His field is Romanticism, and mine is contemporary African American literature. We chatted for a while trying to decide what to say to our students about the election results or whether we should say anything at all. We discussed the fact that many faculty had decided to proceed with business as usual as a way of "helping our students cope." But, at that time, I was the only person of color in my department, and the only full-time faculty member who teaches courses in African American literature, and the ethnic and racial makeup of my classes tend to reflect the demographics of the city of Chicago. I respected the decision of those who chose to go about the day as if nothing had happened, but I could hardly look into the teary eyes of my African American, immigrant, Latinx, Muslim, and White students and pretend that ignoring their fears about their fates over the next four years would be helping them cope. I shared with my Romanticist friend my thoughts about doubling back to a discussion we had earlier in the semester on W. E. B. Du Bois and his writings on the importance of Black political power. My colleague, on the other hand, was in the midst of teaching *Dracula*. For him, pivoting from the plan of the day would require more creativity and, in some ways, courage, given that his approach had been to focus on the more formal elements of the novel rather than the historical circumstances that made the novel possible. Together, we discussed what possibilities might emerge from discussing *Dracula* as an anti-immigration narrative (a common read of the novel) and linking it to some of the concerns of a Trump administration. I mention this anecdote because it exemplifies the necessity of reorienting ourselves to materials that we may have been teaching in the same way for years. The conversation also highlights the possibilities that emerge when we transcend the boundaries of our fields and subfields, and learn from one another how we can work to help produce the kind of engaged citizens we want our students to be.

In this moment, I was reminded of the day I unsteadily walked into my introduction to African American literature course after a St. Louis County grand jury decided not to indict Officer Darren Wilson for the shooting death of the teenager Michael Brown. Judging by the tired, swollen eyes of my students, it was apparent that they, too, had watched the announcement and the ensuing unrest in the streets of Ferguson unfold late into the evening hours. I spent my hour-plus long commute deciding whether to "stay the course" and finish our discussion of Toni Morrison's *Song of Solomon* or address the events of the previous evening. My decision was to stay the course. I had not yet reviewed and processed my own feelings about the St. Louis County grand jury's decision and I had nothing erudite or eloquent to offer my students. But then I saw their faces. Perhaps I was projecting, but as I looked before me, I saw an audience that was both eager and wanting. Maybe I just imagined that they, too, were wondering if I would "stay the course" or if I would take a moment to address the ongoing uprising that was happening in Ferguson, Missouri, at that very moment. In that moment of stillness, I decided that shit had hit the fan, and it was time to throw out the lesson plan.

What We Did

A large part of the dilemma between "staying the course" and throwing out the lesson plan is the fact that when tragedy strikes, we, as professors, have had little time to review and process our own emotions, often just waking to the news that "something" has happened. In the past few years, there have been too many "day afters" to count: the protests in Ferguson and Baltimore in response to policy brutality and killings of unarmed Black men, the video release of the murder of Laquan McDonald by a police officer in Chicago, the shooting of Philando Castile by a police officer during a traffic stop in Falcon Heights, Minnesota, among others. Although we often demand that students get comfortable with being uncomfortable, arguing that such discomfort opens the space necessary for learning to happen, as faculty, we often find it challenging to reckon with our own sense of discomfort. *Difficult Subjects* provides faculty with ways not only to encourage this discomfort among our students but also to embrace this discomfort as educators so that we can create the kind of spaces where intellectual unease translates into generative dialogue and learning.

In Therese Huston and Michele DiPetro's (2007) study of student perceptions of faculty responses to the attacks on the World Trade Center on September 11, 2001, Huston and Pietro found that "[s]tudents often complained when faculty did not mention the attacks at all, and they expressed gratitude when faculty acknowledged that something awful had occurred" (p. 219). We do not want to suggest that September 11, 2001 was an "easy" topic to address in the classroom in the days immediately following the attacks, but it was a tragedy that registered with all Americans, and the attempt to address events that may be more polarizing requires more forethought and risk. Many faculty are hesitant to discuss issues like the Ferguson uprising or the 2016 election for fear that they may alienate students who do not share their political views. Professors should, after all, maintain an affect of neutrality and objectivity. Or, should we?

Boldly Embracing Difficult Subjects

This book is a collection of essays from scholars across disciplines, institutions, and ranks that offers diverse and multifaceted approaches to teaching about subjects that prove both challenging and often uncomfortable for the professor and the student alike. It encourages college educators to engage in forms of pedagogical praxis that do not pretend that teachers and students are unaffected by world events and incidents that highlight social inequalities. Readers will find the collected essays useful for identifying new approaches to taking on the "difficult subjects" of race, gender, and sexuality. Perhaps the collection will also serve as inspiration for academics who believe that their area of study does not allow for such pedagogical inquiries to also teach in ways that address difficult subjects. Contributors to this volume span a range of disciplines from criminal justice to gender studies to organic chemistry, and demonstrate the productive possibilities that can emerge in our classrooms when we consider identity as constitutive of rather than divorced from our academic disciplines.

The urgency of this book has become even more prescient in the wake of the 2016 presidential election as demonstrated by the abundance of crowd-sourced resources now available to faculty that are dedicated to Teaching Trump, or the now-popular Facebook group Teaching in the Aftermath, which has, to date, close to 1,500 members. It is encouraging to see so many faculty concerned about how the current political and social climate will change the way our students understand themselves and the environments in which they exist. It is even more promising to witness faculty who were previously disengaged from "politics" now taking an interest in broaching these difficult subjects in the classroom. If these weren't already difficult subjects to teach, our current social and political realities now mandate such attention even in disciplines in which politics plays no obvious role. Although Trump's victory allows for the opportunity to discuss broader issues around class politics, race and racism, immigration, misogyny, gender, and sexuality, it is important for college educators to engage in mindful and intentional considerations of pedagogical choices.

The contributors acknowledge the pedagogical challenges of confronting issues like social inequities, race and racism, gender, sexism, and sexuality in college classrooms, particularly within a challenging and often overwhelming political climate. The concept of *difficult subjects* points to the ways in which professors who address these issues in their teaching are often deemed difficult or hostile, or even racist, and thus become the targets of conservative political groups and student organizations, as well as university administrations tasked with maintaining the status quo while presenting an image of valuing diversity. In fact, at a recent conference roundtable that focused on the issue of teaching race, gender and sexuality featuring scholars in this volume, an audience member (and registered conference participant) identified himself as a journalist from a conservative student news outlet. Upon hearing that he would be in the audience, the panelists expressed discomfort and announced their refusal to speak while he was in the room. Eventually, he left. However, his presence made the issues discussed in this volume (and at our roundtable) ever more vital and marked, in an immediate sense, the dangers and risks of teaching "difficult subjects."

As this collected volume acknowledges, *diversity* has become a loaded and contested word among academicians. As Sara Ahmed (2012) has persuasively argued, *diversity* is a word that conceals rather than resolves social inequalities and conflicts. To effectively address and deconstruct such problems would require acknowledging that such issues even exist, but too often, faculty are nervous to invite potentially polarizing discussions into the classroom because they don't want students to feel uncomfortable, nor do they want to feel uncomfortable themselves. As Ahmed (2012) noted, "to speak of racism is to introduce bad feeling" (p. 47). Perhaps this is the reason why many faculty avoid "difficult subjects" in the first place. To introduce such topics would mean potentially opening up the classroom to "bad feeling." The fear is real and so are the implications, particularly for pretenure and contingent faculty. In many cases, *bad feeling* equals bad evaluations, which can result in the failure to earn tenure or a contract renewal. But the reality is that the bad feeling is already there.

We cannot assume that the bad feeling we prefer to avoid in our college classrooms is not already part of the classroom dynamic in ways that might be invisible to the professor. Even though not every student who goes to college is interested in learning about identity politics, increasingly, we and our students are bombarded by the news of world events and troubles by social media and other forms of constant communication. Is it not our responsibility as educators to help students make sense and meaning of the world, and to develop problem-solving and critical-thinking skills to confront social dilemmas and conflicts?

In recent years, college student activists across the country have demanded inclusion of curriculum addressing racial inequalities as part of their protests renewing demands for racial equity and diversity on their campuses, concerns that are connected to the ills of the world around them both on and off campus. Arguably inspired by the broader Black Lives Matter movement, these students are calling on their colleges to be places of transformative education, responsive to the challenges in the world around them. In their campaigns and actions echoing the Third World Liberation Front and Ethnic Studies Strike of 1968 (Rojas, 2007; Umemoto, 1989), they are rightly calling for increased diversity in student enrollments, faculty and staff hiring, and a relevant curriculum for addressing social problems.

Although the professoriate remains stubbornly White and male, the racial and ethnic demographics of college students have been shifting relatively rapidly over the last four decades. According to the National Center for Educational Statistics (NCES, n.d.), there were just over 7.3 million undergraduates enrolled in postsecondary education in 1970. By 2013, this number had grown by over 238% to 17.5 million. Students of color and women contributed the most toward this upsurge in college enrollment. Latinx students saw the fastest rate of increase, growing from 4% to 16% of the U.S. undergraduate population between 1976 and 2013. In this same time period, Asian Americans and Pacific Islanders increased from 2% to 6%, African American enrollment went from 10% to 15%, and American Indian and Alaska Natives rose from 0.7% to 0.8%. White students, in contrast, declined in their proportion of the undergraduate population, from 84% to 59%. Additionally, the number of women enrolled in postsecondary education has exceeded the number of men since 1988. Given the changing demographics among college students, it is not surprising to see students calling for organizational, curricular, and cultural changes at their postsecondary institutions.

Although the most frequent demand from student protests was to hire more racially diverse faculty with the assumption that diverse faculty would lead to a more critical curriculum, this promises to be a long and arduous process, given the well-documented inequalities in educational pathways (Flaherty, 2015). At the same time, it is important to note that not all faculty focus their scholarship and teaching on topics related to their personal identities, and to assume so is a reductionist presumption. Moreover, changes in curriculum should not be contingent on the slow struggle to racially diversify college faculty.

Therefore, this volume is intended to be a resource for faculty who choose to courageously engage in teaching difficult subjects in the college classroom. Each chapter confronts unique challenges in teaching such classes across a range of disciplines and institutional types. The chapters are arranged in three thematic sections. In (Dis)comfort, Fragility, and the Intersections of Identity, the contributors explore notions and challenges of comfort and discomfort in the classroom. Embracing Embodiment and Emotion as Pedagogical Praxis features essays that center human emotion, experience, and affect as key components to powerful pedagogies. Finally, the chapters in Radical Pedagogy in "Neutral" Places bring attention to teaching difficult subjects in unexpected fields and disciplines like the STEM disciplines, which are often presumed objective or political neutral.

Collectively, the perspectives on pedagogy in this volume seek to embolden college educators who wish to advance a development of critical literacy among their students. According to Ira Shor (1999), critical literacy

> challenges the status quo in an effort to discover alternative paths for self and social development. This kind of literacy—words rethinking worlds, self dissenting in society—connects the political and the personal, the public and the private, the global and the local, the economic and the pedagogical, for rethinking our lives and for promoting justice in place of inequity. . . . Essentially, then, critical literacy is language use that questions the social construction of the self. When we are critically literate, we examine our ongoing development, to reveal the subjective positions from which we make sense of the world and act in it. (n.p.)

Pedagogies for critical literacy essentially contribute toward the health of an active democratic society concerned with combatting dehumanization and enabling collective movements for justice. Too often, academic contemplations of social justice ideals are simply that—theoretical ideals. Our intention and hopes for this volume are that the perspectives and tangible examples of pedagogical praxis presented here will inspire, support, and empower college educators to engage in more classroom conversations, teaching and learning about difficult subjects to open possibilities of a more just society.

References

Ahmed, S. (2012). *On being included: Racism and diversity in institutional life.* Durham, NC: Duke University Press.

Berg, M., & Seeber, B. (2016). *The slow professor: Challenging the culture of speed in the academy.* Toronto, Canada: University of Toronto Press.

Duncan-Andrade, J. M. R. (2009). Note to educators: Hope required when growing roses in concrete. *Harvard Educational Review, 79*(2), 181–194.

Finley, A. (2009). Women as contingent faculty: The glass wall. *AACU: On Campus With Women, 37*(3). Retrieved from http://archive.aacu.org/ocww/volume37_3/feature.cfm?section=1

Flaherty, C. (2015, November 30). Demanding 10 percent. *Inside Higher Ed.* Retrieved from https://www.insidehighered.com/news/2015/11/30/student-activists-want-more-black-faculty-members-how-realistic-are-some-their-goals

Flaherty, C. (2016, November 22). Being watched. *Inside Higher Ed.* Retrieved from https://www.insidehighered.com/news/2016/11/22/new-website-seeks-register-professors-accused-liberal-bias-and-anti-american-values

Freire, P. (1985). Reading the world and reading the word: An interview with Paulo Freire. *Language Arts, 62*(1), 15–21.

Freire, P. (2000). *Pedagogy of the oppressed.* New York, NY: Bloomsbury Academic.

hooks, b. (2003). *Teaching community: A pedagogy of hope.* New York, NY: Routledge.

Huston, P., & DiPetro, M. (2007). *In the eye of the storm: Students' perceptions of helpful faculty actions following a collective tragedy.* Retrieved from http://www.bu.edu/sed/files/2013/04/In_the_Eye.pdf

Lazos, S. R. (2012). Are student teaching evaluations holding back women and minorities?: The perils of "doing" gender and race in the classroom. In G. Gutiérrez y Muhs, Y. Flores Niemann, C. G. González, & A. P. Harris (Eds.), *Presumed incompetent: The intersections of race and class for women in academia* (pp. 164–185). Boulder, CO: University Press of Colorado.

National Center for Education Statistics (n.d.). *Fast facts.* Retrieved from http://nces.ed.gov/fastfacts/display.asp?id=98

Rojas, F. (2007). *From Black power to Black studies: How a radical social movement became an academic discipline.* Baltimore, MD: Johns Hopkins University Press.

Shor, I. (1999). What is critical literacy? *The Journal of Pedagogy, Pluralism, and Practice, 1*(4). Retrieved from http://www.lesley.edu/journal-pedagogy-pluralism-practice/ira-shor/critical-literacy/

Umemoto, K. (1989). "On strike!" San Francisco State College strike, 1968–69: The role of Asian American students. *Amerasia Journal, 15*(1), 3–41.

PART ONE

(DIS)COMFORT, FRAGILITY, AND THE INTERSECTIONS OF IDENTITY

Each essay in this section broaches, in a diverse way, how the notion of *comfort* has been deployed to avoid and/or deflect from engaging anti-racist pedagogies. With the advent of *trigger warnings* on syllabi, there has been increased attention to the ways in which students (and university administrations) might perceive certain pedagogical practices and course content as uncomfortable. The parlance of comfort thus has been used as a way to silence or punish faculty who encourage discomfort as a necessary precondition to intellectual and social growth. The essays in this section address the challenges (and successes) of encouraging discomfort as a necessary aspect of the learning process.

This part opens with Rucha Ambikar, Daniel Guentchev, and Dennis Lunt's chapter, "A Conversation on Challenging and Using Comfort-Zone Racism in the Classroom." This chapter presents three experiences on negotiating Whiteness and comfort-zone racism on a rural, predominantly White college campus. It considers the dilemmas and ethics of teaching about Whiteness, race, and racism from the perspectives of an immigrant woman of color, an immigrant White man, and a White American man. The chapter argues for coteaching as an effective strategy for addressing *comfort-zone racism* and how the racialized and ethnic identities of professors can be used, rather than ignored or rendered neutral, to facilitate anti-racist pedagogies. Comfort-zone racism can often be difficult to discern in a college classroom because it typically takes the "form of polite silence or dismissal rather than aggression" (p. 6, this volume).

Cheryl E. Matias and Lisa Silverstein's "When Racially Just Teaching Becomes Your Own Heart: Pedagogical Strategies for Teaching Whiteness" documents the psychical and emotional challenges of two college faculty (one of color and one White) to implement and teach a course on the topic of

Whiteness. This chapter offers pedagogical strategies for teaching Whiteness in the college classroom as well as strategies for overcoming the emotional toll teaching such a course takes on faculty at predominantly White institutions. Through the process of journaling and symbolic pedagogies, Matias and Silverstein argue for embracing emotional affect as part and parcel of racially just teaching.

Teaching the "difficult subjects" of race, sexuality, and gender in the college classroom is often met with resistance by students, particularly in a cultural moment in which anti-political correctness has become an excuse to be racially insensitive, offensive, and even violent. The experiences of faculty of color who challenge the racial status quo and undermine the conventional logic of White, heteropatriarchal norms is often met with opposition ranging from microaggressions to verbal assaults. In her chapter "Addressing Incivility in the Classroom: Effective Strategies for Faculty at the Margins," Chavella Pittman offers applied strategies for how faculty who endeavor to teach difficult subjects might mitigate and counter classroom incivility. Pittman discusses the most frequently suggested practices for student incivilities as well as their promise and limitations for faculty at the margins. This chapter also examines potential consequences of unchecked classroom incivilities for faculty. Most importantly, this essay offers faculty methods to employ—both inside and outside the classroom—to address problematic student classroom behaviors.

David J. Leonard and Paula Groves Price's chapter "Whiteness Matters: Tourism, Customer Service, and the Neoliberal University" makes the case that rather than address the systemic problems of inequality on their campuses, colleges and universities are too comfortable with advancing an illusion of diversity. Leonard and Groves Price argue that doctoring promotional materials like brochures, websites, and so on, gives an obvious recognition that a diverse university is desirable, yet there are fewer efforts to make the actual campus demographics reflect the desirable diversity in their advertising. Their chapter calls on administrators and stakeholders to recall and make tangible once again the public good purpose of universities. Inclusive within that ideal is the imperative to create actual diverse spaces rather than simply imagining them.

In relation to calls for systemic transformation, the impetus of Nicole Truesdell's chapter, "Black Lives, Black Women, and the Academy: 'Doing' Equity and Inclusion Work at PWIs," is to offer insights as to how administrators can avoid the *tourism model* of diversity work by looking to and embracing social justice movements like Black Lives Matter and centering marginalized bodies in White spaces. Truesdell approaches this issue from the perspective of an administrator attempting to change the campus by shifting institutional practices so that university diversity initiatives are more than just lip service to the communities they are supposed to serve.

A CONVERSATION ON CHALLENGING AND USING COMFORT-ZONE RACISM IN THE CLASSROOM

Rucha Ambikar, Daniel Guentchev, and Dennis Lunt

Teaching about race and racism often presents a range of challenges and difficulties. One such challenge is the prevailing ideology of color-blind racism which

Seems like "racism lite." Instead of relying on name calling (n----s, S---s, C----s), color-blind racism otherizes softly ("these people are human, too"); instead of proclaiming God placed minorities in the world in a servile position, it suggests they are behind because they do not work hard enough; instead of viewing interracial marriage as wrong on a straight racial basis, it regards it as "problematic" because of concerns over the children, location, or the extra burden it places on couples. Yet this new ideology has become a formidable political tool for the maintenance of the racial order. . . . color-blind racism serves today as the ideological armor for a covert and institutionalized system in the post-Civil Rights era. (Bonilla-Silva, 2006, p. 3)

Within our specific context of a rural northern Minnesota college campus setting, the ideology of color-blind racism aligns well with a dominant state culture that emphasizes comfort and nonconfrontation. The *Minnesota Spokesman-Recorder* (*MSR Online*), dubbed this localized version of color-blind racism "comfort-zone racism" ("How does the new Jim Crow," 2015). Nonconfrontational by nature, comfort-zone racism relies on avoiding confrontation with people or facts perceived as threatening one's comfort zone of race. People who look, speak, and otherwise carry themselves in a way that makes them appear foreign to White comfort often face exclusion in the form of polite silence or dismissal rather than aggression. Though not unique to Minnesota, comfort-zone racism presents a particular challenge, which manifests differently for faculty with varying identities, for teaching about race and racism.

There are two features of comfort-zone racism that we find relevant to our discussion. First, it leads to an inhospitable environment to those perceived as "others" and different from the White norm. The result is a significant level of segregation, maintained in a seemingly unintentional and nonconfrontational way. Clarence Hightower, executive director of Community Action Partnership of Ramsey and Washington Counties, points out in several contributions to *MSR Online* that Minnesota is often praised for providing a high standard of living for its residents while maintaining a very large gap between the quality of life of White residents and that of people of color. For example, in 2012 the state boasted the highest home ownership rate in the country (77%), whereas home ownership among people of color was well below the national average (41%; Hightower, 2016). Likewise, in spite of evidence that Black Americans are no more likely than White Americans to use marijuana, in Minnesota the former are eight times more likely to be arrested for marijuana possession. Nationally, Black Americans are four times more likely to be arrested for marijuana possession, compared to White people, making Minnesota's numbers even more conspicuous (ACLU–MN, 2014). A recent CBS report confirms that Minnesota has the second-highest level of racial inequality in unemployment and incarceration rate (Wagner, 2017). Second, comfort-zone racism underscores the significant role played by a sense of comfort in governing when, and how seriously, social issues are confronted, as well as who is qualified to confront them. In and out of the classroom, people perceived as "others," especially people of color, must make significant efforts to appear nonthreatening to Whiteness and demonstrate that they fit into the dominant community of comfort in order to receive serious consideration. When they fail, or cannot afford to do so, they face exclusion.

This chapter explores these two features of comfort-zone racism, guided by the following question: What role does the perceived identity of the teacher play in the teaching of race and racism in a classroom? Answering it involves a self-conscious reflection and appraisal of our respective situations as a White man, a White immigrant man, and a woman of color, and discussing the implications of our individual identities for effective teaching strategies. In different ways, our pedagogical techniques address the structural and political character of racism in the United States.

Issues of race and racism are not brought into class discussion only by professors, but also enter our classrooms with our students, with how we define and teach the canon, and with the professors themselves. Our bearing and attitude, and even how we dress and enunciate our words, already make race relevant to the classroom before it is given time to be unpacked through discussion. In our experience, productive questions about addressing race in the classroom have to start from this premise. For this reason, this chapter is written to compare the experiences of three instructors of different racial, national, and social backgrounds. The approaches we have developed for challenging and even using comfort-zone racism are more or less effective because of our personal backgrounds in relation to our students' backgrounds and perspectives. Therefore, in this chapter we consider how our identities and backgrounds equip or limit our strategies for teaching race.

The following mini-essays are not offered as a collection of expert solutions to "problem students." Rather, they are offered as self-reflective analyses of instructors who have tried and sometimes failed to teach about racism at a rural American college. At the same time, we wish to emphasize that this is not an opportunity to gripe about students. When we discuss examples of racism in the classroom, we do so acknowledging the fact that racist acts are often not perceived or intended as such—although, we discuss some examples in which it was quite intentional. Indeed, racism is larger and more structural than individual perceptions. This fact does not excuse racist behavior, but it does mean that racism in the classroom is not reducible to a disciplinary issue. It is an instructional issue, especially in environments that make the teaching of race particularly difficult. Our hope is that our reflective narratives of strategic pedagogical efforts to address comfort-zone racism can offer a starting point for others who also face the challenges of color-blind racism in the classroom and wish to disrupt the comfort found in this dominant ideology. Each of our individual narratives discuss the implications of how our personal identities interact with student perceptions, and how keeping these interaction effects in mind lead us to specific teaching strategies, which have resulted in varying degrees of pedagogical success. In the end, we argue for the importance of having faculty of diverse identities teach about race and racism in multiple ways and classrooms.

Daniel Guentchev: Comfort as Obstacle and Resource

I was born and raised in Bulgaria, and in my students' eyes I am unmistakably White. This, combined with the fact that I am a man, lends me an air of objectivity when discussing issues of race (see chapter 6 by Estill). Although I am a White man, my experiences of migration and my Bulgarian identity give me some insight into marginalization and the experience of being told what you are by others. Part of the Ottoman Empire for five centuries,

Bulgaria lost much of the physical evidence of its history. Bulgarian cultural identity, fragile for centuries, required reconstruction. Given this context, I know what it is like to have much of my history written by outsiders, often in very dismissive terms. Crossing a European border in the 1990s, I was made aware that others did not consider Bulgarians to be real Europeans. Bulgarians were often treated as dangerous, exemplified by contemporary rhetoric in the United Kingdom that paints Bulgarian immigrants as invasive and threatening, notions exacerbated by the Brexit referendum. Although not on the receiving end of racism in the United States, I can, at times, articulate what it is like to be the subject of certain types of exclusion, such as xenophobia. Because few in the United States are aware of Bulgaria's history and the social status of Bulgarians, in the classroom context I have the luxury of choosing when to evoke my personal background and experiences of exclusion and marginalization.

Given my personal background, my pedagogical strategy attempts to turn student comfort from an obstacle to an entry point into discussions of race. There are several senses in which comfort is an obstacle to teaching and learning about race. First, some students are put off by the distinctive vocabularies of writings that challenge the Eurocentric status quo of texts accepted as canon. In the context of comfort-zone racism, some students dismiss such vocabularies as less intellectually valid. Second, students in this context may devalue works by authors challenging dominant notions of race and other ideas as having an axe to grind, and thus lacking objectivity. For example, while teaching Richard Mohr's (1992) "Gay Basics: Some Questions, Facts, and Values," an essay that includes a significant amount of statistical data, a student objected to the text, arguing that it lacked the philosophical authority of other works containing primarily a priori arguments that defended opposing viewpoints. Third, recognizing the cost of White comfort to people of color is a common challenge. This failure of recognition is often brought to the foreground by class discussions of Derrick Bell's (1992) "The Space Traders."[1] Bell poses the question whether, given the opportunity, the United States would revoke the civil rights of its Black population for the sake of economic and ecological benefits to its White population. When I ask the question in class, the most common response is silence or fervent denial that something like this would happen. When I press students in class, asking for evidence to substantiate their belief, reminding them that we predict the future on the basis of historical precedent, they merely insist that things have changed and that the racial divide is not as bad as Bell describes. No evidence is offered by these White students in the classroom discussions. In private though, a few White students have admitted to me that they would surrender their Black friends in exchange for benefits similar to those in the short story. Bell confronts students, through his work on paper, and invites them to confront their belief that the comforts they enjoy are shared by people of color, and that their communities offer fair treatment. Even in the face of this mild confrontation, the majority of students initially resist serious discussion of a grim prediction expressed in the form of fiction.

My teaching experiences have challenged me to work toward turning comfort into a resource for teaching about race and racism on a predominantly White campus. Informed by my own undergraduate experiences, I often begin with a discussion of works that are recognized as canonical and then employ their own language to highlight underlying Eurocentrism in these very texts. Attending a private liberal arts college, my education emphasized figures who critiqued the philosophical and educational canons of the West. As a student, I grew resentful of these texts, seeing them as primarily reactive and limited to objecting to specific issues. I wished to learn the canon, or solid philosophy, as I saw it then. During my graduate career, I focused on studying the canon. As I focused on the history of Western philosophy after studying dissenting voices, I became increasingly aware of the racial element inherent to texts that are often accepted as the canon. It became apparent to me just what marginalized voices critiqued and what role their vocabulary and style played in their projects. Because most students have been trained to take the White philosophical canon more seriously, I begin with it. Along the way, I make sure to expose the ways in which race and racism function within canonical writings.

As I did as an undergraduate, many students in my classes today often view White European thought and philosophical texts as objective and uninfluenced by race. My goal, thus, is to show that this assumption is, for the most part, mistaken. For example, after reading *An Essay Concerning Human Understanding* (1690) we discuss Locke's conclusion that a superior human mind is marked by its ability to isolate an object's perceived qualities and to create ideas of new objects by composing new combinations of qualities. This process of mental dismantling of objects is related to the physical dismantling of natural resources and their recombination into previously nonexistent objects. In his *Second Treatise of Government* (1689), Locke claims that a wise government empowers citizens to derive more conveniences from the land it secures. Conveniences are the products of extracting, dismantling, and recombining natural resources, selected because they possess particular qualities that we wish to isolate and use. Students quickly catch on that for Locke, cultures that do not place a premium on the extraction and recombination of natural resources (as Europeans do) are inferior because they fail to utilize the human mind's full potential. Already familiar and comfortable with Locke's vocabulary, students are able to use his very words to trace and analyze his logic and its implications for non-Europeans, revealing the Eurocentric underpinnings of his work. This process bears fruit in discussions of many philosophical texts, authored by White men, which are unquestioned as canonical. My perceived Whiteness leads many students to take criticism of the canon more seriously than if it had been presented by a teacher who was not White. This White privilege allows me to then highlight the significance of the linguistic and stylistic choices of marginalized voices.

I have found that taking the first step of critiquing European ideas of progress by using their own language disposes students to take issues of race more seriously and be charitable about the more radical critiques. For example, the gravity of the narrative of *Basic Call to Consciousness* (Notes, 2005), a series of papers presented by an Iroquois delegation to a United Nations convention in New York, becomes more apparent in light of already identified issues in the European ideas of progress. The authors claim that, from the standpoint of self-identified Neolithic peoples, each stage in the ever more aggressive utilization of resources (large-scale agriculture, urbanization) is a step closer to disaster. This understanding of history and progress sharply contrasts with Locke's. Understanding the problems of Locke's narrative assists with understanding the significance of the Iroquois narrative. Through this pedagogical method, I have had some success with students discussing the Indigenous text without an outright dismissal of it.

There is a danger in my method, however, and it is something I continue to work on. I concede to student comfort and comfort-zone racism. I reinforce the habit of not taking the critiques of marginalized voices seriously without listening to the internal critique first. The internal critique here is the utilization of the canon's vocabulary for the purpose of self-criticism by a White male instructor. This process continues to center Whiteness. The legitimacy of marginalized voices hinges on the canon's admission of its own mistakes. At this stage, one cannot repeat enough that what the canon has recently admitted to has been apparent to the marginalized all along. Thus, my strategy is most effective when it is one of several strategies employed simultaneously, when students are exposed to other pedagogical methodologies, and often shocked out of their comfort, rather than eased into different perspectives.

Rucha Ambikar: The Outsider Perspective

I grew up in India in fairly privileged circumstances where I could access every educational opportunity I wanted. So, when I moved to the United States for graduate studies, I certainly did not expect to assume any sort of identity that would portray me as an underprivileged minority. I have been teaching about race and racism for a while now, but my experiences since I joined our university in rural Minnesota have made me see my own identity and pedagogy in a wholly different light.

On the second day of my new job in this university, a student sought out the provost and complained that I had sworn in class. I had not. I marveled at both the manufactured complaint and the fact that although I hadn't even had the time to Google the provost, a student had taken the time to seek him out and lie about me. I was full of anxiety until the university administration helped me figure out what was happening, suggesting that they imagined this was the nameless student's way of dealing with difference. "Our students," they tried to explain, "lack exposure. They are not bad people, they just aren't used to somebody like you!" This was an "aha" moment for me. It hit me then that, more than what I was going to teach, I needed to pay attention to how students perceived who I was.

I obviously don't look like I have White or European heritage. I sound different than most Minnesotans, and I teach things that disrupt their comfort zone. As Daniel points out in his section, comfort-zone racism means that the students' sense of comfort significantly influences when and how seriously social issues are confronted—as well as who is qualified to confront them. I've come to realize that many students either expect outsiders to appear nonthreatening and demonstrate that they fit into a White norm or tend to dismiss this outsider as having nothing useful to teach them. When I teach, I teach from this outsider perspective.

As a woman of color and an Indian immigrant, I am always marked as an outsider; I use this to disrupt students' expectations. One of the ways in which I do this is by pointing out that because I am from somewhere else, I did not have the same life experiences as most of their classmates. I then ask students to articulate the reasons behind their opinions about particular issues and ask them to critically examine why they think in these ways. For example, in introductory classes, I often teach about globalization and describe the global competition that students will face in their own job searches as I explain the basics of capitalism. I then ask students if I, an immigrant woman, should be teaching them. After some humor and cajoling, one or two students will usually say "no" and admit that they feel an American, which is often popularly understood as a White American (Frankenberg, 1993), should hold my job.

This answer helps the students identify the anti-immigrant or unconscious bias that may be prevalent in class. I ask students to do some self-reflective writing at this point, which helps them explicitly identify their own unconscious and conscious biases—about race, immigration, and gender, in this case. It is a self-reflective, analytical path that they might not otherwise take. At this juncture, I explain the open and competitive recruitment process through which I was selected for this job. Explaining that anybody who has the right combination of qualifications, experience, and willingness would be eligible to compete for this job allows for students to realize that although they may think that American jobs are being taken away by foreigners, their comprehension of the situation is not necessarily correct.

My teaching strategy, however, does reinforce my foreignness, which means that students may sometimes dismiss me as an outsider and comfortably ignore the content of my teaching. One way I deal with this is to mark my expertise in the subject by presenting data and facts as part of my pedagogy. However, sometimes, this strategy might still not be as effective for me as it might be for White male professors. Even the facts I present are often questioned, because students may not trust the facts that somebody they have marked as other will provide (Ambikar & Lunt, 2016).

In my classes I grapple with what students will think is sufficient evidence of the existence of racism. Exercises such as Peggy McIntosh's (1990) Knapsack of White Privilege, which identifies some of the daily effects of White privilege in people's lives, start students thinking about some of these things. However, in the end, adjudication of what counts as evidence is itself an exercise in racial superiority. Nothing is sufficient proof of the continued existence of racial discrimination for students who may not be willing to go beyond their own experiences. These same students may not feel the need to offer proof when they assert that racial discrimination is a thing of the past. Whereas making fact-based arguments, continually reinforcing the scientific method that seeks proof beyond the anecdotal, may set students on the path to learning, it is important to admit here that the comfort zone of racism that students may operate in means that, perhaps, women of color professors are generally taken less seriously than their White male counterparts (Bachen, McLoughlin, & Garcia, 1999).

Students, especially some White students, may take the existence of White privilege more seriously when it is pointed out by a professor who is like them. As Dennis will discuss in the next section, the opportunity to be taken seriously as an objective expert is not equally available to all of us. And this raises the very important limitation that I always face as I teach about race and racism. I cannot teach in isolation. At this point, I may need to acknowledge that perhaps the insider is the only one who can break through the comfort zone in which many students on predominantly White campuses operate.

Sometimes, though, the comfort zone is not simply limited to the students and the classroom. It permeates much of the institutional climate in the university. Let me give you an example: I once accepted an invitation to a senior (White, male) colleague's classroom as he was teaching a topic vaguely related to my area of expertise in India. Sadly, my presence did not contribute much to the students' learning because he had created no space to for me to enter the class discussion. It became obvious that I had been invited as garnish to the classroom to essentially lend credence to the professor's pronunciation of Indian names.

At one point, students split into groups for discussion and the professor decided to regale me with his wit. Sotto voce he said, "My wife has a fun way of distinguishing between two kinds of Indians. You ask the Indian in front of you whether they are the dot kind or the feather kind." I was taken aback. He laughed alone at the racist punch line, and I felt angry as I contemplated this professor's contribution to the students' psyches.

In the end, my participation in this class is something that I am ashamed about. I grew angry at the professor's "joke"; but I did nothing to call him on it. Was it any wonder that the students felt so comfortable ignoring racism and refusing to discuss White privilege if this is the attitude that some of their faculty displayed? I wondered if this sort of racism permeated institutions because faculty like me chose not to point out instances of racism when they happened. Students, too, could choose to retreat into classes offered by faculty they found comforting, and any real chance of engendering a critical view of racism may then be lost.

This experience has challenged me to be more willing to speak up when I experience situations that occur due to comfort-zone racism. In the end then, I have to do better at calling out these instances of racism whenever I encounter them—to seek to interrupt the comfort-zone racism of not only the students but also other faculty and at an institutional level. If anything, a chapter like this shows that no single faculty can do it alone, but together, we may have just enough arsenal to change the conversation on race and racism.

In Table 1.1, I identify and summarize both positive aspects and drawbacks of the three pedagogical approaches to teaching about race and racism that I take as a female professor of color. There remain some serious shortcomings to each approach to teaching race and racism presented in our three narratives. Each of us fulfill student expectations of how we should teach, given their racialized perceptions of us as individuals. As philosophers, Daniel and Dennis must first fulfill their obligation by teaching the "real" (i.e., White male) philosophers. If they manage to then raise the point that canon is itself based in culture and history they may have successfully taught their students to exhibit critical-thinking skills. As an anthropologist I may only limit myself to being exotic while I talk of exotic cultures, but am rejected as a legitimate scholar and professor when I start talking about race and racism in the United States. Given who we are, and given our teaching goals, we may be limited in our pedagogical approaches as individuals. What

TABLE 1.1

Pedagogical Approaches to Teaching About Race and Racism

Pedagogical Approach	Positive Aspects	Drawbacks
Outsider seeking cultural insight	Students identify and reflect on their own biases. Facts and analysis can then be used to teach students.	Instructor of color may reinforce or remain an outsider and hence not be trusted or respected.
Seeking allies among fellow faculty	Reinforcing this pedagogy on race and racism may help students learn by starting from a place of comfort. There can be a concerted effort at change with like-minded faculty and can affect overall curricular redesign.	Faculty on campus may not be interested in this alliance or they may be unwilling to engage in this pedagogy. Faculty teaching about racism may feel isolated.
Interrupting structural racism	Engender conversations of how institutions and/or fellow faculty may be reinforcing comfort-zone racism. Seek to interrupt these structures that reinforce comfort-zone racism.	Faculty may feel isolated, and may face indirect penalties for insisting on these conversations. This interruption cannot happen in isolation.

might work is for all of us work in tandem. When all of us, in different contexts and in different classes reinforce the message, we might be successful in disrupting this comfort zone of racism.

Dennis Lunt: A White Guy Teaches Du Bois

I do bring texts that are considered marginal by most philosophers to center stage. These are the difficult texts in my curriculum, because they touch directly on the comfort zone of White privilege that I and many of my students bring into class. I include myself because my "insider" status is usually taken for granted. I grew up near Cincinnati, Ohio, a White man from a Baptist family. Although my beloved Cincinnati chili does not always sit well with Minnesota palates, my Midwestern mannerisms and evangelical upbringing do translate, and I benefit from that shared language in ways I cannot always control or perceive. For instance, although I take a professional tone in class, I do swear occasionally (usually unintentionally). The occasional strategic swear can enliven discussion and sometimes make me more approachable. In contrast to Rucha's experience, my students have yet to lodge a complaint with me, let alone with my provost.

I would like to use one "difficult text" as an example of the situation of a White teacher trying to interrogate Whiteness. W. E. B. Du Bois's "Souls of White Folk" (1920) is a good example, because it discusses and creates a confrontation with White privilege. Du Bois (1996) begins the essay with a characteristically florid picture of that privilege: "Of [White folk] I am singularly clairvoyant. . . . And yet as they preach and strut and shout and threaten, crouching as they clutch at rags of facts and fancies to hide their nakedness, they go twisting, flying by my tired eyes and I see them ever stripped,—ugly, human" (p. 497).

Those "rags of facts and fancies" he mentioned are the collage of pseudo-science, ad hominems, and tu quoques that are used to avoid hard questions about racial privilege. It is when a White student says "Don't the Black kids say it?" after being told they cannot use the n-word, or when scientific studies that challenge racial stereotypes are dismissed with an anecdote about someone they knew in high school who fits a stereotype. Comfort-zone racism is a much more complex performance than I expected it to be when I began teaching. I often think of it as having two "modes" or "gears." First gear is the tendency we've focused on, to solve problems in a self-contained discussion of White thinkers and White categories. (In first gear, one does not see the racialization of ideas and thinkers used to solve social problems, but sees them instead as neutral and normal.) Race and racism are often outside the social problem-solving of many White folks, in that questions in and out of the classroom are not answered with explicit reference to racial categories or the history of race relations. In fact, it is the absence of such references that leads many of us to uncritically assume that we are not *really* racists.

When we are forced to respond to examples of racism—say, by an instructor—there is a loose collection of non sequiturs and anecdotes that can be readily deployed to, as Daniel noted in his narrative, dismiss a voice from "outside" as angry or hyperbolic. Second gear, as I call it, is an orderly retreat back into the comfort zone, using a few ready-to-hand arguments to avoid the full force of an injustice. For instance, in class, I may invite discussion on the fact that African Americans in Minnesota are eight times more likely to be arrested on a marijuana possession charge than White people (despite evidence that the latter are as likely or more likely to actually use marijuana). When I discuss this fact in class, many White students stay in first gear, declining to engage. Others shift into second gear and avoid the topic with an ad hoc example of an African American they knew who was not arrested, or by deflecting to class divisions.

Du Bois spoke from the perspective of someone excluded from White privilege, hence "singularly clairvoyant" about its inner workings and blindnesses. When us White folks teach Du Bois or Anzaldúa or Yancey, it is tempting to appropriate that clairvoyance for ourselves. In class discussion, Du Bois is then read as a window into the perspective of a victim of racialization. In my first few lectures on Du Bois and his contemporaries, I found myself speaking *as* Du Bois, talking about what "we"—Du Bois and I—can see about racial privilege from where he stands. After all, I was the expert, there to explain and defend Du Bois's thinking.

Role-playing is a natural enough strategy when we cover authors who are unfamiliar to our students. The problem with this strategy is that my own racial background, and the racial divisions that shape my classroom and community, drop out of the discussion. When I speak as Du Bois, I cannot also speak as someone heir to the privileges he is questioning. I would be questioning racial privileges, but not *my* racial privileges or *our* racial privileges, because I read Du Bois as translating his experience for me.

Du Bois himself never promises to take White folks by the hand and show them how the world looks to a Black person, like some kind of intellectual Willy Wonka showing us how the candy really gets made. Du Bois is not translating his experience for a neutral White audience. He is engaged in two efforts: building consciousness and consensus among a Black audience, and interrupting the "rags of facts and fancies" that White privilege sews for itself. In this situation, what is the most professional, effective tone for a White instructor to take? Instead of trying to speak from the community that Du Bois wanted to build, today I find it more constructive, and truthful, to talk about how Du Bois's text confronted his own political situation—and my political situation today.

Having tried some dead-end strategies, I feel more confident when speaking on what has not worked than on what will. My goal as a teacher is not to overcome (or worse, ignore) the differences between Du Bois (or Darwish or hooks or . . .) and I, to reach a neutral perspective on race. This idea that I can, at will, suspend centuries of racism to reach a neutral place where Du Bois and I have the same interests and the same perspective is part of the problem.

For today, my plan is, rather, to model the transition out of my comfort zone—a transition in which Du Bois's writings were a factor. Put differently, if Du Bois was writing (in part) to interrupt that comfortable racism of his White audience, then a White instructor teaches him best by modeling how to listen and not talk over him, and how to be interrupted without immediately retreating to an easy answer. Table 1.2 summarizes this metaphor.

TABLE 1.2.
Avoiding Easy Answers

NOT	*BUT*
Putting marginalized voices at the end of a curriculum, as an outside perspective on the self-contained conversation of White voices.	Placing marginalized voices in their historical spot in the canon, so that their ideas can be read as a direct confrontation with or interruption of the canonical White texts.
Translating marginalized texts into the form and vocabulary used by canonical White texts.	Discussing the importance of why and when the form and vocabulary of marginalized texts deviate from that of canonical White texts.
Placing all the risk of being perceived as racist on my students, by asking them to respond to me and Du Bois (who are subtly identified).	Inviting questions about how a marginalized text confronts the White comfort zone by first talking about how the text affects me resists assumptions that I and other White folks (some canonical) took for granted.
Talking about the transition out of my White comfort zone as a finished conversion.	Attempting to model a willingness to doubt, to be subject to the logic and force of marginalized texts, just as with the canonical White texts.

I have focused on Du Bois, because he was an early touchstone for my own thinking on race, racism, and Whiteness, but I believe these strategies may apply to many other marginalized thinkers, and to contested topics.

The Palestinian poet Mahmoud Darwish once said, "Sometimes I feel as if I am read before I write. . . . When I write a poem about my mother, Palestinians think my mother is a symbol for Palestine. But I write as a poet, and my mother is my mother. She's not a symbol."[2] There is a risk in refusing to hear and read the political force of marginalized voices, and there is a concomitant risk of not allowing marginalized voices to speak of anything but their political situation. I do not have a reliable chart for guiding teachers and students between these two misreadings. But I think a responsible pedagogy must include a cultivated habit for reading what the author has written, before reading the author, so to speak. Creating this kind of space, where the text is equal to us, is a challenge on most days.

Concluding Remarks

Based on our reflective narratives about the advantages and disadvantages of our personal identities and how they influence our pedagogies, we suggest that engaging in a group effort is key to confronting comfort-zone racism. If White faculty like Daniel and Dennis are not aggressively demanding that race and racism be discussed, then they are contributing to experiences like Rucha's. We know that some students squirm their way through discussions of race with faculty of color, and then retreat to classes with White faculty who do not demand attention to racism. The results would be, and often are, not only the isolation of faculty of color who teach about race and racism but also a reinforcement of comfort-zone racism and what Bonilla-Silva (2006) has defined as *color-blind racist ideology*, because the division would reinforce a key racist assumption: that race is only a topic for angry others who do not belong as "we" White Americans do. The other key factor, which we have not discussed at length, is the role of students of color in confronting comfort-zone racism. Minimally, we owe our students of color an environment that does not fixate on either the privileges or problems of White students, which would perpetuate a centering and privileging of Whiteness. Likewise, even the most fine-tuned pedagogy can only meet students halfway, because it depends on their cooperation. Education on race finally depends on the students' willingness to engage with it.

The strategies that we have shared are by no means the only viable ones, and they certainly do not apply to all faculty and academic institutions. As we point out, each strategy has shortcomings. When used in isolation, their effectiveness is quite limited. Often the shortcomings of one strategy are addressed by others. Thus, these strategies are most effective when students are exposed to multiple approaches to teaching race and racism. We see that the instructor's background can play a significant role in the choice of pedagogical strategies. As Kenneth Stickers (2014) writes, White faculty must listen long and carefully before speaking on the subject. They must take seriously the experiences of faculty and students who suffer from racism, but also of those who engage in the discussions to better themselves. The availability of multiple strategies relies on the availability of faculty of various backgrounds. Successful academic discussions of race and racism are therefore the result of not only faculty effort but also the campus as a whole.

Notes

1. In the story, aliens offer the United States the technology to solve economic and environmental issues in exchange for the Black population without knowing their fate. Bell follows the discussions and policies enacted during the 40-day deliberation period. The closing scene is of shackled Black people loaded onto space ships. The unstated question at the end of the story is whether, given the opportunity to

benefit the White population so much, the White establishment would sacrifice all rights of Black people.

    2. Shatz, A. (2001, December 22). A Poet's Palestine as a Metaphor. Retrieved from www.nytimes.com/2001/12/22/books/a-poet-s-palestine-as-a-metaphor.html

References

Ambikar, R., & Lunt, D. (2016, May 15). How the teacher's race affects the teaching of race. *The Chronicle of Higher Education.* Retrieved from http://www.chronicle .com/article/How-the-Teacher-s-Race/236446

American Civil Liberties Union of Minnesota (ACLU–MN). (2014, June 4). In Minnesota, Black people found to be 7.81 times more likely to be arrested for marijuana possession than White people, despite equal usage rates. *ACLU–MN,* p. N4. Retrieved from https://www.aclu-mn.org/news/2013/06/04/minnesota-black-people-found-be-781-times-more-likely-be-arr

Bachen, C. M., McLoughlin, M. M., & Garcia, S. S. (1999). Assessing the role of gender in college students' evaluations of faculty. *Communication Education, 48*(3), 193–210.

Bell, D. (1992). The space traders. In *Faces at the bottom of the well: The permanence of racism* (pp. 158–194). New York, NY: Basic Books.

Bonilla-Silva, E. (2006). *Racism without racists: Color-blind racism and the persistence of racial inequality in the United States* (2nd ed.). New York, NY: Rowman & Littlefield.

Du Bois, W. E. B. (1996). Darkwater: Voices from within the veil. In E. J. Sundquist (Ed.), *The Oxford W. E. B. Du Bois reader* (pp. 481–623). New York, NY: Oxford University Press.

Frankenberg, R. (1993). *White women, race matters: The social construction of Whiteness.* Minneapolis, MN: University of Minnesota Press.

How does the new Jim Crow work? Study Minnesota. (2015, September 2). *Minnesota Spokesman-Recorder.* Retrieved from http://spokesman-recorder. com/2015/09/02/new-jim-crow-work-study-minnesota/

Hightower, C. (2016, April 28). Yet another Minnesota first place in racial gaps. *Minnesota Spokesman-Recorder.* Retrieved from http://spokesman-recorder.com/ 2016/04/28/yet-another-minnesota-first-place-racial-gaps

Locke, J. (1689/1980). *Second treatise of government.* Indianapolis, IN: Hackett.

Locke, J. (1690/1998). *An essay concerning human understanding.* New York, NY: Penguin Classics.

McIntosh, P. (1990). White privilege: Unpacking the invisible knapsack. *Independent School, 49*(2, Winter), 31–35.

Mohr, R. D. (1992). Gay basics: Some questions, facts, and values. In R. M. Baird & S. E. Rosenbaum (Eds.), *Bigotry, prejudice, and hatred: Definitions, causes, and solutions* (pp. 167–182). Buffalo, NY: Prometheus Books.

Notes, A. (Ed.). (2005). *Basic call to consciousness*. Summertown, TN: Native Voices.

Stickers, K. (2014). ". . . But I'm not racist": Toward a pragmatic conception of "racism." *The Pluralist, 9*(3), 1–17.

Wagner, Jeff. (2017). "Minnesota ranked 2nd worst in US for racial inequality." CBS-Minnesota. Retrieved from http://minnesota.cbslocal.com/2017/08/22/minnesota-racial-inequality/

2

WHEN RACIALLY JUST TEACHING BECOMES YOUR OWN HEART

Pedagogical Strategies for Teaching Whiteness

Cheryl E. Matias and Lisa Silverstein

Teaching about race or racial justice—one that seeks to dismantle the manifestations of Whiteness and White supremacy in the U.S. educational system—in a predominantly White institution (PWI), taxes the hearts of those educators who teach it (Matias, 2012; Stanley, 2006; Williams & Evans-Winters, 2005) and is also highly dangerous (Matias, 2016; Smith, 2014). From racial battle fatigue that stems from constant racial microaggressions from students and colleagues alike to the outright threats from the public on educators' lives, racially just educators in the academy are experiencing record high numbers of emotional, physical, intellectual, and spiritual assaults (Matias, 2013). Despite this, racially just educators are steadfast in promoting a more racially equitable educational system, often finding new ways to engage topics that many White folks find "controversial." One such controversial topic is teaching the *emotionalities of Whiteness*—meaning, racialized emotions, otherwise sentimentalities, of White folks that get expressed in a way that operationally silences the emotional traumas of people of color's experiences with White supremacy and racism. These sentimentalities are used as a mechanism to errone-ously recenter Whiteness at the core of racial trauma. These emotionali-ties of Whiteness are ever-present in education, especially within a field like urban teacher education, because most of the educators believe themselves to be well-intentioned, liberal White females (Matias, 2013; Sleeter, 2001) who claim to care for students of color (see Matias & Zembylas, 2014).

The question then is how does one teach and research the emotionalities of Whiteness in an institution that believes it is already unbiased, diverse, and inclusive?

This chapter documents the emotional struggle and survival of two college educators (one of color and one White) in their ceaseless efforts to implement and teach the university's first course on the topic of Whiteness, Problematizing Whiteness: Educating for Racial Justice. We offer our journey as both a caution and a possible roadmap for other racially just educators at PWIs. Essentially, this chapter is a *testimonio* (Huber, 2009) whereby we, the authors, share excerpts from our journal entries written throughout the course and our reflections as a way to "disrupt the apartheid of knowledge in academia, moving toward . . . racial and social justice" (p. 640). Additionally, we draw from critical race theory's methodology of counter-storytelling, which counter majoritarian stories (Solórzano & Yosso, 2002). In doing so, this chapter artistically weaves in these counterstories to illuminate its pedagogical innovations, and thus the narrative between authors will change throughout the chapter. In the end, however, our unified voice will return.

Chronology of a Whiteness Course

Cheryl first introduced the course Problematizing Whiteness: Educating for Racial Justice in 2012 as a doctoral course under the name Critical Whiteness Studies in Education. Although Cheryl was initially informed that the course needed 6 to 8 doctoral students to enroll in order for the course to proceed, that enrollment minimum was later raised to 12 students when that initial 6-student enrollment number was met. As a result, the course was cancelled and was reoffered in 2013 as an independent study—a course that did not count toward faculty load. By 2015, other departments, student groups, and campus organizations recognized the importance of studying race and thus asked Cheryl to resubmit the course, offering it to both undergraduates and graduate students. Because the Whiteness course was not considered a required or an elective course for any education programs, Cheryl had to attract students from outside the school of education. Working in collaboration with several departments across campus, the course was then reoffered to the entire university as a cross-listed course among 6 different departments. It was even adopted as a required course for one master's program. Consequently, enrollment increased from 7 to close to 50 students, most from outside of the school of education.

Our Story

We thought that offering a course on racial justice would be a good thing, especially for a school of education that commits to social justice. After all, don't we hold true that all humans are created as equal? Or were those just words in the wind, mere rantings from our country's forefathers' pen, meaningless in fruition? In our experiences, especially with developing this course, words like *race*, *racism*, *Whiteness*, and *racial justice* became as fashionable and as uncomfortable as skinny jeans: one which people would sport in public but detest in private. Meaning, just as the 2016 postelection results showed that despite White women's public rejection of Trump a majority of White women voted for him in private, certain persons would also publicly claim support for the course but then privately sabotage it.

For one, because there had never before been a course specifically on Whiteness on our campus, which is home to three different educational institutions (one community college and two state universities), we figured the course would benefit students from all three campuses. In fact, because the course's final project was to organize a community-wide event that promoted racially just education as a way to both learn about racial justice and enact racial justice, the course highly appealed to socially just-minded students from all three institutions. Thus, we wanted to offer the course tri-institutionally. From the onset we got much support from all three campuses. Some faculty members from all three institutions were so excited about the course that they began asking if they could sit in on the course. Despite the growing support from students, faculty, and staff, our attempt to offer the course tri-institutionally was denied. Oddly enough, there have been other courses that have been offered tri-institutionally, yet our course was not one of them.

Notwithstanding this decision, we found a way to work with the community college registration process. There were counselors and associate deans at the community college who supported the course and encouraged their students to enroll, so they registered students under a first day add-in process. Because of this, the course ended up with a unique mix of undergraduate students from both the community college and the state university. In addition, it had graduate students from the state university. The unique blend of students greatly contributed to the depth of understanding for the material.

Because this was one of the first courses on Whiteness ever offered at the university, we, as educational researchers, were interested in examining its pedagogical effectiveness (ie., what works when teaching about Whiteness?). As such, we submitted a proposal for our study in fall 2015. Yet, there were many roadblocks to our proposed study. Before we share some of them, we must first discuss the proposed study.

The proposed study was to focus on our pedagogies and student work to decipher which pedagogies were most effective for students. There were no focus groups or interviews, nor were any of the students' names to be used. In fact, it was indicated in our proposal that we would obtain student consent, de-identify all student work, and give students the option to withdraw at any point of the study. Initially, there were verbal and written statements supporting our study. However, in the end there were so many roadblocks that as of winter 2017, the study is still pending approval on claims that the topic of Whiteness is "high risk" and may potentially "traumatize or hurt the reputation" of the students. Essentially, by claiming that learning about Whiteness would "traumatize" students, which served as the rationale for a deeper medical review of our study, Whiteness was center yet again, particularly because most students who feel discomforted by learning about race are White (see Matias, 2016; Rodriguez, 2009; Tatum, 2003). And, such a maneuver inadvertently categorized Whites who may feel traumatized by learning about Whiteness as a special group in need of additional protection and consideration. Plainly, the underlying message was that Whites who study race and feel discomfort are a more "vulnerable" population and thus are in need of additional protection from the university, hence the demand for deeper review, a consideration not often afforded to White researchers who conduct research in communities of color.

Although we had many more challenges, we share the following two examples to remind those who are interested in teaching about Whiteness that they will face many more hurdles, especially during a time when conservative social media promotes public "watchlists" of academics who challenge racial norms.

Cheryl's Story

I always considered myself a passionate educator who wholeheartedly believes in racially just education. So, when the opportunity arrived for me to teach a course that centers on what I specifically research—emotionality of Whiteness—I could not pass it up. Based on society's misunderstandings of what racism is about (see Blauner, 1992), especially regarding how various racial groups define (or misdefine) *racism*, I knew understanding one's emotions within the hegemonic framework of Whiteness would also be instructive in how we respond to learning and talking about race. As an educator, this is necessary to understand, because how can educators teach about race if students, particularly White students, are too emotionally reactive to the content of race? In fact, in a field like teacher education in which the teacher candidates and professors alike are mainly White, how can an educator engage in racial justice or teach about it if the topic of Whiteness is too disconcerting to them? That's like talking about how sexism impacts women but never engaging the topic of patriarchy itself. Although some people negatively react to my work, especially when merely saying the words *Whiteness* and *emotionality*, their reaction proves the significance of my work. For why would one negatively react to something they claim they do not know much about or cannot see due to being "color-blind"?

Despite my passion to use education as a racially just tool to push society into a deeper critical consciousness of race, I too was attacked in fall 2015 when one of my published articles got into the hands of ultra-conservative bloggers. The blogs went viral and I, in return, received countless pieces of hate mail threatening my career, my life, and my family's life. I was quickly engulfed in a whirlwind of university public relations, law enforcement, and social media associated with hate groups and White supremacists. By the time I began my Whiteness course, I was concerned, to say the least. I say this not to scare away those individuals who are also interested in teaching racial justice, specifically on Whiteness. Rather, I want to remind those individuals of the real sacrifices and dangers of staying committed to racial justice during a time of emboldened racism. In fact, in my first journal entry for the course I wrote the following:

Journal Entry, January 21, 2016

Well I went into the class a bit stressed because . . . last fall's hate mail and threats against my teaching, scholarship, career, and safety were looming over [my] head. I was unsure as to how I would protect everyone.

According to campus law enforcement, the only things I could do to protect my students and myself was to preplan for an attack, especially in Colorado where (a) one is legally allowed to conceal and carry firearms on campus grounds, and (b) there is a history of mass shootings made by White perpetrators—many of whom were deemed emotionally distraught. Specifically, they recommended I share a YouTube video with my students on how to protect ourselves during a campus shooting and to predesignate a spot where the students and I could convene if such a campus shooting occurs. Such advice was offered to me after bearing witness to the slew of hate mail I received in response to the topic of Whiteness. None of it made me feel comfortable. In fact, I instructed my teacher assistant to park in the lot closest to the building, which was considerably higher priced than student parking. To financially support her, I proposed that the department pay for her parking to ensure both her and my safety to and from our night course. Additionally, the campus offered to place an armed officer near the classroom, which, in actuality, never took place. Needless to say, one of the biggest challenges to the course was the looming threat of White supremacy that we all know has a history of violence on those who challenge it.

Teaching race, racism, and Whiteness always conjures up discomfort, so to assuage that, I do the following: (a) acknowledge that such discomforting emotions will surface and explicitly lecture to the students how it will feel; (b) engage my own stories of my own privileges to better explicate how Whiteness operates, especially drawing from other systems of oppression like patriarchy, ableism, and capitalism, so that they see how each system operates similarly, albeit with specificity; and (c) use humor (see journal entry that follows). In fact, on the first day of class, I had to loosen them up, so I taught all 50 students how to dance Bachata while singing aloud words such as *racism*, *Whiteness*, and *White supremacy*, just so they would not be afraid to say such words. Such an exercise had them laughing and, more importantly, made them realize that the emotions bound up within such words are ones we all have concocted and thus must really deconstruct. This is shown in my journal reflection.

Journal Entry, February 3, 2016

I felt I needed to give that lecture [on White privilege] and I noticed that the students were sucking it all in and really engaged. I noticed them laughing, and participating when I solicited for commentaries. Perhaps, they need more then? I notice I alleviate tension with my humor and personal stories. Meaning, I can really sense the vibe of the class and notice when things get tense I take it upon myself to model my own privileges through my stories. In doing so, students can relate and realize that privilege and power are within us all, although more so for some than others.

One such story I relayed to the students to help them better understand how Whiteness and racism is beyond intentionality was a story from one of my previous students, Jane. Jane's husband moved using a wheelchair. One time, Jane and her husband parked in a disabled parking spot at a shopping center. Once parked, Jane immediately jumped out of her car and started yelling at the driver of the car parked next to her. The woman who Jane was yelling at appeared to be an innocent mother of two kids who just finished shopping. Surprised by Jane's vehement name calling, the mother quickly got into the car and drove off. Jane later described how the woman had parked over the line and by doing so, Jane's husband, (the passenger) did not have enough room to get out of the car. The point of the story was that, although seemingly innocent and with good intentions, the mother partook in a behavior that supported ableism—that is, when a person has the privilege to not even consider the experience of another who may have to struggle in response to the privileged person's actions, thoughts, and demeanor. Telling this story allowed students to better understand how racism can happen beyond intentional maliciousness, and that, whether intentional or not, it can still have negative effects on those who do not have the same privilege.

One way I teach students to be aware of their and other people's racialized emotions is through my lecture on Uncle Joe. I confirm that everyone has an Uncle Joe who will react negatively if you bring up the topic of racism. Often in this negative reaction, Uncle Joe will employ typical Whiteness rhetoric, such as "it's not an issue because I'm color-blind," "I'm Irish and overcame prejudice so why can't they," or "'they' are just complaining, 'they' want a free pass, and I shouldn't feel guilty because I never owned slaves." I ask the students why they would not want to tell Uncle Joe about taking this course or talk to him about what they learned in this class. I list their responses on the board and have them write the responses down in their notes. Often, my students respond saying they wouldn't tell Uncle Joe because he may do the following: reject or dismiss everything, demand proof, get angry, say racism is irrelevant nowadays, scream, refuse to believe, completely shut down, get belligerent, feel uncomfortable, start blaming others, find alternative explanations, and so on. I then have them read each one of their responses aloud. Then I remind them that anytime they feel uncomfortable, angry, or refuse to acknowledge points made during class discussions and online postings or when reading articles about Whiteness, they are engaging in the emotionalities of Whiteness just like Uncle Joe and, in doing so, are inhibiting their ability to learn about Whiteness. Explicitly detailing how they will feel gives them a baseline to recognize their own emotionalities and places the onus of learning on themselves instead of their emotions. That is, instead of reacting and allowing their reactions to stop their learning, they are forced to metacognitively investigate why they are reacting or feeling the way they feel when learning about Whiteness.

When teaching the course I noticed there were many students who wanted to discuss their own experiential stories of Whiteness and racism. I quickly nipped that in the bud, telling the students that until they have mastered the vocabulary that can best communicate their critical understanding of racialized experiences, they are not to begin ranting about what was or was not racist in their lives. Some students were taken aback by this, assuming the course would be open to this. This is one of the greatest challenges of teaching racial justice. If the course focuses too narrowly on personal experiences of racism and Whiteness, then the academic learning of racism and Whiteness will either not happen or will be viewed as abstract instead of relational. Or, as documented in Matias, Viesca, Garrison-Wade, Tandon, and Galindo (2014), Whites will misuse racially just vocabulary to erroneously deem themselves the "true" victims of racism. This is seen in semantic moves like "I'm the only White person in my urban classroom and the students of color are racially microaggressive to me." Therefore, I begin the course with exercises on how to deconstruct Whiteness in various social media, film, tweets, and online Facebook challenges. One example I used was reading through the social media responses to Beyonce's 2016 Super Bowl perfor- mance that paid tribute to the Black Panthers 50th anniversary. Students formed groups and were asked to select three responses and then use the texts and articles from the course to provide a rationale behind the responses. For example, one social media commenter wrote about his distaste for Beyonce's overt display of Blackness because he is German and would be considered rac- ist if he were proud of his White heritage. The students then used Thandeka's (1999) book *Learning to Be White* and chapters by critical Whiteness scholars such as George Lipsitz (2005), Karen Brodkin (2006), and David Roediger (1999) to describe how White ethnics have historically shed their ethnicity to be racially accepted as White, and how in doing so, they confuse ethnicity for raciality and feel ashamed for their loss of ethnic heritage, and thus, react negatively when others proclaim pride in their heritage.

Only when students can master concepts and vocabulary to describe the Whiteness they identify in social settings can they apply them to their own lives. Additionally, the course needs time for the students to gain trust with each other. In fact, I write in my journal entries how this strategy was beneficial.

Journal Entry, February 10, 2016

I like how into the conversation they were. Some were ready to jump on in. The fact that Lisa and I are bringing in videos, cartoons, and current events into the class makes the students come alive. I think it is always important however that we first model how to deconstruct then have them practice deconstruction of their own social text.

Journal Entry, March 16, 2016

I could sense the class was becoming more trusting of each other and that we were developing as a familia. As such, I knew it was time to open our personal stories with whiteness which I knew would have a lot of emotions.

Using this strategy was helpful because students learned how to iden- tify and deconstruct Whiteness in society using their knowledge gained in the course thus far. I did, however, offer an outlet for some students to begin sharing their personal experiences with racism and Whiteness online. Students were instructed to (a) apply the same academic reasoning regarding how Whiteness was being exerted and (b) respond with a heartfelt message to someone who has been hurt by Whiteness. This allowed for deeper trust among the students, such that in the summer after the course, they were organizing class reunions together and even developed a Facebook group pages for all students who take the course. I also lectured at length about vulnerability, how it can only be felt if it is reciprocal, and how it will initially feel discomforting but, if we stick together, it will transform into a collective strength. To illustrate this, I asked them to think about a time when they had a major conflict with a friend, partner, sibling, or parent, and how they took the opportunity to talk it out. I asked them how they felt going into the talk and during the talk. Often, students respond to this question with descriptions of how nervous they were or how the conversation got really heated. I asked the following of students who "stuck with it" and came to a point where both parties felt they had fully disclosed their discontent: How did both parties feel at the end of the talk? Many reported that they felt they had a stronger bond, as if they both went through the struggle together. After this, I reminded them that is how vulnerability transforms into a collective strength.

A little past mid-semester I conducted a round table discussion to test reciprocal vulnerability. In this discussion, I instructed that only the students of color were allowed to speak about their experiences with Whiteness. To this, one African American student began openly describing how much Whiteness has made her hate her Black skin. Another Latina described feeling inhuman and overlooked and constantly trying to be heard. Many students either cried or shouted angrily, like David did when describing what it means to be American in the film *Color of Fear* (Wah, 1994). After that session, many students reflected on how powerful it was and they showed a level of engagement that far surpassed any course I'd taught. This is shown in the following journal reflection.

Journal Entry, March 16, 2016

Last week's class session was so vital. It was emotional, raw, and, yet an explicit display of beautiful family and humanity. My thoughts here will be jumbled as I try to best capture all that has moved me from the course thus far. Anyhow, last class was definitely a turning point for the class and judging on the amount of e-mails and texts I received praising last week's class, I believe it was a success. . . . From these texts, and overcrowded office hours I knew the students were ready to bare their hearts and trusted the class and me enough to do so. So began last week's class with a lecture on how one becomes vulnerable, which is a necessary feeling one must have in order to do this kind of work. The class talked in length as I scribed their ideas on the board.

Many of my students have said that the course was life-changing for them, but needless to say, it was life-changing for me as well. In fact I wrote the following journal entry:

Journal Entry, February 18, 2016

I can finally breathe. I've been at [this university] for 6 years, hired specifically because I study race and offered to bring in the study of whiteness
to urban teacher education. Therefore, based on our contract, I moved
1,000 miles away from home, away from family, and away from any of my
friends. I do not have a single family member in this state. I did not have
a single contact in this state. In fact, I had never been to this state before I
moved here. But I gave everything up simply because, as their job call so
stated, they were ready to learn about race and whiteness so that the possibility of social justice and educational equity in urban school can manifest
more deeply. . . . So when I teach this course 6 years after I began at [this
university] I feel finally free. I feel I can teach what I am so known for and
why I moved here. These are not students who are resisting race, refusing
to talk about race, or are too emotionally unfettered or privileged to engage
the topic of race. These students are who I came and moved all this way for.
I just had to fight, let them know I was here, and never give up.

In this entry one can see how much the students in this course gave meaning to my life. Meaning, although it took years to get the course up and running and we faced many challenges in that process, in the end, it was worth the emotional investment. Within this struggle I found within me an emotional fortitude that outshined the challenges that sought to dull our hope. In his book *Power, Privilege, and Difference*, Allen Johnson (2001) described the concept of time constancy in relation to object constancy. Just like object constancy whereby a baby first learns that mommy is still behind her hands during peek-a-boo despite not seeing her face, time constancy is acknowledging there will be change despite never seeing it. I guess I did not recognize my emotional fortitude until the course was over. Nor did I realize that, in the end, reciprocal teaching was not only about the learning among my students but also the learning within me.

Lisa's Story

When Cheryl asked me if I wanted to be a teaching assistant (TA) for the new Problematizing Whiteness course, I jumped at the opportunity. As a White, female educator, I wanted to learn more about teaching courses on race, particularly on the topic of Whiteness. The journey started roughly six months before the course began as I was involved in creating the syllabus and reaching out to various departments both within and outside of the institution, when the course was originally slated as a tri-institutional course. I was also involved in discussions about security and the risk involved about teaching on the topic. Controversy was entwined with this course and it had not even started yet. As a doctoral student and emerging critical race scholar, this controversy became a vital part of my own learning. If the upcoming course was causing discomfort and disequilibrium, it was all the more necessary to push forward toward equity.

As Mezirow (1996) claimed, impactful learning often involves disequilibrium, which both the students and I experienced as members of a complex society. As an educator with 15 years of experience in my own classrooms, from middle school to higher education, I feel confident in my teaching, seeing myself as a facilitator, with a cache of activities to open up students for discovery. However, I was quite nervous about this endeavor, the new challenge of learning with Cheryl, and the students in the course, about what it means to walk the walk and talk the talk about how to decenter Whiteness in our society. I rolled up my sleeves, put my fears aside as much as I possibly could, and got to work with a leading expert in the field, who wanted me to stand alongside her.

As the TA for the course, an emerging race educator and a White woman, I noticed these three things during the semester: (a) I am hyper aware of my own Whiteness, that this is constantly checked, and shared, as the educator and facilitator in the room; (b) the idea of safe space *will* come up in a course on this topic and the way in which it is managed must be intentionally shared with students; and (c) there is a balancing act performed when engaging students on the topic of Whiteness as awareness is quite varied between students of color and students who are White. The students who enrolled chose to take the course, to talk about race, and do something about it. This vulnerability and openness among students, and us, created a space encouraging transformation that occurred both individually and as a community.

I was one of the facilitators for the course, and when it was my turn to lead, I looked out into a class of undergraduates and master's and doctoral students who were also my peers. In essence, I was working on learning some of the course content alongside the students in the class and needed to be upfront and honest about this. I had to be myself, often referring to bell hooks's readings as a place of grounding (see hooks, 2014) in my own transition, while also standing in strength for others. After one activity I led during the third week of the course, I documented the following:

Journal Entry Week 3, February 5, 2016

I started class off with an activity about white privilege moving into whiteness [using an animated cartoon comic and an audio excerpt from the O.J.
Simpson case]. With my own privileged lens, some of the pieces in the
podcast I had to listen to more than once to truly get the meaning behind it
all. I wanted to know where the students were with this part and how many
of them could identify the whiteness within the podcast.

As the facilitator during this activity, I knew there was a possibility that
students might identify deeper complexities in the activity than I originally
did. This was an activity for them to do the discovering, so I did not share
what I already found. My philosophy and practice was to facilitate, I did not
need to be the expert and this was helpful to remember as I led the activity
(Mezirow, 1996).

I met with students outside of class on occasion, as some wanted to
process the course readings and discuss the transformations they were experiencing. In one particular journal entry, I noted the following after a meeting
with a student:

Journal Entry, March 2, 2016

I was authentic with [the student], letting her know that I am learning
too, so opening up myself in this way made it easier to talk through. I tried
this in class the week before as well and this really helped me to be more
confident on the topic.

After our meeting, the student shared that she wanted to meet more
often, as processing helped her not only with the material but also with her
own awareness and personal navigation in society. Meeting with students
individually and in small groups allowed me to discuss the topics with more
confidence. It also gave students a chance to talk more personally, as there
were quite a few of the White students who wanted to process their own
stories based on what they were learning in class. Office hours and meetings
outside of class gave students an opportunity to talk through their thoughts
without detracting from class time.

The ability to articulate the topics and concepts was important in building a foundation for discussion and space among the class community. Some
students were more comfortable with this than others. A student who was
White often spoke about personal events in her life around race during class.
She was quite comfortable in the space created, although she frequently dom-
inated the discussion by taking the focus away from the topic at hand and
redirecting the focus on her. What did this do for the students of color? The

course aimed to critique/deconstruct Whiteness, yet sometimes Whiteness still had a way of dominating. How does a race educator address this? We addressed it in a large discussion in class about love. Cheryl led the discussion, opening the floor to the students of color first. This is captured in the following journal entry.

Journal Entry, March 10, 2016

A student mentioned that this may feel like a safe space for some, but as a person of color she has a distrust of whites, so this space doesn't feel safe to her. I've wondered how the students of color in the class feel about the topic, because they know and experience what is discussed, when the white students in the class are having various "epiphanies" and in turn working out their own traumas. . . .

This opened a door for students of color to speak, and for the white students who talk often to keep quiet and listen. Some of the comments that stood out to me (from students of color):

- Whiteness is a CONSTANT pressure.
- You are never enough. It's [whiteness] like a pest.
- Have to be better than [what/whom] to still be judged as less than [what/whom].
- It's a REAL fear. Just living as a person of color among whiteness means legitimately fearing for life on a daily basis, beyond microaggressions that are also felt daily. For whites it is "uncomfortable" but there is no fear of life for people of color.
- Feel less than just for being [existing].
- Grasping onto whiteness [in order to feel accepted] but hate for it to show.
- Acceptance in society is conditional.
- I want to peel my skin off, but I can't.
  I want to peel my skin off too . . . .

After this particular class discussion about love, where students of color spoke first and the White students listened, the community changed. It was this discussion, and the moment that a student of color said she did not feel like the class was a safe space, where real, palpable change happened within the students. The objectives and goals of the course about understanding the emotionalities of Whiteness were becoming more internalized by many of the students at this point. The students truly felt the *pain*, and then the *love*. This is what race education is about, and how we turn Whiteness on its own head. Students of color spoke more, there was ownership, and it decentered Whiteness.

At the end of the semester, Cheryl encouraged me to find new symbolic pedagogies that encapsulated our learning. I mean, she is the professor who, on the first day of class, noticed how discomforted students were when talking about Whiteness. Thus, she taught us how to Bachata dance in class while singing words like *Whiteness, White supremacy, racism,* and *race* just so we would realize they, too, are just words and are not too scary to say. Following her pedagogically innovative lead, I facilitated a spider web activity in lieu of a lecture. To begin the activity, we all went outside, where the class split into two groups, forming two circles. In the circle, a ball of string was tossed from student to student while they shared their discomforts throughout the course and where they were on their racial justice journey. As each student shared, they took hold of the string so that after everyone shared, a spider web was constructed in the middle of the circle. The web symbolized how the learning—complete with all its discomforts—was what was connecting each student to one another. Essentially, the spider web represented the love and support among our class community, or as we called it, our familia, and that our educational journeys were indeed connected. To unravel the web, each student shared what he or she wanted to do moving forward beyond the semester. This activity was symbolic of our inclusive community, a space where love of humanity (complete with all our discomforts and struggles) trumped the hate inside White supremacy. And, in doing so, Whiteness finally took a back seat.

Reflective Analysis

Teaching is emotional work, and at the root of urban education are social constructions of race that are used to justify violence in racism. To work through student emotions, an educator must understand their own. Through this experience, we needed the emotional fortitude to combat the "perceived threat" of teaching about Whiteness. Students who choose to study race and enroll in a class about Whiteness are ready to talk about it. Through challenges, the course became a reality, where students had a dedicated place and time to learn together, transforming one another. Administrators spoke of necessity and interest in the course, although the actions of some showed otherwise. There was a disconnect between what was assumed and perceived by the administration and what really took place in the course. If the administration had taken a moment to enter the classroom and see for themselves what was taking place, many of the challenges might have dissipated.

Surviving the journey of creating a Whiteness course amidst the hegemonic intoxication of Whiteness in the academy was only bearable because there were two of us involved in creating the course. At times, we relied on each other to heal our hearts and encourage us to forge ahead. From this experience, it is clear that doing this work alone would have been too overwhelming for either one of us. Before we started the course, we agreed to have weekly debriefing sessions, expecting that we would encounter many barriers. This became a vital component because it gave us an outlet for our own emotional work during the semester. Debriefing sessions also provided a way to learn about our teaching styles, and how we approach race education through the lens of a teacher of color and of one who is White. The debriefing sessions also offered mentorship for Lisa as an emerging race educator. Journaling allowed us to process our thoughts individually and come together to share them afterward. This practice provided deep reflection about student learning.

A group of students regularly attended office hours to engage in additional reflection outside of class. In these office hours, students had the opportunity to reflect on the readings, ask questions, and push their own understanding of race, racism, and Whiteness. These weekly meetings spilled over into the classroom, where the students who came to the office hours had more to offer in class discussions, often taking a leadership role in small group conversations. These students pulled from the readings in their comments, becoming role models for other students, evidencing their own deeper understanding of the content and reflecting this in how they conducted themselves in the classroom community. As a result, more and more students attended the office hours as the semester progressed.

Because more students started attending the office hours, we had to provide additional office hours. The students were so engaged they even started meeting outside of class to host more dialogues about what they learned. In fact, one ethnic studies student told us how she kept referencing our course in her other courses, which made other students want to sit in on a few classes.

Recommendations and Effective Classroom Practices

Based on our experiences, to replicate a course about Whiteness and race education we recommend the following:

1. Race education is a transdisciplinary topic that needs administrative support. In order to get such support, it is vital to work across various departments in an institution. Often, departments are grouped into silos in higher education institutions (Kezar, 2005). To discourage this fragmentation, a transdisciplinary course on race is one way these silos can be broken down.

2. The course needs to count toward a student's degree or program requirements as either an elective or mandatory course. Such institutional val-

idation of a course provides encouragement for enrollment, meaning, and applicability of the course campus-wide, and will better encourage enrollment across disciplines.

3. Connecting the course to a student organization that focuses on race, like Research Advocacy in Critical Education (www.facebook.com/ ResearchAdvocacyinCriticalEducation) helps boost visibility and serves as a "safe space" where graduates from the course can maintain the dialogue. In order for race education to be translated outside of the classroom walls, it is important that individuals have a community with shared ideology in order to enact racial justice. It is in these spaces where the conversations continue past the course's academic term that the real work on decentering Whiteness is done.

4. We highly encourage instructors to conduct invited lectures around campus beforehand to increase a new consciousness of race inclusive of Whiteness studies. This allows the instructor to build connections across the institution and trust among students, faculty, staff, and administration. Developing a new consciousness about race—one that does not quickly rely on Whiteness rhetoric such as color-blindness, or the presumption that racism is a thing of the past—is vital if one wants to open a course on Whiteness on campus.

We also offer these three classroom practices we found to be effective in teaching about Whiteness:

1. Focus on vocabulary and terminology and less on personal experience so students can better communicate their critical understanding of racialized experiences. Give students ample opportunities to refer to their course readings to describe their thoughts on the concepts learned. When students can master concepts and vocabulary to describe the Whiteness they identify in social settings, then they can apply them to their own lives. The use of current social media, videos, music, and so on, is a helpful tool for students to deconstruct Whiteness while applying the course readings to support their explanation of the concepts they identify.

2. In large discussions, open the floor for students of color to speak first, to decenter Whiteness. Even in a course titled Problematizing Whiteness, Whiteness can still have a way of dominating.

3. Use the course online platform as an outlet for students to share their stories if they feel the need. Setting up a discussion forum provides students a place to process and practice using the terminology and concepts with one another.

Conclusion

Educators already know that teaching is a labor of love, yet what is not fully understood is how that love is felt. Instead of romantic notions of love that superficially rest on feelings of contentment and self-gratification, the love in teaching is raw; vulnerable; and at times, rough. Teaching a class on Whiteness was exactly that labor of love because as we taught the course we, too, were experiencing the painful reality of race once again. Despite the discomfort in reliving some of our own traumas and insecurities about race, it was necessary; for, in modeling our honest vulnerabilities, a stronger, more cohesive class emerged, such that they still have class reunions. Cheryl informed all of us (the students and the TA) that we would experience great discomfort, but she urged us not to steer clear of that discomfort. In fact, she admitted that she, too, as a professor, would experience discomfort, and begged us to not leave her hanging alone. In her words, "Do not leave me hanging. If you truly want to understand race you cannot leave the table once it gets tough. Please stay with me and we will get through this together." Too often, scholars talk about teaching as care (Noddings, 2013), love (Nieto, 2003), and courage (Palmer, 2010), but rarely does the literature talk about what those feelings entail beyond a feel-good moment. Because the pursuit of racial justice is about our human existence, teaching race is not just about learning about our society; rather, it is about learning about our own hearts, and how we can better take care of each other. Simply put, when racially just teaching becomes our own heart, the class will finally beat as one.

Special Note

To the first Problematizing Whiteness course familia/pamilya, a community of learners who did the hard work of digging deep within in their commitment to a more racially just society, we love you.

References

Blauner, B. (1992). Talking past each other: Black and White languages of race. *The American Prospect, 10,* 55–64.

Brodkin, K. (2006). How Jews became White folks and what that says about race in America. *Race and racialization.* New Brunswick, NJ: Rutgers University Press.

hooks, b. (2014). *Teaching to transgress.* New York, NY: Routledge.

Huber, L. P. (2009). Disrupting apartheid of knowledge: Testimonio as methodology in Latina/o critical race research in education. *International Journal of Qualitative Studies in Education, 22*(6), 639–654.

Johnson, A. G. (2001). *Privilege, power, and difference*. Boston, MA: McGraw-Hill.

Kezar, A. (2005). Moving from I to, reorganizing for collaboration in higher education. *Change: The Magazine of Higher Learning, 37*(6), 50–57.

Lipsitz, G. (2005). The possessive investment in Whiteness. In P. S. Rothenberg (Ed.), *White privilege: Essential readings on the other side of racism, 2,* 67–90. New York, NY: Worth Publishers.

Matias, C. E. (2012). Beginning with me: Accounting for a researcher of color's counterstories in socially just qualitative design. *Journal of Critical Thought and Praxis, 1*(1), 9.

Matias, C. E. (2013). On the "flip" side: A teacher educator of color unveiling the dangerous minds of White teacher candidates. *Teacher Education Quarterly, 40*(2), 53–73.

Matias, C. E. (2016). *Feeling White: Whiteness, emotionality, and education*. Boston: Sense Publishers.

Matias, C. E., Viesca, K., Garrison-Wade, D., Tandon, M., & Galindo, R. (2014). "What is critical Whiteness doing in OUR nice field like critical race theory?" Applying CRT and CWS to understand the White imaginations of White teacher candidates. *Equity & Excellence in Education, 47*(3), 289–304. doi:10.1080/106 65684.2014.933692

Mezirow, J. (1996). Contemporary paradigms of learning. *Adult Education Quarterly, 46*(3), 158–172.

Nieto, S. (2003). *What keeps teachers going?* New York, NY: Teachers College Press.

Noddings, N. (2013). *Caring: A relational approach to ethics and moral education*. Berkeley, CA: University of California Press.

Palmer, P. J. (2010). *The courage to teach: Exploring the inner landscape of a teacher's life*. San Francisco, CA: Wiley.

Rodriguez, D. (2009). The usual suspect: Negotiating White student resistance and teacher authority in a predominantly White classroom. *Cultural Studies ↔ Critical Methodologies, 9*(4), 483–508.

Roediger, D. R. (1999). *The wages of Whiteness: Race and the making of the American working class*. New York, NY: Verso.

Sleeter, C. E. (2001). Preparing teachers for culturally diverse schools research and the overwhelming presence of Whiteness. *Journal of Teacher Education, 52*(2), 94–106.

Smith, W. A. (2014). "Foreword." In K. Fasching-Varner, K. A. Albert, R. W. Mitchell, & C. Allen (Eds.), *Racial battle fatigue in higher education: Exposing the myth of post racial America* (pp. xi–xii). Lanham, MD: Rowman & Littlefield.

Solórzano, D. G., & Yosso, T. J. (2002). Critical race methodology: Counterstorytelling as an analytical framework for education research. *Qualitative Inquiry, 8*(1), 23–44.

Stanley, C. A. (2006). Coloring the academic landscape: Faculty of color breaking the silence in predominantly White colleges and universities. *American Educational Research Journal, 43*(4), 701–736.

Tatum, B. (2003). *Why are all the Black kids sitting together in the cafeteria? New York,* NY: Basic Books.

Thandeka. (1999). *Learning to be White: Money, race, and God in America.* New York, NY: Continuum.

Wah, L. M. (Director). (1994). *The color of fear* [Motion picture]. USA: Stir-Fry Productions.

Williams, D. G., & Evans-Winters, V. (2005). The burden of teaching teachers: Memoirs of race discourse in teacher education. *The Urban Review, 37*(3), 201–219.

3

ADDRESSING INCIVILITY IN THE CLASSROOM

Effective Strategies for Faculty at the Margins

Chavella Pittman

S tudent incivility in college classrooms is more common than people may realize. In fact, it is increasing. This uncivil behavior is not aimed only at other students, as faculty are often the target of the worst class-room behavior by students. Although all types of faculty face classroom inci-vility, faculty with marginalized identities and social status are more likely to be frequent targets of student incivility.

At its most innocuous, student incivility is disruptive to the learning environment and inhibits the effectiveness of the faculty member's teach-ing. At its worst, student incivility turns the classroom into a site of frequent bullying and a toxic work environment that can eat away at the mental and physical well-being and health of faculty. Thus, it is imperative for college educators to address, rather than ignore, classroom incivility to ensure an environment in which students can learn, where their efficacy is maximized, and that is not toxic to faculty well-being.

What can be done to address classroom incivilities? There are a set of common strategies suggested by the scholarship of teaching and learning that faculty can use to address incivilities. Proposed as effective methods to deal with classroom incivility, their use has some limitations and challenges for faculty with marginalized social status. A few additional strategies, par-ticularly suited for these faculty, are suggested that can be used to attend to classroom incivilities.

In short, this information should help faculty with marginalized status understand this aspect of their classroom experiences. In particular, it should contextualize these student interactions within the scholarship of teaching and learning, providing a broader framework rather than viewing incivilities as an individual level phenomenon and thus an individual problem. This information also provides strategies noting their limitations while suggesting other potential actions for dealing with student incivilities.

Classroom Incivility

What Is It?

Classroom incivilities have been defined in various ways in the scholarship of teaching and learning (e.g., disrespect for standards of classroom behavior as posted in the syllabus; disruptive behavior that hampers the ability of instructors to teach or students to learn; Berger, 2000; Clark, 2008; Feldmann, 2001; Morrissette, 2001). At its most base level, classroom incivilities are student behaviors that inappropriately disrupt the learning environment. These can be indirect behaviors such as sleeping in class, texting, silence, eye rolling, late arrival, making excessive noise, and the like. They can also be direct behaviors like verbal outbursts, offensive language and comments, failing to respect the rights of other students to express their viewpoints, and refusing to comply with faculty direction, among other disruptive acts. More extreme examples of classroom incivility might include the verbal abuse or harassment of the instructor or students, physical confrontations, aggressive dispute of the instructor's judgment, authority, or expertise (e.g., frustration over a grade or other instructor decision).

Why Does It Occur?

Faculty incivility is one possible reason for student incivility. That is, when faculty are discourteous or rude in the classroom, it is thought that this leads students to behave in a similar manner. Although this is a possibility, most of the reasons for student incivilities are outside the control of individual faculty (Berger, 2000; Boice, 1996; Lippmann, Bulanda, & Wagenaar, 2009; Nilson & Jackson, 2004). For example, students being treated by universities as consumers is believed to lead to classroom incivility. The consumer mentality may result in students making inappropriate demands and believing they should be treated as "always right." Thus, they may become uncivil when their wants and demands are refused as they do not fit what the faculty knows is best for student learning. In addition, the relatively recent practice of faculty asking students to call them by their first name may contribute to incivility. This acceptable practice has changed the nature of the institutional climate for even those faculty who do not choose to participate, creating the illusion that students and faculty are equals—leading to corresponding student behaviors that cross the real and actual boundaries between professor and student.

Several explanations for student incivility are linked to the most recent student generations. For example, some argue that changes in parenting may have resulted in fewer precollegiate academic challenges for this generation than the prior one (Berger, 2000; Boice, 1996; Nilson & Jackson, 2004). As such, some students of this generation may behave inappropriately when the classroom environment, content, assignments, feedback, and expectations are demanding or require more than what they have had to do in the past. Research suggests the current generation does not have respect for authority (Lippmann, Bulanda, & Wagenaar, 2009; Nilson & Jackson, 2004). This can result in uncivil classroom behavior as students inappropriately challenge faculty because they believe their "opinion" has equal status with faculty "expertise." Another reason for incivility might be an increase in entitlement—"a sense that [students] deserve what they want because they want it and want it now" (Lippmann et al., 2009, p. 197). Often entitlement results in uncivil behavior when students make disruptive demands in the classroom for grades they have not earned. Finally, the distraction of modern technology has been listed as a reason why students might disruptively be on social media, make phone calls, and send texts in class when they should be otherwise engaged in learning activities.

Can I Just Ignore It? No!

Institutions should be involved in a systemic effort to encourage civil student behavior and address student incivilities. Briefly, here are a few steps institutions can take: Work to understand and acknowledge student incivility, especially that it is not an "individual faculty" problem; create a campus culture that discourages grade inflation; do not promote a "student as consumer" perspective; support and back up faculty policies about uncivil student behavior; and set expectations for civil classroom behavior at orientation.

Beyond institutional efforts, faculty may think ignoring classroom incivilities is better than drawing (more) attention to them. Unfortunately, these incidents are distracting to students and thus interfere with their ability to learn. In addition, ignoring incivilities breeds more incivility such that the classroom environment gets worse and students use that growing power to silence and intimidate faculty further. Thus, it is important for faculty to respond to incivilities to protect both the learning environment and themselves (Berger, 2000; Hirschy & Braxton, 2004; Morrisette, 2001).

Faculty Experiences With Classroom Incivility

Research and Recent Findings on Incivility

Unfortunately, incivility in the college classroom is not uncommon (Morrisette, 2001; Nilson, 2003). In fact, student classroom incivilities have increased and are continuing to increase. In recent studies, 60% to 75% of faculty and students report witnessing incivility in their classrooms (Royce, 2000). Although all types of faculty across all disciplines experience classroom incivilities, faculty with marginalized status are more likely to experience classroom incivilities than their White, male, hetero, native-English speaking faculty counterparts (Nilson & Jackson, 2004). In addition, faculty with marginalized status experience the same indirect incivilities as their mainstream peers, yet are also more frequent targets of the direct and aggressive forms of incivilities. To provide more background on what direct incivilities might look like in a college classroom, here are a few illustrations from Berger (2000):

- A student walks into class 10 minutes late and slams his backpack down on his desk.
- A student's cell phone goes off in the middle of class and the student proceeds to have a 5-minute conversation.
- After receiving his grade on his midterm exam, a student raises his hand and states belligerently, "This exam sucks and this course sucks."
- In the middle of a lecture, a student stands up and says, "We're not paying you to read to us and put us to sleep!"

In addition to these direct incivilities, research on marginalized faculty's classroom experiences reveals specific challenges to their authority, disrespect for their scholarly or teaching expertise, and threats to their personal safety and professional career (Gust, 2007; Moore, 1996; Pittman, 2010; Russ, Simonds, & Hunt, 2002). At the core of these particular incivilities is the student's belief that a faculty member is not a legitimate scholar or teacher. They may think a faculty member is teaching a political stance or has an "agenda" rather than a scholarly topic. This incivility can be worsened if the student or others complain in a campus climate where marginalized faculty's scholarship is indeed viewed as personal and "controversial" rather than protecting these faculty with the academic freedom supposedly afforded to all academics. If students believe the faculty member is not intelligent or credentialed, they may feel qualified and justified in correcting and directing the course content. Or, students might doubt marginalized faculty's ability and authority to assess their work and thus dispute a grade. These types of student incivilities might also be reflected in the following incidents:

- A student interrupts and yells "That's not true/accurate!/I don't agree!" and proceeds to aggressively argue with the faculty member about the accuracy or veracity of the course content instead of respecting their teaching skill and knowledge (challenging teaching expertise).
- While complaining loudly about an assignment grade, a student stands physically close to a faculty member and then takes a step forward even as the faculty member steps back (challenging authority/ safety threat).
- During a class discussion, a student blurts out, "We're not paying you to share your personal/political opinion!" (challenging scholarly expertise).

Faculty with marginalized status also face incivilities squarely based on their status: Women faculty may be physically intimidated by male students; faculty of color might be accused of being racist against and by White students; hetero students may state that a gay faculty member is trying to "convert" them; students might criticize the accents of faculty for whom English is a second language. It is important to highlight that faculty expect and want students to ask questions and grapple with the course material. Thus, it is the manner/tone and nature of questioning and challenging that is at issue. Thus, standards of civility expect students to ask questions in a way that is not disruptive, not threatening, and which is grounded in the disciplinary scholarship of the course material.

Classroom incivility has negative consequences for both students and faculty. Leaving it unchecked erodes the learning environment and student perceptions of a faculty member's teaching effectiveness. Although faculty may think that addressing it might bring attention to incidents that students may not otherwise notice, this is not the case. In several studies, students had higher reports of incivilities as they were more astute at noticing and identifying the problematic behaviors of their peers. Students not only notice the classroom disruptions but also want faculty to address them swiftly and firmly. When students see faculty ignore these incidents, it decreases the confidence they might have in their teaching ability and their ability to manage a classroom, teach them, and so on. In these ways, students learn less in classrooms with student incivilities.

There are consequences for faculty, too. Indeed, student incivilities are often reflected in teaching evaluations, which are worse for marginalized faculty who receive lower and more negative teaching evaluations (Lazos,

2012; Miller & Chamberlin, 2000; Pittman, 2010; Rubin, 2001; Russ et al., 2002). In addition, it is less than ideal for faculty to have prolonged exposure to such a classroom environment that might be linked to stress, burnout, disillusionment, lowered morale, the desire to leave academia, and negative physical and mental health outcomes (e.g., Castro, 2010; Schneider, 1998). Given that faculty with marginalized status spend more time on teaching activities than their mainstream peers, it is important that they have options to increase their ability to act to reduce classroom incivilities. For all of these reasons, faculty should act to address classroom incivilities.

Responding to Student Incivility: Strategies to Address Classroom Incivility

Unfortunately, yet understandably, there are faculty who ignore incidents of classroom incivility. Faculty feel as though they are not prepared to respond to the unexpected. Some are stunned into silence by the uncivil behavior. Some may believe the incidents are not serious enough to warrant time or energy. Others do not respond to classroom incivility due to fear of student backlash and retribution (e.g., teaching evaluations, complaints to administrators). Whatever the reason, to improve/preserve the learning environment, reduce faculty stress, and improve teaching evaluations, faculty should respond to student incivilities. If you feel physically threatened by a student, use your best judgment on how to get to a safer environment, then immediately call the police. For nonphysically threatening incidents of student incivility, the most commonly suggested strategies, from the scholarship of teaching and learning (Berger, 2000; McKeachie & Svinicki, 2006; Morrisette, 2001; Nilson, 2003; Nilson & Jackson, 2004), to deal with incivilities can be organized into three categories: anticipatory, indirect incivilities, and direct incivilities.

Anticipatory

One way to deal with indirect and direct classroom incivilities is to set up conditions that reduce their likelihood, prevent them, and head them off before they occur. As such, there are a few strategies that can be put into place before the course begins. One suggestion is to model civil behavior for students. The advice is for faculty to treat students with respect by not belittling them or their ideas. Another is to use a student-generated code of conduct. This can be done with an in-class activity where students choose the ground rules or guidelines for classroom behaviors and ways to address transgressions of them. Syllabus policies can communicate the expectations for students' classroom behaviors. They can also include policies for attendance, assignment submission, late or missed work, grievances, cell phone/tablet/ laptop use, and so on. These policies promote an early understanding of what students need to do to be successful in the course and should reduce common situations that can result in student incivilities. The syllabus policies are the documentable response to any actual student incivility. Faculty are also encouraged to establish authority by dressing professionally and having students refer to them using the titles "Dr." or "Professor." Finally, to reduce incivility from students, uphold teaching standards. That is, do not give in to unreasonable student demands for easy work, higher grades, less responsibility, no accountability, and so on. Doing so may result in more student incivilities as students see that their pressure successfully gets their demands met by faculty. These anticipatory strategies make expectations for classroom behavior transparent through particular faculty behaviors (i.e., model civility, establish authority), policies (i.e., student-generated code of conduct, syllabus policies), and consequences for not adhering to these behaviors (i.e., uphold teaching standards).

Indirect Incivility

For student behavior like texting, eye rolling, and other indirect incivilities, the scholarship of teaching and learning (Berger, 2000; McKeachie & Svinicki, 2006; Morrisette, 2001; Nilson, 2003; Nilson & Jackson, 2004) recommends the following strategies. Faculty can comment to the class about the uncivil behavior rather than to an individual student. For example, a faculty member could say "Please stop packing up your belongings to reduce noise level for the remaining five minutes of class," instead of calling out the one or two students who are loudly shuffling papers and loading materials into their backpacks. When a student is engaging in an indirect uncivil behavior, one suggestion is to make eye contact with the student until they stop the unwanted behavior. Another approach is to continue leading discussion, lecturing, answering a student question, and so on, but at the same time physically move toward the student's area of the classroom. For example, if a student is texting or engaging in other uncivil behavior, keep doing whatever you are doing but walk in the student's direction until he or she stops the problem behavior. The final suggestion is to stop talking until the incivility ceases. The silence highlights to the class that something is amiss and might get errant students back in line so the class can continue. These strategies for indirect incivility allow the faculty member to subtly let the student know that he or she is aware of the disruptive behavior. Each of these strategies increases the disruptive student's awareness of the faculty member's surveillance of the behavior. Usually, this apparent surveillance results in students ending the indirect uncivil behavior.

Direct Incivility

For direct incivilities (e.g., verbal outbursts), the scholarship of teaching and learning suggests the following strategies. Although direct incivilities often involve students behaving aggressively, faculty are directed to listen without being defensive. Perhaps if the student sees that his or her concerns are being heard the student will calm down. Faculty are also encouraged to be calm and not aggressive while the student is expressing the concern to keep the uncivil situation from escalating. To address a direct incivility, faculty can talk with the student outside the classroom. However, be sure to do so in a public and safe space. If you meet in your office, leave your office door open and inform a colleague about the meeting. For each of these strategies—listen, remain calm, talk with the student outside class—faculty are to address the student concern while also advising the student that the behavior is disruptive (e.g., yelling, acting hostile, being disrespectful) and thus not appropriate. Finally, faculty can firmly ask the student to stop disruptive behavior or risk disciplinary action like being asked to leave the class or being escorted out by security. For example, faculty might ask the student not to interrupt, to physically take a step back, to take a phone call outside of the classroom, not to make a personal attack, or to use a professional tone when making a comment or asking a question. These strategies for direct incivilities recommend that faculty manage their impression (i.e., listen, be calm) to shift or redirect student's aggressive behavior (i.e., talk outside of the classroom) to address the concern and end (i.e., firmly ask the student to stop) the uncivil behavior.

Caveats for Faculty With Marginalized Social Status

Each faculty member has to assess or determine which strategy might work best for each specific situation of uncivil behavior. In addition, he or she will have to determine which strategies fit with the teaching style, pedagogy, course content, disciplinary department, or institutional norms. In addition to those assessments and choices, it is important for faculty to be thoughtful about the strategies in the context of his or her marginalized status. I will expand on some of these specific considerations next.

Anticipatory

Some of the anticipatory practices assume faculty power and authority. However, we know this is not a given for faculty with a marginalized status.

For example, syllabus policies may not work to establish classroom expectations with students who do not recognize the faculty member's authority. Rather than follow these expectations, they may test them by complaining about points deducted for late work, pressuring faculty to arrange for them to take a make-up exam for an unexcused absence, texting during class, and so on. Similarly, establishing authority by dressing professionally likely will not work for these faculty. That is, putting on a suit does not give a Black or woman or gay faculty member the power that society does not afford. Finally, it may not be possible to command the attention of students who disregard faculty authority. In short, these strategies rely on the assumption that faculty have power—recognized by students—to determine how the classroom will be managed. Again, this is not about power in an absolutist way but in a way where they get to use their expertise to decide if the class will be student-centered, participatory, and so on. Faculty need recognized authority to make *any* decision about the classroom. If students do not recognize faculty authority, they will disregard faculty's choices about classroom expectations as well.

In addition, faculty should clarify with students that the generated code of conduct is *not* meant to create the illusion of "safe space" (Aroa & Clemens, 2013). It is unreasonable to set the expectation that a classroom space is safe. The faculty member cannot know the totality of each student's experiences to anticipate what might be upsetting to any one of them at any moment. To be protective about seemingly "agreed upon" upsetting topics privileges and protects some students to the disadvantage of others. Instead, the faculty member can highlight that course topics will be discussed critically and fully and make students aware of the potential discomfort of challenging ideas and the campus support services they can access if necessary. Thus, the purpose of the student code of conduct is to increase the transparency and commitment to behaviors that support the exchange of diverse ideas that lead to learning.

The remaining anticipatory strategies make assumptions about how students will perceive the behavior of faculty with marginalized status. This is problematic as research (e.g., Lazos 2012) demonstrates that students can negatively misattribute the behavior of marginalized faculty (e.g., perception about student evaluations, beliefs that faculty are trying to "convert" them to ideologies, sexual orientations, etc.). Specifically, these anticipatory strategies ask faculty to model civil behavior and uphold teaching standards. To model civil behavior, the scholarship of teaching and learning (Berger, 2000; McKeachie & Svinicki, 2006; Morrisette, 2001; Nilson, 2003; Nilson & Jackson, 2004) suggests that faculty treat students with respect and not belittle their ideas. When these faculty teach topics that do not affirm students' opinions, they may perceive them as uncivil even if they are indeed modeling civil classroom behavior. That is, students might perceive the faculty member as belittling and not respecting their ideas (e.g., claims of "no safe space") just by teaching content that challenges mainstream and "accepted" knowledge. For example, a student might believe faculty are uncivil when they engage in scholarly discussions of marginalized topics, interpreting them as—one example—racists against Whites due to their teaching about structural racism. Along the same lines, faculty who maintain academic standards in response to student incivility may be perceived by students as biased against and punishing majority (e.g., White, male, hetero, Christian) status students. Thus, these strategies, which depend on student interpretations of faculty behavior, may not work for faculty who are members of marginalized groups.

Indirect Incivilities

Many of the strategies for indirect incivilities also make use of the assumed faculty power and authority that is not guaranteed for faculty with marginalized status. For example, faculty indirectly commenting to the class about an uncivil behavior strategy is intended to be a gentle reminder to students that their behavior is being surveilled. However, students might expect an authority figure to plainly ask a specific student to stop the disruptive behavior. Students who already do not recognize the authority of marginalized faculty may interpret the use of this strategy as a passive admittance/confirmation of his or her lack of classroom power and authority. Similarly, eye contact and silence may not encourage a student to stop texting during class—"So what if you are looking or silent? Suits me."—if they do not acknowledge the authority of faculty with marginalized status. Again, these strategies only work if students acknowledge faculty authority and thus will respond to the surveillance by adjusting their behavior to be in line with classroom expectations.

The final suggestion for indirect incivility further highlights the importance of considering faculty social status regarding incivility. It suggests that faculty move toward the area where the student is engaged in the indirect incivility. A male faculty member moving into the physical space of a female student may result in her feeling like she is being sexually harassed. Doing the same to a male student might escalate the indirect incivility into a direct one if the student perceives the faculty movement as a threat. A male faculty member of color moving toward the physical space of a White student could have even more dangerous outcomes for faculty in the current racial climate. So a strategy might not reduce student incivilities due to social status; rather, it might produce unintended and undesirable consequences for both students and faculty members.

Direct Incivility

The direct incivility strategies are similarly based on factors beyond faculty's control. The first two suggestions, to listen without being defensive and to be calm without aggression, may not be effective. If faculty are teaching content with which a student does not agree, the student may interpret continuing to teach this content as faculty trying to "defend their opinion" when they are merely presenting the appropriate and relevant scholarship. Again, depending on the course material being taught, students might consider adherence to that scholarship as threatening/aggressive to their majority group (e.g., male, White, conservative).

In addition, as previously mentioned, students may incorrectly perceive the behavior of faculty with marginalized status (e.g., Lazos 2012). This means that students may think these faculty are being defensive even if they are not behaving as such. Marginalized faculty may be calm yet the student might incorrectly perceive the faculty member as agitated, due to prevalent stereotypes and implicit bias. Similar to comments in the prior section, a faculty member's social status (e.g., men of color) may result in students thinking the faculty member is being aggressive no matter what he or she is actually doing, given the problematic connection between race and perceived physical threat—in particular—in U.S. society.

The other two suggestions for direct incivilities rely on assumed faculty authority: Talk with the student outside class and firmly ask the student to stop disruptive behavior. These strategies work only if the uncivil students recognize the authority and power of the marginalized faculty member. Only then would they adjust their behavior to be in line with the faculty's classroom expectations. Otherwise, students who do not view these faculty as having authority will continue their disruptive behavior. As mentioned previously, how these strategies are perceived by students may be dependent on the faculty's specific social status and could escalate the incivility. For example, a male student might be angered that a female faculty member (who—in his eyes—has no real authority) had the audacity to reprimand or attempt to remove him from the space/voice that he feels entitled to occupy/use. Or an office room chat might be perceived as threatening or including unwanted sexual advances or as anti-Christian.

Of particular concern is the potential for escalation that might make these strategies dangerous for faculty if students do not recognize their authority, expertise, or scholarship. Indeed, this faculty group already reports threats of violence and threats to their careers because of student backlash to their assertions of authority. Faculty have to use and assert their authority to be effective teachers. However, these seemingly simple strategies for direct incivilities—based on authority—can be complicated for marginalized faculty.

Closing Thoughts About Strategies for Classroom Incivility

It is naïve to assume that broader social patterns of inequality and oppression do not enter the classroom. These societal dynamics are likely to have consequences for faculty who have marginalized status (especially if they also teach marginalized topics) regarding the occurrence of and how they address student incivilities. For example, faculty from those groups not afforded legitimacy or authority in society are less likely to have those privileges in their classroom. The scholarship of teaching and learning provides a range of strategies for faculty to deal with student incivility. However, they should be used (and their effectiveness assessed) in the context of faculty's social status.

The first issue is that although authority seems like a simple given, it is *not,* as the authority of faculty of color (and other marginalized faculty) is what is most challenged by students (Moore, 1996; Pittman, 2010; Russ et al., 2002; Stanley, 2006). Given this particular and specific issue of challenged authority, the suggested anticipatory, indirect, and direct civility strategies—syllabus policies, eye contact, requests to stop behavior—may be less effective at reducing incivilities in marginalized/faculty of color's classrooms. The second issue is that many of the strategies rely on students' ability to correctly perceive and interpret faculty behavior, because these strategies ask faculty to manage the impressions and perceptions students have about them personally—being calm, not being defensive, listening, being civil. These strategies reveal that sometimes the source of incivility is not faculty teaching behavior but student perception. Still, these suggestions are less likely to be successful for marginalized faculty given how students perceive their marginalized status.

Responding to Student Incivilities: Faculty With Marginalized Social Statuses

Unfortunately, student incivility might be viewed by colleagues or students as bad teaching or the faculty member's inability to manage the classroom properly. Thus, it is important to remind faculty that they cannot fix classroom oppression. No amount of good behavior by faculty will fix the sexism, racism, heterosexism—any form of oppression—in their classroom. Although faculty should act to address classroom incivilities, they should *not* spend an inordinate amount of time and energy doing so. In light of giving attention to power and authority, and the complexity of marginalized social status, a few additional strategies for classroom incivility are discussed next. They can be used by any faculty to address incivility but they may be especially useful for marginalized faculty whose power, authority, and correct "reading" by students in the classroom cannot be assumed. The following suggestions for addressing incivility are organized into two categories: inside the classroom and outside the classroom.

Inside the Classroom

One strategy for classroom incivilities is to use student-centered and active teaching. Faculty might use more small-group discussions, creative problem-solving exercises, simulations, and/or fewer lectures. Student-centered and active learning are good teaching practices proven to improve student learning (for a review, see Prince, 2004). They have the added feature of involving students with the course content so that they are less focused on who is delivering it. For example, if a woman faculty member is teaching about feminism, her use of active learning will help focus students on the theory, the reading, and engaging with the course material and with one another, rather than on her social status. Of course, students are aware of faculty's social status; however, their involvement in active learning may mean they may have less time and energy to focus on the marginalized status of faculty, which may reduce student incivilities.

Another suggestion is to use peer review and self-evaluation for some of the course grading. For example, peer grading can be used for low-stakes assignments, quizzes, drafts, and presentations. When executed properly, use of peer grading is a proven classroom practice where classmates give and receive solid and useful feedback (Dochy, Segers, & Sluijsmans, 1999). Similarly, faculty should have students engage in a self-evaluation of their classroom performance (e.g., regularly attended class? completed readings? visited office hours?). This process provides students with an assessment of their performance in relation to their own self-reported effort. Asking students to reflect on their own and their peers' performance shifts faculty from the center of the evaluation process. Peer reviews and self-reviews position students as efficacious evaluators of the quality, features, and content of student's academic work. Indeed research does suggest that students who conduct peer reviews view themselves as more responsible for their own learning (Dochy et al. 1999). This shift might result in increased focus on the actual course work and less student resistance and reaction to marginalized faculty's grading.

The reasons for suggesting active learning and peer/self-review classroom practices are threefold. First, they are best teaching practices. Although there is no guarantee that they will reduce classroom incivilities, a faculty member's teaching quality—despite student incivilities, complaints, and backlash sourced in their marginalized status—can be argued/supported by the use of teaching widely accepted as effective for student learning. Second, the suggested strategies are student-centered rather than faculty-centered. They allow the faculty member to use his or her authority and power to direct students' focus and efforts on the course content rather than inappropriately on his or her social status. Faculty may feel these strategies may further make them invisible or disempower them in their classrooms. While acknowledging and understanding that perspective, the suggested strategies affirm that these faculty have and use a lot of classroom power as they are the ones choosing the course material, planning the active-learning activities, giving short lectures, facilitating classroom discussions, evaluating student work, and so on. Finally, these classroom practices are suited to the current generation of learners. Given that these students prefer classroom environments that are active, collaborative, and participatory (Price, 2009), using these strategies might offset the incivilities assumed to be sourced in generational differences.

The final suggested strategy is to establish and use a disruptive behavior policy that provides students with descriptions of disruptive behavior and the levels of response for them (e.g., warning, being reported to a higher-up, dismissal from class). This policy's primary intent is to anticipate and prevent incivility by establishing classroom behavior expectations. It also provides a procedure for addressing both indirect and direct incivility. For example, the procedure might include a written notice documenting the student's disruptive behavior with a reminder of the next step/outcome for future similar behavior. The next step might be a meeting with the faculty member, the department chair, and/or the dean. Given the persistence or nature of the uncivil behavior, the policy might involve a complaint about the student to the student affairs office as a violation of the student code of conduct.

Outside the Classroom

Many faculty are uncomfortable when classroom incivility occurs. One way to reduce discomfort is to be as prepared as possible by choosing a few strategies and practicing them. For example, faculty might choose one of each type—one anticipatory (e.g., syllabus policies), one indirect (e.g., silence or peer review), and one direct (e.g., disruptive behavior policy)—and role play using each strategy with different types of student incivility. If faculty know how they will deal with disruptive behavior before it occurs, they may feel more comfortable responding if they have already picked a couple of strategies and know that is how they could respond if incivility occurs.

Faculty might also log incidents of classroom incivility as they occur. In this log, the faculty member should document everything by writing down what the student did and said and how he or she responded—either/both in the moment or as a follow-up to the incident. The faculty member should also write down the outcome of the interactions pertaining to each incivility situation. This log will help faculty identify patterns in student behavior, how that disruptive behavior was addressed and that strategy's effectiveness, and ideas about future strategies that might be used in similar situations. The log is the record that can help faculty assess their current needs, support, and institutional fit regarding teaching. Its contents can also support a faculty member's claim about a student's disruptive behavior if the faculty member has to refer the situation to another office in the institutional power structure.

Students may complain to others (department chair, dean, provost, president, etc.) about faculty who have maintained the learning environment, upheld teaching standards, or asserted that students must exhibit civil classroom behavior. In these situations, students and others are actively creating a narrative about faculty members' teaching without their lens or input. Instead, faculty should tell their own teaching stories with appropriate context. This can be done in two ways. First, share narratives of incidents of classroom incivility with colleagues. For example, a faculty member might briefly mention to a colleague in passing that "Student X was disruptive in class today when s/he was doing Y." The purpose of this interaction is to shape the conversation around student incivilities rather than around the faculty member's teaching as deficient. The second way faculty can tell their teaching stories is to provide research about classroom incivilities and marginalized faculty's experiences to their colleagues. The purpose of doing so is to place faculty's teaching experiences in the context of the research that connects student incivility to larger societal patterns regarding faculty with marginalized status. Whereas it would be ideal if collegial support or empathy results from these interactions, it is okay if that does not occur. The real goal of these strategies is faculty's active involvement in the narrative being told about their teaching and a narrative that connects their experiences to broader patterns.

Conclusion

Student incivilities are common and on the rise for a variety of reasons outside faculty control. This is especially troubling for underrepresented faculty who have frequent and acute experiences of student incivilities likely related to their marginalized status. The commonality of student incivilities means that all faculty should know how to deal with and address them. However, it is especially important for faculty with marginalized status because they experience more and the most severe forms of student incivility. If faculty do not know how to address these incidents, then the classroom is not ideal for student learning. It also means considerable time spent by marginalized faculty in a hostile classroom with all of the related potential consequences (e.g., negative mental and physical health, lower teaching evaluations, threats to job security).

To help faculty address student incivilities, the scholarship of teaching and learning commonly poses a variety of strategies. They range from anticipatory strategies like student-developed classroom expectations, subtle faculty behaviors like making eye contact with the uncivil student, to faculty explicitly asking students to stop the disruptive behavior. These suggested strategies provide a solid starting base of ideas for faculty figuring out how to address and reduce student incivilities. At the same time, however, many of these strategies' effectiveness is limited by their reliance upon assumed features of faculty's classroom experiences. That is, for faculty with marginalized status faculty authority is not a given and is indeed frequently challenged by students. In addition, faculty's marginalized status results in student errors in perception and interpretation of faculty behaviors—not only weakening the effectiveness of strategies but also potentially leading to increases or escalated student incivility.

As some of these "best practices" may not work for faculty with marginalized status, a few additional strategies are offered for dealing with student incivilities. The strategies are grounded in the scholarship of teaching and learning as effective classroom practices that enhance student learning. Specifically, these student-centered and active pedagogies might reduce incivility by concentrating student effort on the course material, which may reduce their reactivity to faculty's marginalized status as conveying that content. These strategies affirm and maintain faculty authority and expertise as faculty remain actively in control of the classroom content, the teaching activities, facilitating discussions, and assigning grades to students. Another suggestion for marginalized faculty is the use of a disruptive behavior policy. This policy specifies expectations of behavior and the levels of actions students can expect in response to transgressions of them. The levels of response begin with the faculty but should extend to institutional others because they are also responsible for maintaining a climate where students can learn classroom environment. Faculty are also encouraged to increase their comfort addressing student incivilities by practicing these strategies and keeping a log of their use and effectiveness. Finally, faculty should be actively involved in shaping the conversations about their teaching quality by discussing student disruptions in the context of the larger patterns identified in research on both incivility and faculty with marginalized status.

Colleges and universities should be proactive at creating and maintaining an environment that encourages student civility and discourages student incivility. In the context of this structural support, once faculty have affirmed that they are not engaging in incivility, they should act to address student incivility in their classroom. Given the many factors that appear to contribute to classroom incivility, it is more likely in marginalized faculty's classrooms. These faculty should be aware of the potential strategies they can use, as well as how the effectiveness of these strategies might vary based on their status. To supplement these strategies, faculty with marginalized status might be able to reduce classroom incivilities with student-centered pedagogy. Faculty who choose and practice a few strategies should feel more prepared and become more comfortable addressing student incivilities. In addition, these faculty might benefit from sharing research on student incivilities as well as documenting and sharing narratives about their own classroom experiences with student incivilities.

References

Aroa, B., & Clemens, K. (2013). From safe spaces to brave spaces: A new way to frame dialogue around diversity and social justice. In L. M. Landreman (Ed.), *The art of effective facilitation* (pp. 135–150). Sterling, VA: Stylus.

Berger, B. A. (2000). Incivility. *American Journal of Pharmaceutical Education, 64*, 445–450.

Boice, B. (1996). Classroom incivilities. *Research in Higher Education, 37*(4), 453–486.

Castro, Corrine. (2010). *In the margins of the academy: Women of color and job satisfaction.* In S. E. Moore, R. Alexander, Jr, and A. J. Lemelle, Jr. (Eds.), *Dilemmas of Black faculty at predominantly White institutions in the United States: Issues in the post-multicultural era* (pp. 135–157). Lewiston, NY: Edwin Mellen Press.

Clark, C. (2008). The dance of incivility in nursing education as described by nursing faculty and students. *Advances in Nursing Science, 31*, E37–E54.

Dochy, F., Segers, M., & Sluijsmans, D. (1999). The use of self-, peer and co-assessment: A review. *Studies in Higher Education, 24*(3), 331–350.

Feldmann, L. J. (2001). Classroom civility is another of our instructor responsibilities. *College Teaching, 49*, 137–140.

Gust, S. W. (2007). Look out for the football players and the frat boys: Autoethnographic reflections of a gay teacher in a gay curricular experience. *Educational Studies, 41*(1), 43–60.

Hirschy, A. S., & Braxton, J. M. (2004). Effects of student classroom incivilities on students. *New Directions for Teaching and Learning, 99*, 67–76.

Lazos, S. R. (2012). Are student teaching evaluations holding back women and minorities: The perils of doing gender and race in the classroom. In G. Gutiérrez y Muhs, Y. Flores Niemann, C. G. González, & A. P. Harris (Eds.), *Presumed incompetent: The intersections of race and class for women in academia* (pp. 164–185). Logan, UT: Utah State University Press.

Lippmann, S., Bulanda, R. E., & Wagenaar, T. C. (2009). Student entitlement: Issues and strategies for confronting entitlement in the classroom and beyond. *College Teaching, 57*(4), 197–203.

McKeachie, W. J., & Svinicki, M. (2006). *McKeachie's teaching tips: A guidebook for the beginning college teacher* (12th ed.). Lexington, MA: D.C. Heath.

Miller, J., & Chamberlin, M. (2000). Women are teachers, men are professors: A study of student perceptions. *Teaching Sociology, 28*(4), 283–298.

Moore, V. A. (1996). Inappropriate challenges to professional authority. *Teaching Sociology, 24*, 202–206.

Morrissette, P. J. (2001). Reducing incivility in the university/college classroom. *International Electronic Journal for Leadership in Learning, 5*, 1–12.

Nilson, L. B. (2003). *Teaching at its best: A research-based resource for college instructors.* Boston, MA: Anker Publishing Company.

Nilson, L. B., & Jackson, N. S. (2004). *Combating classroom misconduct (incivility) with bills of rights.* Paper presented at the International Consortium for Educational Development, Ottawa, Ontario, Canada, June.

Pittman, C. T. (2010). Race and gender oppression in the classroom: The experiences of women faculty of color with White male students. *Teaching Sociology, 38*(3), 183–196.

Price, C. (2009). Why don't my students think I'm groovy? *The Teaching Professor, 23*(1), 7–10.

Prince, M. (2004). Does active learning work?: A review of the research. *Journal of Engineering Education, 93*(3), 223–231.

Royce, A. P. (2000). *A survey of academic incivility at Indiana University: Preliminary report.* Bloomington, IN: Center for Survey Research, Indiana University. Retrieved from http://www.spea.iupui.edu/documents/Incivility%20at%20IU.pdf

Rubin, D. L. (2001). Help! My professor (or doctor or boss) doesn't talk English. In J. N. Martin, T. K. Nakayama, & L. A. Flores (Eds.), *Readings in cultural contexts* (pp. 127–140). Mountain View, CA: Mayfield.

Russ, T. L., Simonds, C. J., & Hunt, S. K. (2002). Coming out in the classroom . . . An occupational hazard?: The influence of sexual orientation on teacher credibility and perceived student learning. *Communication Education, 51*(3), 311–324.

Schneider, A. (1998). Insubordination and intimidation signal the end of decorum in many classrooms. *Chronicle of Higher Education, 44*, A12–A14.

Stanley, C. (2006). Coloring the academic landscape: Faculty of color breaking the silence in predominantly White colleges and universities. *American Educational Research Journal, 43*(4), 701–736.

4

WHITENESS MATTERS

Tourism, Customer Service, and the Neoliberal University

David J. Leonard and Paula Groves Price

Once described as "an idyllic place, neutral and untarnished by the ugly inequalities that mar the 'outside world'" (Stockdill & Danico, 2012, p. 1) today's colleges and universities have undergone dramatic changes over the last 75 years. With increased access to higher education, student populations have diversified to include more first-generation college students, women, and students of color. Perhaps never the idyllic place of intellectual pursuits commonly romanticized within American popular culture, today's colleges and universities mirror, and perhaps are even driven by, "ugly inequities" and ideologies of White supremacy and global capitalism. Despite the widespread rhetoric of the progressive, liberal, leftist, and postracial university (Ahmed, 2012; Giroux & Giroux, 2004; Stockdill & Danico, 2012; White & Hauck, 2000), American higher education institutions remain hostile environments for many students of color. Microaggressions in classrooms, Blackface parties (Ross, 2016), affirmative action bake sales (Lewis, 2016), backlashes against faculty who speak truth to power (Grollman, 2015; Nwanevu, 2016), and the erection of "Trump Walls" on campus (Weigel, 2016) are commonplace practices that are a part of today's university landscape.

Mainstream American universities have always been and continue to be places where the needs, desires, and fragility (DiAngelo, 2016) of Whiteness are central. This is evident in marketing approaches, where diversity is superficially imaged in viewbooks as not only about demographic numbers and inclusion but also about the range of experiences brought onto a college campus. Even food preferences and allergies are included as part of the diversity matrix. University "free speech" doctrines are often utilized to protect Whiteness while making vulnerable students more vulnerable. Hollow definitions of *diversity*, the widespread failure to address inequity on campuses across the nation, and the refusal to embrace antiracist approaches to education all speak to the centering of Whiteness in American higher education.

In this chapter, we discuss the myriad ways neoliberalism shapes university culture, further centering Whiteness at the expense of democracy, public good, equality, and diversity. We critique university tourist and customer service tactics to privilege the White gaze, and the ways conservative right-wing organizations exert increased power and influence to support White supremacy on campuses. In the Trump era, where the "alt-right" is now the mainstream power structure, it is imperative that colleges and universities revisit their missions to be institutions of democracy that serve the public through teaching and research for the public good (Giroux & Giroux, 2004; Seligsohn, 2015). We contend that faculty and higher education institutions must actively dismantle White supremacy and heteronormative patriarchy to serve the needs of an increasingly diverse student population instead of the needs of corporate interests.

A Tourist Destination: The Neoliberal University

At the same time that universities have increased access and diversified to include more communities of color, governments have systematically divested from higher education. This divestment is coupled with a marked shift in discourse where higher education is no longer understood and discussed as a public good, but rather as an individual one (Carlson, 2016). These ideological shifts can be traced to the then Republican California governor Ronald Reagan, who boasted that taxpayers should not be "subsidizing intellectual curiosity" (Selingo, 2015b). Researchers from the Georgetown University Center on Education and the Workforce note that it is no coincidence that this ideological shift and public policy change occurred precisely at the time that higher education institutions began to diversify. Leading economist and director Anthony P. Carnevale told *The Chronicle of Higher Education*, "White people my age [70] are not going to vote to educate Hispanic or Black kids. All of the great advances in education—like the Morrill Act to create land-grant colleges in 1862 and the GI Bill to educate veterans of World War II—have come when there was a strong white majority" (Carlson, 2016). Similarly, the Harvard Institute of Economic Research concluded that Americans do not vote for welfare-state funding for public goods such as education because of racial animosity (Alesina, Glaeser, & Sacerdote, 2001; Carlson, 2016). Whiteness and anti-Black racism are very much a part of the trend to cut funding for public goods such as higher education, although it is rarely acknowledged as such.

The steady reduction in state support for public higher education is a part of a larger neoliberal agenda that Lipman (2011) describes as "an ensemble of economic and social policies, forms of governance, and discourses and ideologies that promote individual self-interest, unrestricted flows of capital, deep reductions in the cost of labor, and sharp retrenchment of the sphere" (p. 6). Neoliberalism guides White supremacist global capitalism under the guise of color-blind economics. A central feature of neoliberalism is the privatization of social goods under the premise that competitive markets are more effective and efficient. In universities today, we see these ideologies and practices permeate all facets of university life. Faculty lines are increasingly replaced with adjuncts that are paid minimal wages without insurance; tenure track-positions require securing external grant funding for promotion and tenure; and the language of capitalism guides faculty expectations in what many universities call the *research enterprise*.

In this privatization context, American colleges and universities increasingly rely on funding from various customers to function (Selingo, 2015b). The market-driven university emphasizes strong partnerships with industry and corporations, donors, and foundations not only as sources of cash but also as principal partners in establishing the mission and vision of the university (Slaughter & Rhoades, 2009). As a result, the needs and ideologies of key stakeholders anchor the modern university, jeopardizing the larger public good. Henry Giroux (2013), in "Public Intellectuals Against the Neoliberal University," highlights how the focus on market and hegemonic needs shapes whose voices are heard and whose are rendered as background noise:

> In a market-driven system in which economic and political decisions are removed from social costs, the flight of critical thought and social responsibility is further accentuated by what Zygmunt Bauman calls "ethical tranquilization." One result is a form of depoliticization that works its way through the social order, removing social relations from the configurations of power that shape them, substituting what Wendy Brown calls "emotional and personal vocabularies for political ones in formulating solutions to political problems." Consequently it becomes difficult for young people too bereft of a critical education to translate private troubles into public concerns. As private interests trump the public good, public spaces are corroded, and short-term personal advantage replaces any larger notion of civic engagement and social responsibility.

The erosion of the "public" and larger notions of social responsibility within higher education has consequently shifted the expectations of the student body. Unable to provide a degree that will guarantee a career, even as tuition prices have steadily increased, universities are increasingly about "selling" an experience to its "customers," and keeping those customers happy. According to Guy Debord (1973), "Tourism, human circulation considered as consumption is fundamentally nothing more than the leisure of going to see what has become banal" (p. 168). A diploma and even the education are secondary to the fun, the experiences, and the excitement that defines college. Universities, especially at elite institutions, feel the pressure to provide students with a fun-filled experience that includes football games, parent weekends, Greek life, state-of-the-art recreation facilities, and tourist trips abroad. Institutional or ideological investment in critical learning and social transformation does not fit within this program (Selingo, 2015a, 2015b).

As with discourses that surround tourism, which reflect the politics of traveling, universities, as neoliberal corporatized spaces, are all about "transporting" students from reality into places of excitement. This emphasis on tourism contributes to a culture of faux diversity and multiculturalism. Part of what today's universities are selling is the opportunity for (White) students to learn within a space of diversity that neither threatens the status quo nor questions the power and privilege of Whiteness.

Authenticating narratives of racial progress, and the benevolence of Whiteness ("some of my best friends in college were minorities") is also part of this process. Colleges and universities sell diversity as part of the touristic experience through brochure diversity (Osei-Kofi, Torres, & Lui, 2012). In 2000, Diallo Shabazz, then a student at the University of Wisconsin, entered the admissions office where one of the admission counselors excitingly noted, "Diallo, did you see yourself in the admissions booklet? Actually, you're on the cover this year" (Prechep, 2013). Confused and unclear as to the reason for excitement, Shabbaz examined the booklet. Immediately, he knew something was wrong. There was one major issue with him gracing the cover, sitting among his peers rooting for the Badgers' football team: He had never been to a football game. His image had been photoshopped into the sea of Whiteness that was the Wisconsin student section. Without changing policy or climate, Wisconsin had become diverse, allowing the university to sell an experience otherwise unavailable.

In their examination of admission viewbooks, Osei-Kofi and colleagues (2012) argue that colleges and universities use these promotional materials to sell a particular image that emphasizes their diversity. "By appearing progressive and racially/ethnically tolerant, institutions such as these render inequity and White privilege invisible" (p. 401). Beyond reaffirming color-blindness and meritocracy, this representation of university life renders racial and ethnic differences as superficial and not impacting life's opportunities:

> Through digitized racial diversity, celebrating diversity, rather than substance, takes center stage. Bodies of color are stereotyped, objectified, and commoditized, used as possessions that can be manipulated with a couple of keystrokes and moved around a page to construct an imagined racially diverse campus community. This imagined community is where interaction has no import and the myth of self-segregation among students of color is perpetuated. (p. 395)

According to Tim Pippert, a sociologist at Augsburg College in Minnesota, "Diversity is something that's being marketed. They're trying to sell a campus climate, they're trying to sell a future. Campuses are trying to say, 'If you come here, you'll have a good time, and you'll fit in'" (as cited in Prechep, 2013). Joining several researchers, Pippert conducted a study of more than 10,000 pictures found within America's college brochures, juxtaposing those numbers with the actual diversity at these institutions. Rather than reflecting the racial demographics of their specific schools, much less the authentic experiences of students of color, schools perpetuated the illusion of diversity. The authors concluded that "the whiter the school, the more diversity depicted in the brochures, especially for certain groups." Pippert argued, "When we looked at African Americans in those schools that were predominantly White, the actual percentage in those campuses was only about 5% of the student body," he says. "They were photographed at 14.5%" (as cited in Prechep, 2013).

For colleges and universities, a picture is worth thousands of dollars. The value of presenting itself as a "modern" change agent, as progressive, and as leading to a new America is priceless. This image, and the commodification of colleges and universities as touristic destinations, as places of diversity allowing for dominant students to experience difference in an empowering and affirming way, not only contributes to a culture of brochure and superficial diversity but also shapes the racial landscape in the classroom (Ahmed, 2012; Osei-Kofi et al., 2012; Stockdill & Danico, 2012).

At the same time, these pictures aren't based in reality, but instead perpetuate a false sense of diversity and a belief that the job of a college and university ends once "diversity is achieved." This "achievement," however, does not necessarily translate into a university commitment to diversity that impacts hiring practices to increase the number of faculty of color (Matthew, 2016) or attention to campus climate. As Sara Ahmed (2012) writes, "For a commitment to do something, you must do something 'with it.'" (p. 120). If the goal is to be diverse and nothing more, rather than a starting point to do something, students of color and gay, lesbian, bisexual, transgender, and queer students will likely be seen as little more than objects, flattened pictures or notations on a chart rather than understood or heard. The humanity, the voices, and the needs of students of color and other marginalized students are pushed to the side. Stacey Patton (2015) discusses the false consciousness supported by touristic diversity:

> The irony is that many predominantly White colleges and universities appear to have the signs of progressive campus cultures with healthy race relations, especially in comparison to their 1950s predecessors. As Mary-beth Gasman has noted, most universities have all the ingredients needed to produce a post-racial promise land—diversity offices, glossy brochures and admissions materials with a sprinkling of multiracial faces, cultural centers, administrative diversity positions, and diversity programs infused throughout new student and parent orientations and student-affairs activities. The problem is that they are signs of an alleged commitment that is rarely realized, and they give the false, and dangerous, impression that race relations on campus are much better than they really are. It is no wonder that so many universities lack even the basic data on faculty diversity or a plan to address systemic racism (much less define it). HSWIs [Historically and Still White Institutions] are too busy cashing in on the commodity of their diverse bodies to actually invest in addressing the experiences of students and faculty of color on campus.

In "The Difference Between Equity and Binders Full of Anybody," Rinku Sen (2012) notes the problem is focusing exclusively on diversity, which fosters a culture of tokenism, without any efforts to foster justice and equity. "Diversity is about variety, getting bodies with different genders and colors into the room. Equity is about how those bodies get in the door and what they are able to do in their posts." The focus on satisfying White students mandates surfaced diversity; equity is antithetical to a touristic experience (Ahmed, 2012; Osei-Kofi et al., 2012; Trott, 2014). Although university culture is not mentioned, Sen's assessment is apt for critically examining the racial culture and climate of today's universities:

> After nearly 50 years of applying anti-discrimination laws, American work-places are still dominated by White men. Men of color and all women have more access to some jobs than they used to, but the ranks of decision-makers come nowhere close to reflecting our numbers in the nation as a whole. This is the root of the "tokenism" complaint that I hear constantly as I travel the country. Tokenism means that you can come to the meeting, but no one will pay any attention to what you say. It means that the work-place will open the door to you, as long as you look (to the extent possible)

and act just like the White men who are already there. It means that you'll get invited to the party, but you won't be allowed to make any requests of the DJ or help set the playlist. I've seen dozens of "diverse" workplaces in which all the people of color are in the manual jobs and all the women are doing clerical work. All work has dignity and value, but no one should be stuck in a position they've outgrown because employers segregate their workers by race and gender. Diversity is a start, a good start even, but it cannot be our end goal. The end goal has to be shared power, responsibility, and reward—in short, equity. To get to equity, we have to promote fair treatment both before and after hiring.

For colleges and universities, where power and influence rests in the hands of corporate partners, donors, and a student body that expects to be treated as customers, equity is rarely realized. Equity requires valuing the lives of students of color before and after admissions; in the classroom and in the campus commons; in the curriculum and within the faculty ranks; during the week and on the weekend. Demanding that lives of color matter, not just for brochures, not just on the diversity chart, not only in the appropriation of color, but also in every aspect of campus life, defines *equity*. Moving beyond the touristic experience, demanding justice, and realizing true diversity has been central to protest movements on campuses across the country. From #ConcernedStudent1950 to the "I too am Harvard movement," from Yale to UCLA, students are making clear that they will not be tokens, or tools as part of a White, cisgender, male touristic experience.

Often dismissed as "kids being immature," outside the reach of the university ("it was an off-campus party"), a teachable moment, or as evidence of the higher education unfettered protection of free speech and the exchange of ideas, the entrenched racism within university culture undermines the educational experience of students of color. Yet, despite all of the evidence that points to how racism produces a substandard educational and social experience (a less valuable commodity/product), we have seen little effort to address racial climate in substantive ways.

For example, in the days following the 2016 election, amid reports of increased hate crimes (Gilbert, 2016) and clear discord on America's college campuses, Washington State University (WSU) President Kirk Schulz (2016) released a statement expressing the university's commitment to "Diversity, Inclusion, and Opportunity to All." What was striking about the statement was how *diversity* and *inclusion* were defined:

Regardless of how you feel about the election results, I want to remind you that WSU embraces diversity, inclusion, and opportunity for all.

The foundation of our university is built on those principles. We do not—
and will not—tolerate expressions of hate, prejudice, or injustice.

As a university, we also respect differences of opinion about topics
ranging from music and sports to favorite foods and fashion choices. We
encourage debate and the exchange of ideas. It is a founding precept of our
country and a core WSU value as well. (Schulz, 2016)

Evading the issues of racial harassment, xenophobia, and other forms of
bigotry, the statement defined *diversity* as simply differences—whether they
are reflected in views about food, fashion, or sports teams. The statement is
not unique and harkens back to superficial understandings and implemen-
tations of diversity through food, dance, clothing, and commodity culture
(Ahmed, 2012; Au, 2014; Trott, 2014).

In recent years, there has been an increased amount of protests from
students of color and their allies regarding the rampant hostility and racial
violence that define university culture. Despite claims of postraciality, the
celebration of diversity, and the handwringing from the Right over political correctness, colleges and universities remain hostile spaces for students
of color and other marginalized and minoritized students.

Forty years of protests, from students at San Francisco State and
UC–Berkeley in the late 1960s, to those at University of Missouri, Yale,
UCLA, and countless others in post-Ferguson America have not spawned
systemic change. Although the increased power of social media has given
voice to the injustices on campus—the daily microaggressions and unbearable Whiteness of university curricula—the experiences for students of
color or White students have not been dramatically altered. The power in
a narrative of racial progress and the centering of the needs of White customers remain obstacles to true progress. We surmise that one of the great
obstacles that undermine change within higher education is the centrality
of a touristic model that perpetuates a status quo that privileges White
experiences.

The Customer Is Always Right . . . Even the Racist, Sexist, Homophobic Ones

In 2016, our university launched the Crimson Spirit Initiative as part of
its commitment to provide "parents, visitors, faculty and staff with positive
customer service interaction" (WSU, n.d.). Offering training for faculty and
staff, the program emphasizes the university's "commitment to our customers" through "giving them our full attention and anticipating their needs."
Its full-transparent embrace of the customer service model approach came

less than a year after WSU was embroiled in an all too common occurrence: a right-wing produced spectacle.

In fall 2015, a "news" report from *Campus Reform*, a conservative online publication, gained national attention, highlighting the course policies of three classes within ethnic and women's studies that defined the acceptable mores, behavior, and language to be used within the classroom. Although standard for any discipline, the *Campus Reform* article framed the issues as one of political correctness, free speech, and the "war on conservative students" (Hasson, 2015). Following outcry from right-wing circles, the university issued a statement:

> Over the weekend, we became aware that some faculty members, in the interest of fostering a constructive climate for discussion, included language in class syllabi that has been interpreted as abridging students' free speech rights. . . . Free speech and a constructive climate for learning are not incompatible. We aim to cultivate diversity of expression while protecting individual rights and safety. To this end, we are asking all faculty members to take a moment to review their course policies to ensure that students' right to freedom of expression is protected along with a safe and productive learning environment. (Bernardo, 2015)

In this statement, although the university acknowledged the importance of fostering "a constructive climate for discussion" and learning, ultimately "students' right to freedom of expression," even if it is racist, homophobic, or sexist, was supported and what clearly mattered. Still, members of the right celebrated the "SMACK DOWN [of] Professors Who Want To CENSOR Politically-Incorrect Language" (Owens, 2015).

The language of "individual rights and safety" did not include those historically marginalized, those students that the faculty sought to protect from racist, homophobic, and sexist language in the classroom. This is exactly what Giroux (2013) means when he discusses the danger of private interest—or in this case, individual rights to "free speech"—trumping the social good and negating notions of social responsibility.

Ethnic studies curriculum that centers "the faces at the bottom of the well" (Bell, 1992) and decenters Whiteness, undermines the narrative of the university as a postracial playground where Whites can simply learn about the Other. Ethnic studies, and similar fields, teach about racism and Whiteness, pushing back at the touristic process of transporting students elsewhere and demanding that students look inward at self and community. It is no wonder that these instructors faced significant public and institutional pressures.

The attacks on faculty who set guidelines in classrooms that would encourage sensitive and respectful dialogue is part of a larger resistance to learning and knowing systems of oppression (Applebaum, 2010). Similar attacks have been waged against faculty in ethnic and women's studies departments at the University of Delaware and the University of South Carolina at Columbia by the right-wing Foundation for Individual Rights in Education (FIRE). About 12 years ago, WSU also faced significant backlash following a report from FIRE on the College of Education's use of professional dispositions. According to Shawn Vestal (2005), the college used "dispositions, in which students are evaluated on their attitudes and behaviors . . . assessing a student's cooperation and willingness to offer help to those regarding respect for 'cultural norms' and diversity." The discourse reframed the issue as one of "individual rights" and "free speech," eliding the issues of pedagogy, professional standards, and best practices for teaching diverse classrooms.

In the end, the university provided "free speech" training for faculty from the state attorney general's office, and the evaluation of the professional dispositions of candidates awarded a state teaching license were changed in significant ways. Instead of requiring students "to evaluate whether a student exhibited an understanding of the complexities of race, power, gender, class, sexual orientation and privilege in American society" (Associated Press 2006, p. C2), faculty were now asked to evaluate "willingness to consider multiple perspectives on social and institutional forces that can impede or enhance students' learning" (WSU, 2006).

Whereas all of these cases are couched as "free speech" and individual rights to use offensive language or resist equity ideologies, Applebaum (2010) reminds us the real issue is not about agreement or disagreement with faculty or the political nature of these courses. She writes:

> While it is important to help all students to recognize the racial effects of practices and discourse, often the needs of systematically privileged students are tended to without consideration of the needs of marginalized students who have the right to be able to be educated in a safe environment free from overt and covert forms of discrimination. (pp. 106–107)

The right to exercise "free speech" takes precedent over the right to be educated or in the case of faculty, educate in antiracist environments. Whiteness remains protected whereas faculty of color and Jewish instructors endure racist and anti-Semitic threats from unnamed and untraceable assailants that respond to the media spectacles created by right-wing organizations. Although the Right routinely focuses on the victimization of (White) conservative students, faculty of color must endure threats and hostile university work environments, and students of color must face the realities of overt racism and microaggressions in campus life. Over and over again, the universities remind students and faculty alike that it is accountable to Whiteness—donors, media pressure, and state officials—before it supports faculty, and even students, particularly those of color.

The importance of wooing corporate dollars and donations from wealthy alumni, alongside the all-important tuition dollars has cemented a university culture that privileges the needs of not only its core customers but also those seen as central to its brand and corporate identity. Dave Schultz (n.d.) in "The Corporate University in American Society," describes this shift as follows:

> As corporatized entities, American colleges and universities are under increasing pressure to emulate other market participants and operate in ways that affect their governance and structure, as well as how they generate revenue. The result is that the new corporate university seeks to jettison many of the traditional manifestations of higher education, such as tenure, academic freedom, and shared governance, and replace them with a business model of management and more adjunct faculty who are viewed as mere employees.

The shift toward cheap and exploitable teachers has empowered universities to foreclose on faculty voices, putting decision-making power in the hands of managers whose primary responsibility rests with protecting tuition dollars (students choosing another school or dropping out is seen as "uncaptured tuition dollars"). Disempowered faculty and students who are seen as little more than free-floating dollar signs define today's university.

Today's universities are selling an experience—one that privileges the majority demographic; one that places their pleasure, joy, and values as not only a priority but also as central to the values of a modern university. The hegemony of market forces and neoliberal logic isn't the only obstacle to racial justice on campus. The increased power of the Right represents another obstacle. The customer is always right, when completing student evaluations, demanding higher grades, fighting for the right to hold Blackface parties, or calling people illegal aliens.

Fox News University

The Right has taken over universities at a structural and discursive level. They have perpetuated a culture wars narrative that White males, particularly conservatives, are under attack in America's progressive and politically correct system of higher education.

In the aftermath of the free speech movement, antiwar campus organizing, and the establishment of ethnic studies as a result of student of color activism, conservatives increasingly focused on reclaiming their rightful ownership of the university from top to bottom, from faculty to curriculum. For example, The Olin Foundation, a conservative organization, distributed $370 million to conservative think tanks, media groups, and others committed to "taking the liberal out of liberal-arts education" until its disbandment in 2005 (Mayer, 2016). William Simon, its one-time president, described its agenda in stark terms, demonstrating its impact on every aspect of university: "What we need is a counterintelligentsia. . . . [It] can be organized to challenge our ruling 'new class'—opinion makers. . . . Ideas are weapons—indeed the only weapons with which other ideas can be fought. Capitalism has no duty to subsidize its enemies." Demanding that conservatives cease their practice of "the mindless subsidizing of colleges and universities whose departments of politics, economics, and history are hostile to capitalism," he called for a new path (as cited in Mayer, 2016). Conservatives "must take pains to funnel desperately needed funds to scholars, social scientists, and writers who understand the relationship between political and economic liberty. They must be given grants, grants, and more grants in exchange for books, books, and more books" (as cited in Mayer, 2016). John J. Miller further identified their work as part of a larger movement to seize control of America's universities: "These efforts have been instrumental in challenging the campus left—or more specifically, the problem of radical activists' gaining control of America's colleges and universities" (as cited in Mayer, 2016).

More recently, the establishment of the Young America's Foundation, which in 2004 had an annual budget of more than $13 million, and the Intercollegiate Studies Institute, another prominent conservative group on campuses, highlights the focus of the Right on higher education. By 2006, "conservative groups" invested "more than $35 million into hundreds of college campuses" (Felsen, 2006).

As of the early 1990s, there were roughly 70 conservative student newspapers published at colleges and universities across the United States, and estimates today put this number much higher. The Collegiate Network provides technical support and financial backing to conservative college newspapers in an effort to "focus public awareness on the politicization of American college and university classrooms, curricula, student life and the resulting decline of educational standards" (The Collegiate Network, n.d.) The organization has more than 102 member papers, reportedly publishing over two million copies per year. These papers take up the cause of defending students who stir up controversy with their racist stunts.

Today, online publications are continuing this work in a way that not only takes advantage of social media but also allows for cross-medium work. Two online publications, *Campus Reform* and the *College Fix*, have become adept at "generating outrage by producing stories" about political correctness, liberal universities, and the assault on conservative students "that spread virally through social media" (Schmidt, 2015). With sizable budgets, a huge network of both correspondents and readers, and an established online presence, these publications are able to generate content that reaches a sizable audience in a short period of time. Within this environment, university administrators find a difficult balance to mediate these controversies. For example, following a report from *Campus Reform* on the creation of a "bias free language guide" at the University of New Hampshire, several other conservative websites, blogs, and news outlets picked up the story. With ultimate coverage from mainstream outlets, the university would experience a media backlash that would generate phone calls and letters from alumni and others in the community. In the end, Mark W. Huddleston, president of University of New Hampshire, would "disavow the guide as unrepresentative of his institution's commitment to free speech and ordered it removed" (Schmidt, 2015). This not only thwarted efforts to create an educational space that is empowering to all, to address the culture of microaggressions and racial hostility, but also furthered a narrative that imagines White heterosexual male students as under attack, as victims of a university culture that neither cares about them nor privileges their needs. The world is turned upside from reality.

At the same time, right-wing media have committed time and resources to exposing the purported "liberal biases" and "anti-American sentiments" of faculty and to protecting the rights of conservative newspapers and students against politically correct multiculturalism. Whereas these "think tanks," media groups, and "watch groups" embrace a mission of protecting the rights of students and exposing taxpayer-sponsored political correctness, at their core, these groups are about the spectacle of White victimhood. Mirroring the discourses surrounding affirmative action, feminism, and political correctness in general, the production of news from right-wing media, particularly new media websites, centers a narrative of White victimization. The examples are endless: A conservative group holds an affirmative action bake sale, builds an immigration wall, holds heterosexual pride events, or brings a hateful speaker to campus, prompting student protests demanding a response from the university administration. No matter the institutional response, right-wing groups and their media partners use these moments to point to the prejudice directed at White, conservative students.

This same scenario takes place in the aftermath of race-themed parties, hate crimes on campus, the creation of safe spaces, efforts to encourage best practices with respect to language in the classroom, and other racial incidents. For each, the conclusion is the same: White bodies, White students, White rights are under attack. Rather than confront these tactics, and expose these ideological media attacks for what they are, university officials have consistently relented, either affirming the rights of some to be racist, sexist, and hateful, or simply remaining silent. This culture of fear, of either bad publicity that invariably follows the Right's smear campaign or of reinforcing the narrative of the university as hostile to White males or conservative students, paralyzes university responses.

Where Do We Go From Here?

The widespread focus on customer service, the retention of students for the sake of capturing tuition dollars, and the importance of providing students with the best possible experience has not translated into responsiveness and accountability to the concerns of faculty and students of color. Ample research, local and national protests, and social media exposure have not prompted colleges and universities to address these "customer concerns." Clearly, not all customers are right or deserving of a response.

Most universities exhibit a systemic failure to address campus climate, to combat the daily microaggressions experienced by students of color and historically marginalized students within the classroom and campus (Solórzano, Ceja, & Yosso, 2000). According to the literature, *microaggressions* are "brief and commonplace daily verbal, behavioral, or environmental indignities, whether intentional or unintentional, that communicate hostile, derogatory, or negative racial slights and insults toward people of color" (Sue, 2010, p. 271).

According to a study by Gray, Vitak, Easton, and Ellison (2013), African American students reported fewer positive social experiences with student peers and also performed slightly lower academically than White students, suggesting that there are multiple facets, such as socialization, that make the transition to college more difficult for students of color. Similarly, Taylor (2006) found that the GPAs of African American students suffer because of racial hostility on campus (Taylor, 2006; also cited in Perry 2015). Leah Kendra Cox (2015) notes, "In unhealthy climates, students—both majority and minority—are less likely to thrive academically or socially" (as cited in Perry, 2015). In other words, microaggressions negatively affect *all* students, because they contribute to a hostile classroom and campus climate. A culture of implicit and explicit bias and microaggressions con-tributes to problems of retention, and equally impacts the health of student populations.

The literature highlights the short-term and long-term effects of implicit bias and microaggressions, noting that people of color who "encounter greater amounts of racial micro-aggressions are likely to exhibit a number of mental health issues, such as depression or negative affect . . . as well as physical health issues such as pain or fatigue. . . . Racial micro-aggressions may also be slowly killing the entire population of people of color" (Nadal, 2012). Despite the embrace of a customer-service model, it is clear that the needs of "customers of color" and the learning environment that students of color are paying for, do not warrant a strong market response from campus leaders.

Faculty, especially those in positions of power and privilege, and the uni-versity as a whole, must exercise courage in the face of racism on campus. Rather than hiding behind glossy brochures, celebratory diversity program-ming, or the hegemony of a narrative of campus liberalism, campus leaders need to actively oppose practices that reproduce everyday microaggressions and structural violence. This requires being proactive, intentional, and cog-nizant of the myriad ways Whiteness and neoliberalism operates in higher education. Although students are leading, and demanding accountability for universities to live up to their mission, faculty and administrators need to be courageous and willing to speak to power. Hate, prejudice, and structures of inequality must be challenged in faculty meetings, the classroom, faculty senates, and across campus.

Rather than hiding behind discourses of free speech, universities must work to create an inclusive environment of empowerment for all students, faculty, and staff. Just as faculty hold standards for appropriate behavior and speech in their classrooms to create the desired learning environment, univer-sities must embrace a similar approach with respect to campus life. Whereas academic freedom and the free exchange of ideas are central to the mission of higher education, speech, actions, and policies that silence, enact violence, and undermine the experiences of students of color and other marginalized students must be challenged. The "free speech card," which is increasingly used to promulgate hate, violence, and microaggressions, must not be used as an excuse to maintain systems of White supremacy and heteronormative patriarchy. We must continue to ask, whose freedom and rights are pro-tected, and at what cost?

It is imperative that universities focus on its educational mission. We are not naïve to wax nostalgically for a previous generation, especially when those previous generations are defined by racial segregation, and denied opportunities to students of color and women. Higher education has histori-cally been an instrument of American empire, slavery, and conquest. In other words, there was no "golden age of higher education." Colleges and universi-ties have always been intertwined with broader political and economic pro-jects at the expense of marginalized communities on and off campus. Yet, the increased focus on the market, and the allegiance universities show corporate interest, alongside state divestment from public education, undermines the mission of higher education.

This means the American people not only must put greater pressure on state legislatures to fund public higher education but also must invest in academic programs that enhance university culture and empower students to be racially literate once they matriculate. If universities are truly invested in diversity, they must invest in programs that are committed to producing a campus that is not only racially divers but also that is empowering to each and every student.

Although research suggests that the everyday toll of campus racism and other forms of violence results in a classroom and campus climate that inhibits students from thriving, negatively impacting student retention and gradua-tion rates, we have seen little efforts to change the culture. In the wake of the 2016 election, colleges and universities have issued statements reassert-ing their commitment to dialogue, free speech, and creating a space dedi-cated to the "exchange of ideas." Yet, given the realities of racism, xenophobia, misogyny, ableism, and homophobia, the "exchange of ideas" and "free speech" are not necessarily equal or empowering to all. These commitments come at the expense of marginalized students, once again demonstrating what is most important to American universities: Whiteness. With the increased power of the Right and the entrenched narratives of White victimhood spreading across campuses, universities and faculty must reaffirm for the larger university community that higher education is a public good. Antiracism and liberation strengthen our democracy, and equity in higher education is essential for the greater good.

Given the current political climate, and the increased divestments from higher education, alongside assaults on "political correctness" and multicul-turalism, change will invariably come from within the classroom. Faculty must have the courage to challenge White supremacy and provide more criti-cal tools for students to recognize and critique the touristic experience sold on many campuses. A focus on critically analyzing the local campus and devising student-driven solutions to support student agency is one approach. Lessons and class projects examining the recruitment brochures and advertis-ing materials on campus have tremendous potential to spotlight the discon-nect between what is being sold through a master narrative of Whiteness, and what is lived on campuses. Likewise, students can develop their own brochures offering counternarratives of their experiences. Rather than highlighting the pristine student recreation center, the modern student union, or even the purported diversity, these brochures might document the hate crimes, microaggressions, hypersegregation, and other obstacles to diversity and equity lived by various communities. Such assignments offer powerful visual representations of student voice that can instigate change and they can be used to exert pressure on campus leaders. Pedagogies of dissent that do not back down to conservative media spectacles, but instead frame these counternarratives and the racist experiences of students as a threat to democracy, liberty, and justice, must forge ahead. This work, however, cannot rest on the backs of faculty and students of color who habitually experience a hostile campus environment. What are frequently referred to as impli*cit bias* and *microaggressions*—terms that support White fragility—must be called out for what they are—tactics of White supremacy. White faculty and students cannot hide behind the cult of innocence when allies step up and engage them in more critical self-reflection in all facets of campus life. White supremacy on college campuses cannot be dismantled amidst the silence of the White majority of faculty and students. This work is not easy, as it is fighting against the grain of the power structures that permeate university infrastructure and society at large. However, if higher education institutions strive to be idyllic places of learning that value knowledge as tools of change and not just commodities for global capitalism, a greater focus on equity and the public good must return to the classroom and experienced in campus life, not just in brochures.

References

Ahmed, S. (2012). *On being included: Racism and diversity in institutional life*. Durham, NC: Duke University Press.

Alesina, A., Glaeser, E., & Sacerdote, B. (2001). *Why doesn't the U.S. have a European-style welfare state?* Harvard Institute of Economic Research. Retrieved from https://ideas.repec.org/p/fth/harver/1933.html#biblio

Applebaum, B. (2010). *Being White, being good: White complicity, White moral responsibility, and social justice pedagogy*. Lanham, MD: Lexington Books.

Associated Press (2006, February 23). WSU replaces evaluation form for education majors." *The Columbian*, p. C2.

Au, W. (2014). *Rethinking multicultural education: Teaching for racial and cultural justice* (2nd ed.). Milwaukee, WI: Rethinking Schools.

Bell, D. (1992). *Faces at the bottom of the well: The permanence of racism*. New York, NY: Basic Books.

Bernardo, D. J. (2015, August 31). *A statement from President Bernardo regarding syllabi.* Washington State University. Retrieved from: https://news.wsu.edu/2015/08/31/public-statement-from-wsu-regarding-syllabi-issue/

Carlson, S. (2016, November 27). When college was a public good. *The Chronicle of Higher Education.* Retrieved from http://www.chronicle.com/article/When-College-Was-a-Public-Good/238501

The Collegiate Network (n.d.). *History and mission.* Retrieved from https://www.collegiatenetwork.org/about

Debord, G. (1973). *Society of spectacle.* Detroit, MI: Black and Red Books.

DiAngelo. R. (2016). *What does it mean to be White? Developing White racial literacy.* New York, NY: Peter Lang.

Felsen, S. G. (2006, January 26). The new face of the campus left. *The Nation.* Retrieved from https://www.thenation.com/article/new-face-campus-left/

Gilbert, D. (2016, November 12). Students confront hate. *Vice.* Retrieved from https://news.vice.com/story/hate-crime-reports-emerge-at-schools-and-universities-in-wake-of-trumps-election

Giroux, H. (2013, October 29). Public intellectuals against the neoliberal university. *Truthout.* Retrieved from http://www.truth-out.org/opinion/item/19654-public-intellectuals-against-the-neoliberal-university

Giroux, H. A., & Giroux, S. S. (2004). *Take back higher education: Race, youth, and the crisis of democracy in the post-civil rights era.* New York, NY: Palgrave.

Gray, R., Vitak, J., Easton, E., & Ellison, N. (2013). Examining social adjustment to college in the age of social media: Factors influencing successful transitions and persistence. *Computers & Education, 67*(September), 193–207.

Grollman, E. A. (2015, May 19). Academic freedom won't protect us. *Conditionally Accepted.* Retrieved from https://conditionallyaccepted.com/2015/05/19/academic-freedom/

Hasson, P. (2015, August 29). Professors threaten bad grades for saying "illegal alien," "male," "female." *Campus Reform.* Retrieved from http://www.campusreform.org/?ID=6770

Lewis, S. (2016, October 28). UT Young Conservatives host affirmative action bake sale. *CNN.com.* Retrieved from http://www.cnn.com/2016/10/28/us/university-bake-sale-trnd/

Lipman, P. (2011). *The new political economy of urban education: Neoliberalism, race, and the right to the city.* New York, NY: Routledge.

Matthew, P. A. (Ed.). (2016). *Written/unwritten: Diversity and the hidden truths of tenure.* Chapel Hill, NC: University of North Carolina Press.

Mayer, J. (2016, February 12). How right-wing billionaires infiltrated higher education. *The Chronicle of Higher Education.* Retrieved from http://www.chronicle.com/article/How-Right-Wing-Billionaires-/235286

Nadal, K.L. (2012, July 22). Trayvon, Troy, Sean: When racial biases and microaggressions kill. *American Psychological Association.* Retrieved from http://www.apa.org/pi/oema/resources/communique/2012/07/microaggressions.aspx

Nwanevu, O. (2016, December 22). Wisconsin republicans want "problem of Whiteness" class cancelled, professor fired. *Slate*. Retrieved from http://www.slate.com/blogs/the_slatest/2016/12/22/wisconsin_republicans_want_problem_of_whiteness_class_cancelled_professor.html

Osei-Kofi, N., Torres, L. E., & Lui, J. (2012). Practices of Whiteness: Racialization in college admissions viewbooks. *Race, Ethnicity, and Education, 16*(3), 386–405.

Owens, E. (2015, September 1). Washington State U. SMACKS DOWN professors who want to CENSOR politically-incorrect language. *The Daily Caller*. Retrieved from http://dailycaller.com/2015/09/01/washington-state-u-smacks-down-professors-who-want-to-censor-politically-incorrect-language/#ixzz4IsCVEKfn

Patton, S. (2015, November 16). Black students don't matter. *Dame Magazine*. Retrieved from http://www.damemagazine.com/2015/11/16/black-students-dont-matter-01#sthash.pKw7mFMF.dpuf

Perry, A. (2015, November 11). Campus racism makes minority students likelier to drop out of college: Mizzou students had to act. *Washington Post*. Retrieved from https://www.washingtonpost.com/posteverything/wp/2015/11/11/campus-racism-makes-minority-students-likelier-to-drop-out-of-college/?utm_term=.3b5d282e568c

Prechep, D. (2013). A campus more colorful than reality: Beware that college. *National Public Radio*. Retrieved from http://www.npr.org/2013/12/29/257765543/a-campus-more-colorful-than-reality-beware-that-college-brochure

Ross, L. (2016). *Blackballed: The Black and White politics of race on America's campuses*. New York, NY: St. Martin's Press.

Schmidt, P. (2015, September 8). Higher education's Internet outrage machine. *The Chronicle of Higher Education*. Retrieved from http://www.chronicle.com/article/Higher-Educations-Internet/232879/

Schultz, D. (n.d.). The corporate university in American society. *Logos Journal*. Retrieved from http://www.logosjournal.com/issue_4.4/schultz.htm

Schulz, K. (2016, November 14). *Supporting a safe campus environment for all: Diversity, inclusion, and opportunity for all*. Washington State University. Retrieved from https://news.wsu.edu/2016/11/14/president-supporting-safe-campus/

Seligsohn, A. (2015, April 29). *An observation about the mission of higher education*. Retrieved from http://compact.org/resource-posts/an-observation-about-the-mission-of-higher-education/

Selingo, J. J. (2015a). *College (un)bound: The future of higher education and what it means for students*. Seattle, WA: Amazon Publishing.

Selingo, J. J. (2015b, February 2). What's the purpose of college: A job or an education? *Washington Post*. Retrieved from https://www.washingtonpost.com/news/grade-point/wp/2015/02/02/whats-the-purpose-of-college-a-job-or-an-education/

Sen, R. (2012, October 18). The difference between equity and binders full of anybody. *Colorlines*. Retrieved from http://www.colorlines.com/articles/difference-between-equity-and-binders-full-anybody

Slaugher, S. & Rhoades, G. (2009). *Academic capitalism and the new economy: Markets, state, and higher education*. Baltimore, MD: Johns Hopkins University Press.

Solórzano, D., Ceja, M., & Yosso, T. (2000). Critical race theory, racial microaggressions, and campus racial climate: The experiences of African American college students. *The Journal of Negro Education, 69*(1/2), 60–73.

Stockdill, B. C., & Danico, M. Y. (2012). The Ivory Tower paradox. In B. C. Stockdill & M. Y. Dancio (Eds.), *Transforming the Ivory Tower: Challenging racism, sexism, and homophobia in the academy* (pp. 1–30). Honolulu, HI: University of Hawaii Press.

Sue, D. W. (2010). *Microaggressions in everyday life: Race, gender, and sexual orientation*. New York, NY: Wiley.

Taylor. R. (2006). *Addressing the achievement gap: Findings and applications*. Charlotte, NC: Information Age Publishing.

Trott, A. (2014, December 8). Sara Ahmed on racism and institutionalized diversity. *The Trott Line*. Retrieved from https://adrieltrott.com/2014/12/08/racism-institutionalized-diversity/

Vestal, S. (2005, October 22). WSU takes hit on free speech. *Spokesman-Review*, A1.

Washington State University (n.d.). *Crimson spirit/customer service*. Washington State University. Retrieved from http://hrs.wsu.edu/resources/customer-service/

Washington State University (2006). *Professional disposition assessment*. Washington State University. Retrieved from https://education.wsu.edu/documents/2015/08/professional-dispositions-assessment.pdf

Weigel, D. (2016, October 25). On campus, Trump loses young Republicans—but gains a flock. *Washington Post*. Retrieved from https://www.washingtonpost.com/politics/on-campus-trump-loses-young-republicans--but-gains-a-flock/2016/10/25/48e874f6-970c-11e6-bc79-af1cd3d2984b_story.html?utm_term=.b3afa6aff60

White, G. W., & Hauck, F. C. (Eds.). (2000). *Campus Inc.: Corporate power in the Ivory Tower*. New York, NY: Prometheus Books.

5

BLACK LIVES, BLACK WOMEN, AND THE ACADEMY

"Doing" Equity and Inclusion Work at PWIs

Nicole Truesdell

> If Black women were free, it would mean that everyone else would have to be free since our freedom would necessitate the destruction of all systems of oppression.
>
> —Combahee River Collective

Jelani Cobb, in his March 14, 2016 article for *The New Yorker* titled "The Matter of Black Lives," stated that many have called the Black Lives Matter (BLM) movement "not your grandfather's civil rights movement" because of its nonhierarchical and decentralized leadership—much like the Occupy Movement that arose in the United States after the economic downturn of 2008. More than that, BLM is a new articulation of a long history of Black liberation movements in the United States. It draws from the herstory of Black feminism, Black intellectualism, Black radical academics, and Black activism. The movement is rooted in local, national, international, and virtual communities—emerging from a combination of online activism and on-the-ground organizing. The hashtag first appeared in 2012 on Twitter when Dr. Marcus Hunter tweeted a shout out to two colleagues' work in *Context Magazine*, and he ended the tweet with #blacklivesmatter (see Figure 5.1).

In 2013, the hashtag emerged once again as a response to the acquittal of George Zimmerman in the murder of Trayvon Martin when Alicia Garza wrote a love letter to Black people on her Facebook page and Patrisse Cullors responded with #blacklivesmatter. From there, Opal Tometti joined in, and all three Black women helped usher in a new movement online. BLM held it first national protest in August 2014 when Patrisse Cullors and Darnell Moore organized a Black Lives Matter Freedom Ride to Ferguson, Missouri, after the killing of Michael Brown. According to the Black Lives Matter website, these three Black women, two of whom are queer, began BLM as a call

Figure 5.1. The first appearance of the Black Lives Matter hashtag.

to action for Black people. BLM is distinct as an intersectional movement in which Black lives are central to discussions engaging anti-Black racism, discrimination, and policing in the United States. BLM acknowledges that it is not just young straight Black men who are the victims of state violence and social, political, and economic inequality. Instead Black women, Black queer and trans people, Black disabled people, Black undocumented people, and those with penal records are all subjected to the same systems of oppression. The movement unapologetically centers the bodies, voices, and experiences of all these Black identities so that the message of and fight for Black liberation is a truly an inclusive one. As Alicia Garza says on the BLM network website, "It is a tactic to (re)build the black liberation movement."

Many of the organizers, activists, founders, and leaders within BLM and other organizations like Black Youth Project 100, Young, Gifted and Black Coalition, and Dream Defenders are and have been Black women, women of color, Black and Brown queer and trans, and Black and Brown feminist men. These group members are leading the charge against police and state violence, economic inequality, capitalism, patriarchy, and institutional racism for Black liberation. These marginalized folks are putting their bodies and minds on the line to locally and nationally help empower their communities and thrust Black liberation issues into the national spotlight.

As a Black woman in the academy I have come to rely on the work of these Black women, Black queer, Black trans, and Black feminist scholars/intellectuals who have done, and continue to do, work around community organizing and activism for Black liberation. Their work has heavily influenced my understandings, definitions, and implementation of diversity and inclusion work within the walls of academia. I am not the only one influenced by these activists, organizers, and thinkers as marginalized students are also taking direction from and being influenced by these larger movements, with some starting their own versions at their various institutions. It is from these understandings and experiences that I argue colleges and universities have to also look to these larger movements and take direction from their leadership in order to truly "do" and embed diversity and inclusion work into their institutional spaces. This means taking seriously the concerns and experiences of marginalized groups on campuses, as many times these are the same people leading the charge for change. In this chapter, I highlight and take direction from the ways in which the work of fierce and brave Black women, Black trans and queer people, and Black feminist men have allowed me to rethink the work I do at my home institution. I also critique the ways higher education seeks to resist systemic change, and offer examples of how I have operationalized Black feminist thought and practice in the work I do as a scholar and administrator who is nontenured to advance social justice work in a way that follows the leadership of these brave organizers for justice.

Primarily White Institutions (PWIs) "Doing" Diversity and Inclusion Work

> Black women's lives don't matter in the academy either.
>
> —Tamara Lomax (2015)

In 2016, Yale University announced their diversity hiring plan, following in the steps of numerous other colleges and universities across the country that have committed to increasing their diversity and inclusion efforts on their campuses in the wake of student demands. What stood out about Yale's $50 million commitment to diversifying their professoriate was the simultaneous news of six high-profile, tenured faculty of color leaving the same institution due to the lack of support they felt they received from Yale for their work (Zhang, 2015). Williams and Clowney (2007) argue that when colleges and universities take a vested interest in diversity and/or inclusion it is usually in a reactive manner after a disruptive event or incident occurred. We saw this in 2015, when a host of students rose up and challenged institutions on their (lack of) diversity and inclusion initiatives after events happened on their campuses. So, Yale is not an exception but instead a shining example of the reactive nature of institutions trying to appear to welcome and promote diversity and inclusion within their walls.

Reactive actions from institutions tend to look like this: An incident(s) happens on campus that sparks student outrage and protests. Administrators convene and decide on some course of action, and the newest buzzwords are used to name a new initiative. The new initiative usually entails some sort of commitment to diversity. The president of the institution or another higher-up commissions a taskforce to examine the problems on campus. The taskforce then embarks on a yearlong quest to uncover evidence and then they produce a report (a report that many times mimics past reports and offers similar if not the exact same recommendations). A few new Black and Brown bodies (students, faculty, and staff) are then introduced to campus the following year and administrators bring in outside consultants to run a couple workshops that speak on implicit bias/stereotype threat/cultural competency. Once the students who protested have graduated or the overall campus climate dies down, many of these initiatives are forgotten about or siloed into an underfunded campus diversity/multiculturalism/inclusion office.

What typically does not happen is a deep interrogation of the structures that have allowed for the perpetuation of these issues to maintain themselves across decades. I ask colleges and universities: What does it mean to have a diversity and inclusion plan when the actual structures in which those plans sit are never examined, interrogated, deconstructed, or even amended? What normally occurs is that institutions just reproduce what was already there. This means many times these diversity and inclusion conversations and initiatives never interrogate institutional investment in Whiteness (Ahmed, 2012) and the desire of those institutions to maintain that Whiteness (Patel, 2015). This further isolates the marginalized bodies and voices who first initiated the protests and demands. Many times these bodies belong to Black women, Black queer, and Black trans students who lead the charge for change, put their personal and academic health at stake, and end up left behind once more.

Charles Blow wrote in a November 16, 2015 *New York Times* article titled "Race, College, And Safe Space" that

> Black bodies are a battlefield: Black folks fight to defend them as external forces fight to destroy them; Black folks dare to see the beauty in them as external forces condemn and curse them. Or worse, most insidiously, Black folk try to calibrate their bodies to avoid injury.

Within these academic spaces, the labor and calibration of Black bodies tends to be overlooked, with the labor of faculty of color in general, and in particular that of women of color, rendered "invisible" (June, 2015). Minority faculty are burdened to not only do the work necessary for tenure (or for those in adjunct positions, the work needed to keep their short-term contract positions) but also are heavily sought after by minority and other marginalized students for help, advice, mentoring, and counseling. This invisible labor includes "diversity" work that assumes all minority bodies are stand-ins and experts on these issues, regardless of training and discipline (June, 2015). Hypervisibility of faculty and staff of color on primarily White campuses means that there is an expectation to be at all events on campus, yet when we arrive we are lucky to be acknowledged in these spaces and/or not confused with other Black colleagues. These bodies, my body, stand out and therefore are burdened with even more service work than the bodies seen/treated as "normalized." Black bodies can be stuck within institutions that are committed to diversity, because Black bodies represent diversity within PWIs (Ahmed, 2012).

Often, this *cultural taxation* (Padilla, 1994, 26) is not considered or counted when one is up for tenure or promotion. Although the number of Black women entering into and graduating from college has increased over the years, their labor is still seen as less valued, or as Tamura Lomax (2015) states, "Black women's bodies and grunt work have held capitalist institutions together for a long time." The academy has a long history of relegating Black women's bodies to the margins while co-opting the work of these women for institutional gain. So again, when we talk about diversity and inclusion in terms of the hiring and retention of faculty of color, what do we really mean if the structures in place within these institutions are not called out and held accountable for upholding White supremacy in order to truly be reconfigured?

My Work as a Black Woman at a PWI

> When someone shows you who they are, believe them the first time.
>
> —Maya Angelou

I occupy two roles on my campus. I am, first, a newly minted administrator in academic affairs tasked with embedding diversity and inclusion within the division. Second, I hold an adjunct assistant professor position in anthropology. As a sociocultural anthropologist, I am trained to examine national and global issues and then understand how they operate at the local level. I do this through *ethnography*, what anthropologist Clifford Geertz (1973) defines as the intellectual effort of "thick description"—which is to describe in rich detail the context and methodology behind research conducted by an anthropologist. Ethnography directs one to seek out local ways of knowing and being that then allow an anthropologist to go back to the larger question/issues as a way to see the dynamic relationships between the national and local.

My ethnographic experience is rooted in the United Kingdom, as I work with a local Black and Minority Ethnic (BME) community organization that is committed to ensuring people in its communities are allowed full access to, and can engage in, their rights of citizenship. For me the big question is pretty simple: Can one be both British and a racial/ethnic minority? I am heavily influenced by one of the fathers of American sociology, W. E. B. Du Bois's (1903/1995) notion of double consciousness—the contentious relationship of being both American and Negro and what that means in terms of one's ability to have access to or fully enact one's rights as a citizen. Although I continue to conduct this work in the United Kingdom, my research interests of race, racism, gender, class, citizenship, nationalism, the modern nation-state, and belonging have easily transferred back to a U.S. context. I use my training as an anthropologist in my new role as a college administrator to critically examine what diversity and inclusion really means in these primarily White institution spaces.

Sara Ahmed (2012) argues, "An appointment of a diversity officer can thus represent the absence of wider support for diversity" (p. 23). This is what I faced when I was asked to take on my new administrative role in 2015. I walked into a new role with little support, even more limited institutional resources, and no real direction of what this role was supposed to really "do." On paper, my role is to embed understandings of diversity and inclusion within academic affairs. When I was offered the role I asked myself and my provost a simple question: What does that even mean? As a former director of the Ronald E. McNair Scholars Program that works with first-generation college, low-income, and domestic minority students who are focused on attending graduate school, I saw firsthand the ways in which the institution pushed aside these high-achieving students and the program in favor of majority White middle- to upper-class students. Federal money absolved the institution from committing funds to these endeavors, but at every turn, many in higher administration felt the services we offered to our students should be made open for all. This always left a sour taste in my mouth, as the dedicated staff and programming developed for students in the program was a direct result of the lack of dedicated time, effort, and resources the college could provide. In McNair we had made a space that centered marginalized students in a middle/upper class White institution and the institution wanted to co-opt that. This is an example of the ways institutions orient themselves around Whiteness and "those who are already in place" (Ahmed, 2009, p. 45).

Understanding this, I thought the best way to "do" my new job was to create a new office that was dedicated to centering marginalized students as a way to both physically create space for them and to use a different paradigm when working with students to ensure they thrived, and not just survived. I placed all existing programs on campus that work with first-generation college, low-income, and domestic minority students and those with documented disabilities under my office. The institution did not have a good track record of oversight with these programs, so I used that as evidence of why an organizational reconfiguration was needed that allowed this transfer to happen.

These programs brought with them their own external funding, allowing the institution to publically show that they were committed to diversity and inclusion without having to financially and structurally "show" they were committed to diversity and inclusion. Yet, students who are from these same demographics who are not served by these federally funded and foundation programs also needed support. With very limited financial resources we developed new initiatives and programming for students not served by these programs that allowed us to also work directly with undocumented and LGBTQ+ students. But to truly institutionalize this work, it needs to become part of what the institution is already doing (Ahmed, 2012). To really ensure our students thrive, a large portion of my role is conducting faculty development around what equity and inclusion look like in the classroom and within advising/mentoring, as a way to "embed" this work within institutional structures.

My office promotes these efforts through an approach we call an equity asset-based framework of student learning and faculty/staff development. What this means is that we see the students we serve as having assets and abilities that brought them to college. This directly challenges the deficit-based model used in the U.S. educational system that assumes students (particularly first-generation/low-income/minority/queer/trans or students with disabilities) are coming into college with a large number of deficiencies because of their cultural and socially differentiated positions and experiences. We recognize and aim to dismantle these structural barriers that prohibit the attainment of our college mission for underserved and underrepresented students. Equity asset-based approaches recognize that students have something to contribute to the college. Students' lived experiences are important and bring value to our work because their experiences, skills, and knowledge can be put to use in creating equitable engagement within the classroom and across campus. We want marginalized students to be in charge of their academic selves and understand how to navigate this space so they can claim ownership. This approach reflects the individualization of the student and not the homogenization of people based on their social identities. For faculty development we focus on their pedagogy and create space for them to rethink how they understand their disciplines, their training, and their classroom as a way to allow faculty to see how who they are and what they experienced in their own training influences their classroom and how they engage with students. This is the approach we take at our institution as we draw on the liberal arts setting of the college because teaching and advising are core components of faculty work.

For my office, this is what it means to operationalize Black feminist thought and practice. An equity asset-based framework entails reforming institutional structures and practices to position underrepresented bodies and their assets (lived experiences, skills, and mind-sets) at the center. My office recognizes, values, and centers marginalized approaches to knowledge production and dissemination. Our work disrupts understandings of what is considered "academic" by focusing on and valuing nonmajority discursive practices and ways of knowing. I unapologetically take this approach because the foundations of higher education in general, and liberal arts colleges in particular, have been to educate and train a particular body. That body tended to be upper middle class, straight, White, and male, and now one can include White females. Times have changed and so has the demographics of students who are entering into higher education. To accommodate these students and ensure that all students have access to and can fully participate in the college experience, colleges need to see all students as assets in this environment. For my office, the work of diversity and inclusion is then always seen and framed through this equity asset-based framework.

Yet, the anthropologist in me knows this is not as simple as it seems. Nationally, higher education is at a crossroad. Cuts in education, research, and training have had tremendous impacts on the ground for K–12 as well as higher education. Liberal arts education is continually under attack as the media questions the usefulness of this type of degree once students graduate. It is not accidental that this critique of the purpose of higher education is coming at a time when intellectualism overall is also under attack, because this questioning is rooted in neoliberal understanding of education. Students are rising up to protest what they are seeing as acute and structural inequalities within these spaces—especially minority and LGBTQ+ students who attend primarily White institutions. What they are protesting is the way in which these neoliberal understandings of race, racism, diversity, and inclusion shift attention away from inherent and deeply embedded structural inequalities that are rooted in an investment and maintenance of Whiteness to a superficial focus on the individual and individual action.

What Happened?

To be a Negro in this country and to be relatively conscious is to be in a rage almost all the time.

—James Baldwin (1962, p. 81)

My administrative position is new, created in May 2015 by the provost of the college. When I talk with people about this new role and who I report to, the first question that usually comes from their lips is, "What happened?"—two short words that deliver a powerful message on the place, space, and (lack of) importance of diversity, inclusion, and equity work within colleges and universities.

What happened was a group of us (Black faculty, staff, and students) came together in December 2014 after the nonindictment of officers in the Eric Garner case. We were angry, tired, upset, and grieving, and found that the space we occupied—a small primarily White liberal arts school—had chosen at that time to not fully engage at all with the national conversation around Black lives and state violence. On campus, we had Black students from Ferguson, St. Louis, Chicago, New York, and Baltimore who were going back to their homes for winter break, and there had been no outreach on campus to ensure they were okay. We had Black faculty and staff who were trying to come to grips with what was going on once again nationally and having to sit in meetings and listen while that conversation was tip-toed around. This was a missed opportunity to deeply engage with the relationship among lived experiences, social identities, police violence, and academic spaces. Instead, the college went on break and left us Black students, faculty, and staff to grieve on our own.

The group of us that came together decided to form #blacklivesmatterbeloit—it was not then or now an official chapter of the movement, but the national movement called us to action locally. Our main question was (and still is): "Do all Black lives matter in this predominantly White space?" For many of us the answer was, "not really." We took matters into our own hands and pushed that question to the forefront through organizing and action, using intellectualism and knowledge production as our weapons. We wanted to emphasize to our campus the need to do a better job of taking care of everyone—but specifically Black and Brown folks. In order to do this, we felt there had to be an open and honest conversation about institutional racism and White supremacy on campus. At the time of our organizing, none of us had tenure (and currently still do not). I was the director of the McNair Scholars Program and so my position was fully funded by federal money with an adjunct status as a faculty member in the Department of Anthropology. The other faculty member working with us was tenure-track (but not tenured) and the two additional staff members were salaried staff in marginal diversity type roles in student affairs. When we came together, we all felt the risk associated with doing this organizing work was more important than us not doing it at all, because this organizing was more important than our jobs.

We started our work during the spring semester of 2015. We wanted to raise racial consciousness on our campus and bring to the forefront discussions and action around race and racism using educational practices to show how it could be, and needed to be, done in these spaces. We coordinated an interactive panel series for the spring semester that delved into issues of activism, racism, the Black body, Whiteness, and the military state. The institution did not support us in any fashion, but we never asked the institution for its permission. Instead we embodied what a liberal arts education is about—innovative thinking, creativity, and imagination, and put that into practice. We sought funding from a human rights organization on campus that gave grants for programming along with tapping into some limited funds a few of us had access to. We used our anger, the way Audre Lorde (2007) asked us to, and channeled it into something we felt was productive for Black people on campus. It was extra labor for us all, especially myself, as I had just given birth in September 2016 and had not healed properly from childbirth. But it was the birth of that child that stirred in me the necessity to do this work on this campus.

After our first panel on social media and activism, the institutional "it" happened that led to the eventual creation of my new administrative role. That "it" was racist hate speech scrawled on a dormitory on the residential side of campus that was accompanied by other drawings of nooses and profanity that shouted clearly to many of us that, no, Black lives do not really matter in this academic space. But, we also knew the work we had started had hit a nerve, as this hate speech was a direct response to the panels and conversations we forced to the center of the campus, so we kept on organizing. Our panels created a space for our students, faculty, and staff of color to unapologetically focus and discuss issues facing Black people through an examination of anti-Black racism. That organizing gave us, the seven who founded the group, a space to breathe and do the work that would rejuvenate us as Black intellectuals in a primarily White space.

Our students voiced their dissatisfaction with the college on issues of race and racism through an organized sit-in with a list of demands at the final faculty senate in May 2015. The demands were short and to the point—students demanded more resources on campus for students of color besides TRIO programs. They wanted better protocols and procedures to deal with hate crimes and bias incidents. They wanted attention paid to the recruitment and retention of students, faculty, and staff who were people of color. And they wanted recurring diversity training for faculty and staff to promote inclusivity within the campus. These demands mimicked the national conversation as students across the country staged a number of protests, sit-ins, die-ins, and demonstrations with demands presented (Libresco, 2015).

What was/is happening at my home institution is just a local articulation of national issues—that is, what does it mean to think about diversity and inclusion efforts within institutions of higher education when nonnormative bodies (i.e., not White, heterosexual, male bodies) are not always wanted or welcomed in these spaces?

The reaction to the campus movement from the administration was the creation of two new positions that would address issues of diversity and inclusivity. The first position was a new associate dean of inclusive living and learning housed in student affairs who reports to the dean of students. The second was my position, a senior director of academic diversity and inclusiveness who sits in academic affairs and reports to the provost. Both new positions would also have a seat on the president's senior staff council to be the "voice" for these efforts in strategic priorities. With the creation of these new positions, both occupied by Black bodies, the college, for the first time in its history, had Black people at the administrative level—myself as the first Black female, and for the associate dean, the first Black male. But we do not report directly to the president, meaning the school has still maintained a majority-White senior administration while giving the appearance of diversity at the top level.

On Being an Intellectual-Organizer/Activist

Each time a scholar of color teaches, works and wakes up that, my friend, is critical activism #blacklivesmatter. Each time the stories and realities of black and brown people are centered with assets in mind by a black and brown scholar that is activism #blacklivesmatter. Each time we colored scholars teach a class and write a book with the PhD-in-hand there is activism #blacklivesmatter. This insight is perhaps why Anna Julia Cooper and W. E. B. Du Bois labored so thoroughly to snatch those PhDs. Education, like our ancestors knew, is the only asset that THEY cannot take from you even in debt.

—Dr. Marcus Hunter, Facebook Post (July 13, 2016)

In 1903 W. E. B. Du Bois asked a simple yet profound question: How does it feel to be a problem? Du Bois's words resonate even more in 2016 as we enter into a post-Trump election era, where violence by the state against Black bodies is not ending, blatant racist/xenophobic and bigoted language is touted among followers of political candidates, and higher education is being challenged in the public sphere by Black students/faculty/staff on campuses that continue to choose to ignore our experiences. We are at a juncture in time where the separation between academic intellectualism and everyday lived experiences influenced by sociopolitical events cannot be maintained. Quite frankly, there has never been a time when the two worlds did not influence and shape one another and Black scholars like W. E. B. Du Bois, Anna Cooper, Ida B. Wells, Zora Neal Hurston, Audre Lorde, and many others have shown us this in their writings and speeches.

How does it feel to be a problem? That is the question I have asked myself over and over again while in graduate school, during my postdoc, and now as an administrator and faculty member at a PWI. When Ferguson erupted in 2014, I knew the country had just tipped into a direction it could not pull back from. The organizers on the ground in Ferguson, Chicago, Baltimore, New York, and San Francisco, along with those at the University of Missouri, Oberlin, Smith, Yale, Harvard, and Beloit, were mainly Black women, Black queer people, Black trans people who put their bodies and hearts on the line for the betterment of their communities. Yet, when institutions reacted to this organizing and put into place measures to address concerns, those doing the organizing and actions were often marginalized once again as the measures did not speak, focus, or reach out to them. It is not enough to just bring in Black and Brown students to increase the numbers of domestic minorities if this shift in demographic is not also reflected in tenured and tenure-track faculty, nonhourly staff, as well as within the upper echelons of administration. That is to say, we must make Black lives present and valued within all levels of higher education.

Looking back on our actions with Black Lives Matter Beloit, what we were doing was taking direction from our Black intellectual foremothers and forefathers and channeling their words in order to actually reimagine what inclusion would, could, and should look like in such primarily White spaces. Our panels were a space that allowed for the unapologetic centering and inclusion of marginalized bodies and knowledge as we examined the ways anti-Black racism operates within society and on campus. That organizing gave us, the ones who founded the group, a space to breathe and do the work that would rejuvenate us as Black intellectuals in a primarily White space. Whereas that burden was placed once again on the back of Black folks, the work itself was also for Black folks, and for us, that was what love looked like at the moment.

In a 2015 *Cosmopolitan* article, Patrisse Cullors, with fellow BLM founders Alicia Garza and Opal Tometti, said that she calls herself an organizer and not an activist because she believes

> an organizer is the smallest unit that you build your team around. The organizer is the person who gets the press together and who builds new leaders, the person who helps to build and launch campaigns, and is the person who decides what the targets will be and how we're going to change this world. (Ohikuare 2015)

She calls this work "beautiful" and "powerful." This resonated strongly with me, as I want to focus on the intellectual-activist but reimagine it as an intellectual-organizer. BLM has forced me and my colleagues to take a hard look at our activism, organizing, and scholarship and come to the realization that they cannot and must not be divorced from one another. We had to confront the myths that we had been taught in our graduate training around acting a certain way until tenured or a more "seasoned" staff member.

Bringing in and bridging theory into practice is not an easy task. As someone who researches the intersections of race, racism, gender, class, citizenship, and belonging in the United Kingdom and the United States, I felt a need to not just write about these things, but to embed this work into my pedagogy, programming, and work on the ground. For me, this is true empowerment as a Black woman who currently works and was trained inside the walls of the academy. In the United Kingdom, I learned how to organize while working within a Black and Minority Ethnic (BME) organization, and I took that knowledge with me when I came back to the United States and started my position. I learned that to do this work, one has to focus on the needs of most marginalized voices within the community and operate from an asset-based perspective. All of us are reminded of this as we see students and young people organizing and protesting for Black lives to matter nationally, as they are demanding the same.

Yet, this is not easy. What I have seen while doing this work in my location is a reproduction of the same hegemonic structures we live in. For example, as the only woman of color as a founding member of #blacklivesmatterbeloit who works with straight Black men I am faced with having to make sure the group remembers, talks about, and truly engages with Black women, Black queer, and Black trans people issues. I am faced with having to justify to my colleagues the importance of intersectionality as a theoretical and practicing orientation that is necessary and vital when doing antiracist work. Even as I organize with other colleagues around BLM, Black women/queer/trans people are pushed to the margins in favor of the more comfortable narrative of police targeting straight Black men who are seen as threats. And the even more comfortable narrative of Black men being the main "at risk" population within education—as illustrated with the Obamas' My Brother's Keeper program. This same rhetoric perpetuates the notion that womanhood is rooted in Whiteness and for White women only and Blackness is for men (hooks, 1981).

Just because the organizers and leaders of these various organizations and movements are focused on an inclusive Black liberation agenda does not mean it is portrayed or understood that way on the national level. The fact that movements like these that are meant to push against capitalist, patriarchal, racist structures while empowering and uplifting their communities means that they do not operate organizationally or ideologically like mainstream groups. This reframing is often used as a reason to dismiss the significance and importance of the work. Even though the larger BLM network was created by three Black women (two queer), the appropriation of the movement is still framed within a hegemonic patriarchal heteronormative structure. In other words, Italian theorist Antonio Gramsci (2005) was right when he explained that even when groups organize and resist against hegemonic forces (what he calls counterhegemonic resistance), you will still reproduce some of the existing structures, for that is all you know. Or, as Audre Lorde said, "The master's tools will never dismantle the master's house (1984/2007, p. 112).

Make Lemonade

When life serves a handful of lemons, all you can do is try to make lemonade, for what better way is there to use the master's tools and repurpose them for your own needs. So, to my Black students I say this: You must continue to organize, and do not divorce your scholarship from your organizing/activist/ social justice work. They go hand in hand, and what better way to use your voice than through the platform of your scholarship. Again, we are seeing the academy is not immune from social critique of inequity and injustice, so lead the way. These deeply inform one another and are interconnected and feed each other. We are seeing the power of students' collective voices throughout the country. Organizing means doing your research, reading the work of those who have been there before, seeing what is missing, coming together in a collective, being cooperative, engaging with others, and pushing against the Eurocentric notions and ideas of individuality, agency, and self-promotion because that is the antagonist to collective activism. And work always from an asset-based model, because your lived experiences matter and those are assets that got you to where you are today, and those assets will continue to transform tomorrow.

To faculty: Citations matter. Right now, there is a movement for scholarly and intellectual reparations to make visible the knowledges of marginalized voices/thought/bodies. This is illustrated by Aldon Morris's (2015) book *The Scholar Denied* about the intellectual theft and lack of recognition of the work of Du Bois and his influence within and outside the discipline of sociology. This case is not unique to Du Bois or to the discipline of sociology. So, I ask you to truly think about your pedagogical foundations and challenge yourself to examine and critique the origin myths of your discipline. Who is on your syllabus? What types of knowledge production do you privilege? Do you draw connections between the texts and what is going on at a national and/or local level?

At my home institution, we are starting to conduct this interrogation. I am leading a pedagogy series with two faculty members (who are tenured) and a postdoctoral fellow where, through guided readings and prompts, we are asking participants to critically think about how they were trained and what types of knowledges were/are privileged within their classrooms and disciplines. The topics we cover are not easy. We start with a general conversation on pedagogy and intersectionality and move into disciplinary histories and genealogies as ways to understand privilege and individualism. For the second half of the semester, we move away from the theoretical to how these issues locate themselves on campus with an interrogation of White fragility, White rage, and institutional racism. Many in the group are pushed past their comfort zones, but no one said this work is, or should be, easy and comfortable. But if faculty are committed to diversity and inclusion, then to make any of these initiatives stick, you also have to be committed to equity. This means being committed to examining structural barriers, and one way to do this is through pedagogical work.

To administrators: Recognize and engage in the conflict that this work brings. Do not shy away from it or think that this work can just happen with a little discomfort—lean into discomfort because this is what many of us as Black academics and administrators have to do on a daily basis. Diversity work is not the work of students, as students come and go in four-year cycles. Instead, an institution must commit itself to interrogate the structures that have prohibited nonmajority bodies from being there in the first place. Deep structural interrogation work will help in the recruitment and retention of faculty, staff, and students of color.

Ask yourselves, who is at the table when these decisions are being made? Who is at the table when priorities and resources allocation are being set? And even if a diversity of people are at the table, is the table set up in an equitable way? Not an equal way, but an equitable way. This is important so that one can begin to decenter whiteness as ones orientating lens. Once this is understood, then one can begin to see the ways institutional spaces were never made for marginalized bodies and start to think of creative ways to make space for students (and faculty/staff) who sit at the margins. Are certain voices and perspectives that can give insight and guidance needed for these changes privileged, or are the voices the same and so conversations are somewhat easy? If the conversations are easy, then you are not doing the work of equity and inclusion.

But really, the question that must be asked is, can this work really be done within the halls and walls of academic institutions? I say, maybe. Some call this work *decolonization*, others *revolutionary action*. One of my professors termed it *subverting the dominant paradigm*. I adhere to all of these terms and would argue, as Robin Kelley does in his 2015 *Boston Review* article "Black Study, Black Struggle," for a liberated university environment that decenters the conversation and action around diversity and inclusion from reproduction of the same structures. In this regard, a liberated university environment is truly focused on and committed to structural upheaval and change. In other words, I ask institutions of higher learning: Do you want to put a Band-Aid on your diversity problems or do you want to cut open the belly of the beast and pull out the tumor so when you close up the hole it is fresh and ripe for a healthier future?

Now is the time for those who occupy positions of power to truly understand and do their work in anti-Black racism if we are ever going to have Black lives matter in the academy. For me, and colleagues like me, our work is different from the majority. As a Black woman working in the academy, I feel my first job is to teach my students radical Black self-love, along with practicing it everyday, as a way to resist the dominant narrative of anti-Blackness in this country. Radical unapologetic Black love is in itself a site and act of revolution. I created my office out of love as a space and resource within the halls of the academy to focus on Black lives through intellectual interrogation and work. This means uncovering the works of Indigenous, queer, trans, disabled people of color and using their words and our lived experiences to work together on the larger goal of Black liberation in a space that was never made for us. In doing this work, I pay homage to the Black women who have influenced me in my organizing, activism, and intellectual work. Without their support, guidance, and mentorship, I could not be where I am today. It is through such truth speak, open sharing, and committed and unapologetic action that we truly can work toward a liberatory space.

Take Homes: Creating Liberatory Spaces In Your Location

There is no one-size-fits-all approach to creating liberatory spaces within an institution. Yet, here are some recommendations of places to start for those interested in this work.

- Citations matter. Think about who you use, not only in the classes you teach but also in the work you publish. Using the work of scholars who sit at the margins is important in order to disrupt underlying assumptions in the classroom and within peer review publications of who produces knowledge. Liberatory spaces should foster the centering of marginalized voices and thought, and citational practices are one way to enact this practice. This does not mean creating a "scholars of color" week, but rather, weaving the voices at the margins into the overall structure of the class.

- Critically engage and critique the cannon. Each disciple has origin myths and "founding fathers" that many of us are taught to reproduce once we step into the classroom. Yet, disciplines are not neutral entities devoid of embedded oppression. Instead, disciplinary canons are ripe locations to walk students through concepts like *Whiteness, masculinity, objectivity, sexuality, power,* and *privilege.* The canon should be used as a pedagogical tool that allows students to see the ways lived experiences and who you are influence and shape the types of questions asked and methods used in research. This then means if your canon is majority White and/or male you can use it to teach Whiteness and/or patriarchy and their influence within knowledge production.

- Do self-reflection. Liberation begins with the self. Disciplines are meant to discipline us into performing in a particular way. By this I mean disciplines have a "common sense" that teaches us how to see and analyze through a specific lens that may or may not align with your own lived experiences of the world, or what Gramsci (2005) calls our "good sense" (p. 323). Ask yourself why you went into your discipline. What has that relationship looked like since you were in undergraduate and then graduate training? What are you reproducing that you did and did not like when undergoing your own training? If you are afraid of making changes or pushing back against this training, where is your fear/resistance coming from?

- Why stay? Finally, why do you stay? During a women of color empowerment development session I was attending at a national conference, the conversation kept centering around the trauma that many of the women in the room experience at their home institutions. This focus kept moving us away from the goals of the day (leadership development) and kept us in a space of pain. Finally, one of the members of the group asked us all to ask ourselves the pedagogical question, why do you stay? This one simple question shifted the room and forced everyone to take a step back and assess what was keeping us in spaces we already knew were not made for us. Although answers varied, the question itself was a pivotal one to redirect us all to do some self-reflection on why we continue to teach and/or do research on difficult subjects that wear on our bodies, minds, and souls. By honestly answering this question, we can begin to see new ways of knowing and being within the academy.

References

Ahmed, S (2009). Embodying diversity: Problems and paradoxes for Black feminists. *Race Ethnicity and Education, 12*(1), 41–52.

Ahmed, S. (2012). *On being included: Racism and diversity in institutional life.* Durham, NC: Duke University Press.

Baldwin, J. (1962, March). The Negro's role in American culture. *Negro Digest, 11*(5), 80–98.

Blow, C. (2015, November 2015). Race, college, and safe space. *The New York Times.* Retrieved from https://www.nytimes.com/2015/11/16/opinion/race-college-and-safe-space.html

Cobb, J. (2016, June 20). The matter of Black lives. *The New Yorker.* Retrieved from https://www.newyorker.com/magazine/2016/03/14/where-is-black-lives-matter-headed

Coffer, J., Beyoncé, Williams, C., Mcintosh, D., Lamar, K., Tirado, F., Lomax, A., & Lomax, Sr., J. (2016). Freedom [Recorded by Beyoncé]. On Lemonade [MP3 file]. New York, NY: Parkwood Entertainment & Columbia Records.

Combahee River Collective (1995). A Black feminist statement. In B. Guy-Sheftall (Ed.), *Words of fire: An anthology of African-American feminist thought* (pp. 235–239). New York, NY: The New Press.

Du Bois, W. E. B. (1903/1995). *The souls of Black folks. 100th anniversary edition.* New York, NY.

Geertz, C. (1973). *The interpretation of culture.* New York, NY: Basic Books.

Gramsci, A. (2005). *Selections from the prison notebook.* Washington, DC: Library of Congress.

hooks, b. (1981). *Ain't I a woman: Black women and feminism.* Boston, MA: South End Press.

Hunter, M. [Marcus]. (2016, July 13). Each time a scholar of color teaches, works and wakes up that, my friend, is critical activism #blacklivesmatter. Each time the stories and realities of black and brown people are centered with assets in mind by a black and brown [Facebook status update]. Retrieved from https://www.facebook.com/profile.php?id=2420421

June, A. W. (2015, November 8). The invisible labor of minority professors. *The Chronicle of Higher Education.* Retrieved from http://www.chronicle.com/article/The-Invisible-Labor-of/234098.

Kelly, R. (2015, March 7). Black study, Black struggle. *Boston Review.* Retrieved from http://bostonreview.net/forum/robin-d-g-kelley-black-study-black-struggle

Libresco, L. (2015, December 3). Here are the demands from students protesting racism at 51 colleges. *FiveThirtyEight.* Retrieved from https://fivethirtyeight.com/features/here-are-the-demands-from-students-protesting-racism-at-51-colleges/

Lomax, T. (2015, May 18). Black women's lives don't matter in academia either, or why I quit academic space that don't value Black women's life and labor. *The Feminist Wire*. Retrieved from http://www.thefeministwire.com/2015/05/black-womens-lives-dont-matter-in-academia-either-or-why-i-quit-academic-spaces-that-dont-value-black-womens-life/

Lorde, A. (2007). *Sister outsider: Essays and speeches*. Trumansburg, NY: Crossing Press. (Original work published 1984)

Morris, A. (2015). *The scholar denied. W. E. B. Du Bois and the birth of modern sociology*. Berkeley, CA: University of California Press.

Ohikuare, J. (2015, October 17). Meet the women who created #BlackLivesMatter. *Cosmopolitan*. Retrieved from http://www.cosmopolitan.com/entertainment/a47842/the-women-behind-blacklivesmatter/

Padilla, A. M. (1994). Ethnic minority scholars, research, and mentoring: Current and future issues. *Educational Researcher, 23*(4), 24–27.

Patel, L. (2015). Desiring diversity and backlash: White property rights in higher education. *Urban Review, 47*, 657.

Williams, D. A., & Clowney, C. (2007). Strategic planning for diversity and organizational change: Effective practices for academic leaders. *A Stylus Briefing, 2*(3), 1–16.

Zhang, A. (2015, November 17). In and out? A revolving door for Yale's professor of color? *Yale News*. Retrieved from http://features.yaledailynews.com/blog/2015/11/17/in-and-out/

PART TWO

EMBRACING EMBODIMENT AND EMOTION AS PEDAGOGICAL PRAXIS

The college classroom is often thought to be a space in which emotions, affect, and the body are deemed irrelevant and even out of place within what many believe should be a neutral/objective learning environment. This paradigm aligns with corporatized notions of teaching and learning, whereby education is disembodied from broader democratic and holistic purposes of education, intended only for narrow vocational skills development in response to labor market needs. However, what often makes the teaching of race, gender, and sexuality, "difficult" is that our understanding of these topics is heavily reliant on the visual and visceral. The essays in this part challenge conventional pedagogical logic by placing the queer, raced, gendered body front and center, and engaging emotion and/or affect as a form of intellectual inquiry.

Adriana Estill's chapter "Feeling Our Way to Knowing: Decolonizing the American Studies Classroom," raises the important question of how White students, in particular, confront and engage with the contemporary realities of racism and other forms of oppression and violence. Foregrounding the the following questions: How do I make sure that this emotional journey isn't a form of tourism for White students? and How do I make sure that this journey is productive and not harmful for students of color? Estill offers several concrete pedagogical tools that demonstrate how embracing emotionality for knowledge can disrupt hegemonic Whiteness in the college classroom.

Esther O. Ohito and Sherry L. Deckman's chapter "Feeling Black and Blue in Preservice Teacher Education: Encountering Emotion and Embodiment in Antiracist Teaching" argues against privileging objectivity and reason in the college classroom as sole epistemological sources in favor of acknowledging the importance of emotion and affect as a sites of knowledge. Ohito and Deckman offer exercises like heartmapping and talking circles as examples of engaging emotions as pathways to thinking critically about race in the classroom.

While Deckman and Ohito point to emotionality as a form of engaged pedagogy, Breanne Fahs's chapter, "Transformational Pedagogies of the Abject Body: An Argument for Radical Fat Pedagogies," looks to the body, specifically the emerging field of fat studies as a model for challenging conservative and conventional assumptions about gender, size, respectability, and marginalization. This chapter is ultimately about the kinds of transformative learning that is made possible when we move beyond acceptance and empowerment and resist assimilation of the status quo.

From the first day, faculty play a crucial role in establishing the culture of the classroom. Erica Chu asks that faculty be attentive to the gendered language they use when addressing students as this has distinct implications for the experience of trans* students in particular. Their chapter, "'The Least We Can Do': Gender-Affirming Pedagogy Starting on Day One, "references the mislabeling of trans* students by faculty as a form of structural violence and offers exercises and opportunities that faculty can employ to avoid marginalizing trans* students and serve as a model for their peers.

Addressing how minoritized students often feel simultaneously stigmatized and hypervisible in the college classroom, Dian D. Squire's chapter, "Creating Inclusive Classrooms: Toward Collective and Diverse Intersectional Success," is cowritten by two undergraduate students, Azura Booth and Brandon Arnold. The chapter models how faculty and undergraduate students can work collaboratively to create classrooms that promote inclusivity and affirm all students at the intersections of their multiple identities especially on predominantly White campuses.

6

FEELING OUR WAY TO KNOWING

Decolonizing the American Studies Classroom

Adriana Estill

This is no ordinary time for American studies. It has never been more difficult—yet never more important—to explain how the abstract idea of "America" works in the world, to analyze the social relations it both enables and inhibits, to examine both the bright promises and the bitter betrayals of egalitarian and democratic aspirations that are voiced in its name. (Tomlinson & Lipsitz, 2013, p. 1)

Let us look at the historical present, manifestly organized by the rhetoric of crisis. We need to reinvent what it means to do engaged, solidaristic work for the current crisis, the spreading precarities, and the insecuritization of all labor contexts. What world are we teaching people for, reaching toward, trying to describe or make? (Berlant, 2009, p. 135)

I warn students on the first day that my classes in American studies are always and persistently steeped in the historical and ongoing structural violence that made the United States possible in its contemporary forms. I invite them—urge them—to learn how to look directly at the crises that we face without making excuses, endorsing narratives of exceptionalism, or slipping into easy platitudes. As Barbara Tomlinson and George Lipsitz (2013) point out, the emergence and domination of the neoliberal state has made a sense of urgency permeate American studies as we struggle to "explain the links between the nation and its imagination" (p. 2) and, in doing so, explore and highlight the erasures that those links perform. Confronting the fallen nation in this way requires persistent affective learning; to wit, many of my students let me know at the end of the course that "American studies is a downer," directly naming the toll of recognizing the distance between our aspirational nationhood and the on-the-ground reality. To be clear, these are not students who refuse to engage with the material; these are majors and other students deeply invested in the topic.

Given their investment, it is important to me that they recognize the toll that this learning takes. In asking them to "not look away," I am striving to "reinvent what engaged, solidaristic work" looks like for the pedagogical world that I want us to inhabit, in the hopes that we make new ways of learning and being in learning community possible for us (Berlant, 2009, p. 135). Not looking away means recognizing the seductive nature of our dominant national stories and their aspirational rewards of belonging, equality, and judicial and state objectivity. Not looking away means not using "trigger warnings" on occasional readings but instead understanding that even the most "neutral" readings unveil deeply painful stories for us. Not looking away means that emotion—theirs, mine, that of the figures in the histories we read—matters, and must become part of the educational terrain that we work through. I have come to believe that centering and highlighting the affective aspects of learning in American studies serves as a core method through which we confront and interrupt the neoliberal logics that haunt and reshape the conditions of our epistemological and pedagogical worlds.

Sophia McClennen (2008), following on Henry Giroux's work, argues that we need to consider neoliberalism as a public pedagogy that, in convincing the public that we have little to hope for from the government, public space, democratic processes, and public education "teaches individuals to live, to understand their place in the world, and to imagine the future" (p. 461) In other words, neoliberal logics individuate and atomize, producing both disbeliefs in structural or societal solutions as well as expectations for autonomy and self-care. Considering how "difference" operates within this order, Grace Kyungwon Hong (2015) argues that neoliberalism is

> an epistemological structure of disavowal, a means of claiming that racial and gendered violences are things of the past. It does so by *affirming* certain modes of racialized, gendered, and sexualized life, particularly through invitation into reproductive respectability, *so as to* disavow its exacerbated production of premature death. (loc. 163–177)

Hong's argument leads to the conclusion that neoliberalism performs erasure of collective histories, struggles, and violences through the very same ways in which it dreams of a personhood that has full freedom, self-reliance, and power, no matter the color, gender, or sexuality.

Neoliberal logics exacerbate the historical privileging of rationality over emotion as ways of knowing in the U.S. classroom. As we bring students into our courses, we implicitly and sometimes explicitly ask them to learn how to "gain distance" in order to learn, often associating "rigor" with neutrality. But this move—one I'd taken for granted for years—means that students who feel particularly affected by a topic like the physical and epistemic violence against people of color in the United States must do much more work to manage their emotions whereas other students skate easily into "rationality." Or as Dian Million (2009) puts it in her work on Indigenous feminist scholarship, "academia repetitively produces gatekeepers to our entry into important social discourses because we *feel* our histories as well as think them" (emphasis in original, p. 54). Million (2009) makes the vital case that, to decolonize our knowledge production, we cannot divorce understanding from feeling; bearing witness—naming and detailing colonial violences—necessarily requires feeling, because feelings are "culturally mediated knowledges, never solely individual" (p. 61). In the classrooms of what sociologist Eduardo Bonilla-Silva has dubbed HWCUs (Historically White Colleges and Universities)—in order to recognize and name the sedimented Whiteness of higher educational spaces—it becomes particularly crucial to understand feelings as "culturally mediated knowledges" because of the way in which "neutral knowing" is always already racialized as White (Chason, 2015). White bodies, as George Yancy (2014) points out, "are always already sanctioned as 'knowers' and are always already known as being at home within disciplinary matrixes of knowledge production" (p. 2).

Million's call—to bear witness, to name, to feel—interrupts and recalculates what Lynn Worsham (1998) names the "pedagogies of emotions" (p. 216) in which we have been collectively schooled and yet which have been unequally engaged and reproduced depending on our social identities and locations. Per Yancy, White bodies get the benefit of conferred neutrality, generally presumed objective; bodies of color conversely become coded as hyperemotional and ever-subjective. And yet, we all have feelings that are culturally and socially produced, felt, and circulated. Indeed, both presumed neutralities and incompetencies are sustained by affective regimes. Lauren Berlant remarks that "by the time you've been in primary school for awhile, or whatever, you have feelings about citizenship, you have feelings about race, you have feelings about gender and sexuality. You've been trained to take on those objects as world-sustaining perspectives" (Berlant as quoted in Seitz, 2013). So interrupting our cherished, affect-laden narratives of Americanness in order to develop strategies to understand how we got to where we are requires the following processes that are critically affective: (a) not looking away, and recognizing that the drive to look away—in whatever way that emerges—is affectively driven; (b) challenging and refusing neoliberal frameworks of education that prioritize rote learning and a focus on "pragmatics," that is, credentialed, possible laboral futures.

Both interruptive processes require us to discard those ideals of the management of the self demanded by neoliberalism: emotional curation and self-care, the regimentation of the neutral self in the classroom; the emphasis on passive consumption and order-following. In doing so, we turn toward the messiness of our affective worlds and learnings, with a willingness to feel our way into knowing how the racialized, gendered, and classed histories of the United States continue to place us in emotional relationship to each other, if only we're willing to hear it and work through it. Asking students to move through our classrooms as if they are emotionless, only objective, and always neutral knowers is counterproductive to the learning that I want them to do around racialized, gendered, and classed processes that have and continue to produce inequities. In this chapter, I argue for the need to make space for emotional responses to the things we learn and for our responsibility as teachers to help students figure out how their emotions provide routes for knowing.

Rational Classrooms and Acceptable Emotion

> This pedagogy [of emotion] mystifies emotion as a natural category and masks its role in a system of power relations that associates emotion with the irrational, the physical, the particular, the private, the feminine, and nonwhite others.
>
> —Worsham (1992–1993, p. 127)

How many times have I choked down tears or relaxed my clenching jaw or softened my gut laughter and instead mastered the wry laugh and the considered nod, somatic signs that my personal feelings are under wraps, in tight reins, within control. Too often I have worked to produce a seamless façade for my students that assures that my intellectual command and investment overshadows the topic's or material's ability to "unhinge" me. Academia's pedagogy of emotion mirrors that of larger society: emotion is an impediment to rationalism and productivity. Like my students, I have been profoundly schooled in this curriculum; the practices, familiar and reiterative in the neoliberal academy, have instilled in us the "valorization of the rational, efficient, 'balanced' (White male) student, a profile that is tied to a strong sense of self-regulation and emotional restraint" (Stenberg, 2011, p. 350). Within this ideological frame, if you cannot discuss and learn a thing calmly, you cannot learn. Emotions must be managed in order to learn appropriately; "emotional intelligence" and training privileges skills that "lend themselves to corporate values" (Stenberg, 2011, p. 353). As Sherri

Stenberg (2011) points out, within this pedagogy, emotions "such as anger, bitterness, and rage" are understood to be "urges in need of control rather than social responses to oppression and exploitation" (p. 354). It needs to be said, however, that these emotions are not just *responses*. They are acts of *knowing* oppression, subordination, and violence.

Looking back now, I can see that one of the things that drew me to women of color writers like bell hooks, Gloria Anzaldúa, Audre Lorde, and Cherrie Moraga as a graduate student was their willingness to name the difficult emotions of their knowing. In describing the borderlands, Anzaldúa (1987) baldly and bilingually cries that the "1,950 mile-long open wound / dividing a *pueblo*, a culture, . . . /splits me splits me /*me raja me raja*" (p. 2), in the process reminding me that geopolitical processes and structures are also embodied and emotional. Audre Lorde (1984) argues that "anger is a grief of distortions between peers, and its object is change" (p. 129), suggesting that it serves as a reaction to injustice but also as a crucial component of a process of knowing, because "to turn aside from the anger of Black women with excuses . . . is merely another way of preserving racial blindness, the power of unaddressed privilege, unbreached, intact" (p. 132). Rather than "urges in need of control," these emotions serve multiple purposes, from early warning systems of relations gone awry to vital lenses that permit greater awareness and knowing (Stenberg, 2011, p. 354). María Lugones (2003) points out that although angers can appear irrational, they are "cognitively rich, the cognitive content understandable only in nonofficial, oppositional communities or universes of sense" (p. 104). Lugones's work suggests intriguingly that emotions can signal a field of "making sense" that is not audible or available within a particular community. The way I think about this is that, in the rational classroom, emotions are often minimized or resisted as ways to knowledge, even as those emotions are making a sense and knowledge that are disallowed in that classroom.

And it is not simply that we, as teachers, privilege rationality and circumscribe emotional knowing. Our institutions train us into these expectations. I still remember the way a conversation with a colleague made me feel—powerless, angry, frustrated—during a pretenure discussion of my class. The way he saw the class dynamics, after one class visit, completely denied and erased the way I saw the student learning. He pointed to the class's "lack of rigor"; the students weren't "reaching high enough." I was fairly sure that if the class had not been 30% students of color, he would not have heard our discussion that way. In my pretenure body, I grew increasingly agitated and, finally, faced with his inability to hear about my priorities and pedagogic aims and my inability to speak "rationally" (i.e., without anger), I leaked tears and finally left his office.

Anger comes up often as one of those forbidden signs of emotionality in relationship to learning, but of course we are trained to understand the pedagogical sphere as forbidding sorrow and, even, joy. For example, have you ever had a student apologize to you for "geeking out" about a topic? I have. So many of them! How is it that learning is carefully manicured and divested of feelings of pleasure? Stefano Harney and Fred Moten (2013) highlight the insidiousness of this as a "naturalisation of misery" in regard to intellectual work: "enjoyment is suspect, untrustworthy, a mark of illegitimate privilege or of some kind of sissified refusal to look squarely into the fucked-up face of things" (loc. 1413). The suspicion of emotional engagement in learning becomes a sign of self-involvement on either side, whether for reasons of marginalization or privilege. Henry Giroux (2008) states, "Higher education now narrates itself in terms that are more instrumental, commercial, and practical" (p. 47). The neoliberal university privileges that "neutral" knower and positions him or her as a pragmatic learner, one who "learns" in order to later "produce." To the degree that neoliberalism expects individuals to "manage" themselves (their labor, their health, their emotions) without structural help, recognition, or support from the public sphere or institutions, it also demands that students take care of any edges that make them harder to teach. Within this framework, student demands for trigger warnings or for institutional language and/or action about structural racism and classism becomes understood as a failure of our students and not the institutions because the students have, as individuals, failed to manage their own affective relationship to the material and to the place.

Refusing the Rational Classroom

What are the groundwork practices of refusing the rational classroom? Of reforming it into a place where affective learning has a role? I've gestured at one of them already: the persistent acknowledgment on my part that what we need to learn is "hard." Indicating that our work takes reservoirs of strength for me—some days more than others—and lets the students know that my learning is not emotionally neutral, nor does theirs have to be. There are risks to being the Latina professor emoting at the front of a classroom at an HWCU, the primary one being the reification of stereotypes of Latinas as excessively emotional. I also share a concern of many female faculty: the possibility that this emotional aperture will place me in a maternal; gendered; and, consequently, less authoritative role for the students. These potential risks rely on students understanding my emotional work in the classroom as stemming from *individual* (maternal) and/or *collective* (as an Other, not White) identity positions, so when I make this move I remind them of the public pedagogy of emotions we are all schooled in and, in this way, try to dislocate emotion from individual subjectivity and/or collective identity and to resituate it as a *social practice*. I ask the students to develop "deliberate attention to how we have developed particular emotional investments over our life histories and how these investments subsequently color the lenses through which we view the world" (Stenberg, 2011, p. 361).

Grounding students in their particular—but deeply socially embedded responses—begins by recognizing discomfort with texts. How does Anzaldúa's use of Spanish make me *feel* as a reader? Exclusion or inclusion into the textual space makes for variant emotional responses that students then connect to particular ideological positions. Recognizing discomfort/comfort with each other's voices in the classroom develops more slowly. After one class on the U.S.–Mexico border, several students trickled into my office, echoing each other unknowingly with comments about how tense the class had been, how anxious they had been as they spoke, as they stayed silent. The curious thing about teaching about race for this long is that I know that although some students felt the tension deeply, other students were "oblivious," by which I mean that they had no sense of the emotional investment that permeated the conversation. These emotional imbalances led to one frustrating postclass discussion for my students, where one student approached the conversation about language from a position of neutrality ("isn't this interesting") and the other student felt unheard and alienated because this presumed neutrality made no space for her anger.

It is important to get students to understand that (a) there may be tensions and emotions in a classroom discussion but (b) listening to these makes for good learning is a course-long project. For students who have accepted and been trained to inhabit the position of the mythic "neutral" learner, emotionally infused knowledge production can feel distracting, indirect, or off-topic. They can resist and refuse to listen when someone gets "emotional." But for other students, who have been failing to cordon off emotional responses, the chance to name and detail the affective engagement with particular readings, discussions, or topics allows them to recenter themselves as knowers.

The Class Contract—Its Potential and Its Limits

One of the hallmark strategies of the discussion-centered classroom that I, and so many other colleagues I know, use, is the group-developed contract. Communally developed guidelines decenter faculty authority and, from the outset, situate students within a Freirian framework for learning where their active participation is necessary and honored. A few items are always brought up by students and, when they don't bring them up, I make sure to get them in our contract: some articulation of the need to share space/time; some recognition of our promise to keep our discussions confidential (the Vegas rule); some statement of our desire to assume best intentions. Through the years, I have assumed that they know what this means; I have assumed that I know what it means. And I have assumed that when our discussions failed to reach honest, emotional communications, it was because of limits we had as individuals rather than because the contract had limits. My assumptions were rocked last spring when, in a midterm evaluation, a student wrote that they had heard people talking about things they had said in class. Invoking their name alongside the utterance. Laughing. Mocking. Judging them.

When I walked into the classroom on Monday, all I knew was that we had to recognize the class failure—even/especially mine—to hold to our contract. I set aside the time for an involved, intense conversation. I steeled myself for what that might and could look like, given the truth I was about to lay on them, a violation of our contract meant that something had broken in who we were to each other as a community.

The Fishbowl—Learning to Listen

Monday's scolding led to some quick realizations on my part. First, it was clear that although we all wanted to "assume best intentions" when listening to others, we didn't always know what that meant. Second, the "Vegas" rule had been easier to break than I would have guessed. Why? What made that part of our social contract so very fragile? Given our large class size (30 students), I decided to use a fishbowl set-up because it can provide some intimacy for a difficult topic while also inviting all to participate. A small group of four to six students sits at the center and begins the conversation. The remaining students sit in a larger circle around them, listening. Students "tap out" participants in order to join the inner circle. I required all students to "tap in" at least once. This process also helped to ensure that those who tended to talk a lot have to, at some point, step back to the outer circle and listen. I asked the first small group in the fishbowl to tackle the following central questions that moved them away from feeling shame or guilt at our broken contract and toward understanding why and how we had done so: (a) What does it *feel like* to assume best intentions? (In other words, how do you notice and pause your intellectual and emotional reflexes as you make deliberate moves toward best intentions?) (b) What are your *best practices* for how you engage in this class with best intentions? What has that looked like? Why has it been challenging?

I stepped out of the conversation and the students stepped in. Although I made the time and space for this conversation and I let them know that we would take the time that we needed to unpack and deal with this issue as a community, the students were the ones who allowed themselves to speak honestly, vulnerably, and, in multiple instances, with deep self-reflection. "I might have been the one who did this," a White male student proclaimed, adding that he had been unthoughtful in a moment of discussing the class with dorm mates. Another student, a White female, said a similar thing, ruefully admitting to sharing and identifying names with the quotes from class. Rather than becoming springboards into guilt, these admissions became opportunities for students to consider why and how they had been unthoughtful and what it might feel like to recognize the "betrayal" of their classmates. In none of the moments where students recognized their complicity in this process was it the students that I expected. (And, of course, this also meant that I learned a great deal about my own "best assumptions" and their limits.)

Everyone stepped into the fishbowl at some point during our 70-minute class; the topics ranged from practical suggestions that were attentive to the emotional risks they were taking (i.e., how to listen when you feel yourself getting angry and/or defensive), figuring out the balance between listening and speaking and note-taking, to self-reflection about the kind of participation each valued and wanted from their colleagues, to considerations about what kept people from feeling comfortable in discussion. To the latter, one student wisely noted that in this large class (30 students!), it was "easy" to not feel like a community. This was not a thought that had ever occurred to me because 30—for an introductory-level class—is not huge. Our circles were, yes, wide, but they weren't unwieldy. But this student spoke, and others nodded along, about feeling that their classmates were *distant* and thus listening took much greater effort. One thing that is important to note—something that I emphasized to them all along, but this discussion made clear, is that listening well takes effort and, yes, practice. The larger classroom clearly exacerbated this difficulty. In this moment there was a recognition on their part that it takes work and effort to recognize the humanity of their classmates in a large group.

Did this intense review of our contract, dedicated to learning how to listen and how to trust, work? Nine out of 30 students spontaneously mentioned this particular class in a final evaluation that invited reflection on communication practices while several others highlighted more generally the struggle of learning to communicate and listen in a large discussion class. All nine pointed to the way that their listening improved after the exercise and that "assuming best intent" was, as a class rule, one that had tested their ability to listen "through disagreement and difference." One student, a White male, recognized that, before the exercise, he hadn't considered the impact of his statements; the fishbowl helped him develop a new relationship to the class and respect other students more fully.

Encouraging students to consider the impact that words have *in* the classroom extends readily to considering the impact that words have *beyond* the classroom. During the fishbowl exercise, students persistently raised the issue of intent versus impact, not surprising considering the current popularity of this aphorism. Once they moved beyond recognizing the importance of owning the impact of their words, they realized that part of the task was to extend emotional awareness—to listen for impact and to not hide behind intent. In other words, recognizing others' body language in the wake of a statement you make is just as important as being willing to listen when someone calls you on what you said. Conversely, they agreed as a group that being able to stay present in moments when you feel impacted also matters. A woman of color articulated it this way: "Assuming best intent is always difficult for me. I know others may not realize how or what they said would be offensive but I would say I could have done a better job on that. With that being said I do think I held space for people's mistakes." For the White man, the fishbowl activity helped him grow more attuned to his impact; for her, it helped her recognize the importance of listening past the mistake and the offense.

Fleshing out how it *felt* to assume best intent or discern impact—recognizing that, as one student put it, that they needed to develop emotional "muscles"—led to one of the most important collective findings of the exercise. Recognizing the role of emotions in the American studies classroom requires a great deal of processing and a need for built-in self-reflection. Indeed, a student mentioned—and several agreed—that the class did not end when our time period ended. The class extended into their lives in complicated and emotional ways; as one student put it, it was "impossible" to stop class at the door. Another complained, "class ends and we're not done yet." Students had several suggestions for each other and for me on how to work through this. Several students mentioned as useful the times when I had ended the class with a quick 2-minute exercise to debrief their learning. Others reminded each other that taking down effective emotional notes (not just the "facts" but also the challenges of learning them) was helpful. Others asked for more processing time throughout, perhaps restructuring class time to promote processing. One suggestion that seemed reasonable but that did not prove successful in reality (with the three weeks of class we had left), was to create online spaces where intense discussions might continue.

In all of these considerations of learning how to process emotional learning, the students were struggling to figure out how to "stay in" the conversation:

[Staying in] means each participant needs to seek to understand what other folks are saying and not to assume that they know in advance what someone means. Staying in the conversation involves giving of self; it involves listening with the heart and being fully present. White students often find this difficult since they tend to characterize courses and conversations that center on race as acts of violence. (Watson, 2014, p. 41)

Staying in is not easy for anyone but, as Watson points out, discussions of race feel more violent for White students. Arguably this is because they need to cede their neutral knowing position and recognize the emotions that students of color are invoking and that the readings are pointing toward.

Not Looking Away

The destroyers are merely men enforcing the whims of our country, correctly interpreting its heritage and legacy. It is hard to face this. But all our phrasing—race relations, racial chasm, racial justice, racial profiling, White privilege, even White supremacy—serves to obscure that racism is a visceral experience, that it dislodges brains, blocks airways, rips muscle, extracts organs, cracks bones, breaks teeth. *You must never look away from this.* You must always remember that the sociology, the history, the economics, the graphs, the charts, the regressions all land, with great violence, upon the body.

—Coates (emphasis added, 2015, p. 10)

The previous section tracks what happens—the spin out and recovery—when we teach from a stance of not looking away. Not looking away means, following Coates (2015), making sure to remember the bodies behind the histories, sociological tracts, literary treatments, remembering, indeed, Anzaldúa's body that screams "*me raja me raja*". And it results in students needing processing time to confront the social practice of their emotional knowing—the way that their racialized, gendered, and other identity commitments position them as knowers in the classroom.

One of the reasons I choose to emphasize everyone's emotional investment and reaction to these painful knowings is that I want to make sure that the emotions of my raced/queer/marginalized students can become radical potential within the classroom as pain, anger, and hope become centered as important routes to understanding. In order for their emotion to be understood as productive knowledge-making, the presumed neutral knowing of the White students must be unbalanced and questioned. Presumed neutrality of Whiteness stands in relationship to the historical ability of Whites in this country to look away: "White ignorance is a form of not knowing (seeing wrongly), resulting from the habit of erasing, dismissing, distorting, and forgetting about the lives, cultures, and histories of peoples Whites have colonized" (Bailey, 2007, p. 85). Not looking away means recognizing White ignorance and making a commitment to remembering.

I must emphasize that not looking away is a privilege. Particularly in HWCUs, students and faculty of color do not have that privilege. In her ethnography of British and Australian universities, Sara Ahmed (2012) uses the concept of stickiness to describe the way it feels, for example, to walk into a meeting and be one of the few people of color: "When you stick out, the gaze sticks to you. Sticking out from Whiteness can thus reconfirm the Whiteness of the space" (p. 41). In a much-used, central Carleton meeting room, paintings of past presidents all look so much alike that, as we sit there discussing campus issues, I cannot help but feel unalike and sticky in the face of this "reproduction of likeness" that Ahmed (2012) argues tends to be assumed as an "institutional given" (p. 38). I try to remember how my students of color feel in this space in order to better understand the emotional residue of not belonging as well as the importance of helping everyone "not look away."

We need to reframe the problem. The problem is not that some students come into the classroom with emotion, but that some come into it unable to access the emotion of knowing. In her article on the Freirian classroom, Kristen T. Edwards (2014) writes beautifully about the importance of this classroom in White spaces so that students of color might there be acknowledged "epistemologically, ontologically, and axiologically" (p. 24). She argues that a resistant raced identity and knowledge must "emerge in loving relation to White identity as an act of teaching and learning for emancipation, not oppression. It must exist in a way that offers access and equity for both White students and students of color to be more fully human" (p. 24). To get here, all of us need to recognize the emotion involved in not looking away.

Halfway through my course on U.S. Latinx literature, a student asked, "do we only read sad stuff?" The rest of the class laughed, wryly. I laughed, wryly. I experience the readings on my syllabus as immensely powerful, offering routes of class and racial identification; visions of renewal and survivance; providing interrogations of the relationship between self and community. Pain lives there too, but it finds respite in the beauty of words, images, and stories. So when the student asked this, I wondered, how do I make sure that, for the White students, this emotional journey isn't *tourism*? How do I make sure that for the students of color, this journey is *productive* and not *harmful*?

As mentioned earlier, Hong (2015) argues that neoliberalism shapes not only the knower but also the ease of access to some knowledges. Indeed, neoliberalism promises us that if we inhabit the forgetting—erasing violences past and present—we get the promise of a cultivated, manicured difference. Manicured difference can lead, I believe, into touristic approaches to the stories and histories I introduce to my students. Instead, I want them to not just perceive the sadness of the literature, but also hear why it is sad for each of them in slightly different ways.

Here I use my body as a first step to help all students see that learning can be deeply emotional and fraught. But I agree with Antonia Randolph (2014) that although we might deliberately use our bodies in our teaching, "it is costly. However, we already pay the price of putting our bodies on the line. We might as well reap the benefits that can come from using our bodies as the line that connects us with students" (p. 38). Yes, it matters that I can articulate how the literature makes me sad in order to dig into the particularities (this family, this community) of the loss as well as the generalities (this humanity) of it.

Let us ask students to not just rote learn and thus "know" a particular subject but instead to inhabit it, feel its meaningfulness on their skin and in the pounding of their heart. Let us remind them that what's at stake in our discussions is not only epistemological but also affective. What I *don't* mean is what students often ask for ("How does this relate to my life?") in some flat and easy way. Rather, I'm talking about the fraught production of emotional investment.

Sometimes it is easier to do this in a classroom filled with Brown bodies, where the work to honor the emotions of knowing is also necessary. In the American studies methods class last year, eight out of nine of us in that room were not White. Watching *12 Years a Slave* (Gardner & McQueen, 2013) in the safety of each other's company, it became a route into cognition instead of needing to cordon off our feelings at the door. Working through *12 Years a Slave*, thinking and feeling about Northup and his powerlessness, opened the door for us to consider the empirical and emotional weight of current judicial and law enforcement systems. It allowed us to make historical connections without collapsing the differences in structure, raced lives, and workings of power in these eras. And although eight out of nine bodies in that classroom were not White, we were not all the same "not White." This made for various moments of cross-racial recognition but also times of productive dissonance, where someone or another's voice would emerge to remind us of multiple silences. We held each other accountable to all of our frames of knowing and feeling.

Watching *12 Years a Slave* in a mixed-race classroom means that there will be White people who see it as history and Black people who see it as *their* history. And that is a simplistic, binary way of naming the complex tensions in the room. Naming the truth of these variously raced and gendered affective relationships to our studies ensures that White students must unlearn the presumed neutrality of their learning positions that has taught them that violent moments of our collective past are done with and therefore no emotion need be experienced. Leaving behind the rational classroom means to recognize that emotion is not "out of place" and that feeling their knowing does not "displace" students from learning.

After the movie was over, I asked whether students wanted to talk, or feel in silence. I like to think I could have asked the same question in a mixed-race classroom and that this would have acknowledged that collectively produced affect mattered, and that we needed to be able to name it and account for it. Processing *12 Years a Slave*, we claimed our entry into knowledge and history, through feeling. But I can't deny that, in these moments of strong feelings surrounded by other people of color, it was a relief to me to feel deeply without the worries that have accompanied me in other moments of racially charged emotional revelation: Will I be seen as irrational? Can you handle seeing all of me?

This Bridge Called My Tears

> Behind my work on affect, historiography, and the social, there is a lesbian crying in bed.
>
> —Love (2011, p. 180)

Behind my work on American studies and feeling to know, there is a Latina reaching her boiling point. Working at an HWCU *me raja me raja*. Doing American studies work in a classroom filled with students of color felt freeing. In that room, my identity was no longer something hypervisible or invisible, it simply was. When talking about discourses and histories of race, class, gender, and sexuality—key topics in American studies—I didn't have to explain, justify, or manage my racialized relationship to my field of study. Unpacking the relationship between Whiteness and citizenship could be done without steeling myself for defensiveness. In moving into a classroom filled with Brown bodies, I realized how much control I had exerted over my emotions—and thus over the classroom's—in the more common HWCU classroom.

Returning to a classroom filled with White bodies, I take the risk of naming the emotional work we have to do as we read and think and develop deeper awarenesses of our tangled and bloody national legacy. From allowing space for emotional readings to acknowledging how our differentiated affective locations shape our discussions and understandings to recognizing that doing this work is challenging, each of these takes transparency and a level of comfort with naming and spending some time understanding the social practice of emotions. In this era of student "unrest," it becomes that much more important to recognize how our classrooms and our campuses, to the degree that they deny collective emotions, continue to privilege neutrality and Whiteness, ensuring that some students have the privilege to feel absolutely content and others gaze up at the paintings of White men and wonder why the place where they came to learn produces in them anger, frustration, and alienation.

References

Ahmed, S. (2012). *On being included: Racism and diversity in institutional life*. Durham, NC: Duke University Press.

Anzaldúa, G. (1987). *Borderlands la frontera: The new mestiza*. San Francisco, CA: Aunt Lute.

Bailey, A. (2007). Strategic ignorance. In S. Sullivan & N. Tuana (Eds.), *Race and epistemologies of ignorance* (pp. 77–94). Albany, NY: State University of New York Press.

Berlant, L. (2009). Affect is the new trauma. *The Minnesota Review, 71–72*, 131–136.

Chason, R. (2015, April 8). After noose incident, faculty illuminate history of lynching. *The Chronicle*. Retrieved from http://www.dukechronicle.com/article/2015/04/after-noose-incident-faculty-illuminate-history-lynching

Coates, T. (2015). *Between the world and me*. New York, NY: Spiegel & Grau.

Edwards, K. (2014). "The Whiteness is thick": Predominantly White classrooms, student of color voice, and Freirian hopes. In G. Yancy & M. Davidson (Eds.), *Exploring race in predominantly White classrooms: Scholars of color reflect* (pp. 17–30). New York, NY: Taylor and Francis.

Gardner, D., et al (Producers), & McQueen, S. (Director). (2013). *12 years a slave* [Motion picture]. USA: Fox Searchlight.

Giroux, H. (2008). Academic unfreedom in America: Rethinking the university as a democratic public sphere. *Works and Days, 51/52–53/54* (26–27), 45–71.

Harney S., & Moten, F. (2013). *The undercommons: Fugitive planning and Black study* [Kindle Fire version]. Retrieved from http://www.minorcompositions.info/wp-content/uploads/2013/04/undercommons-web.pdf

Hong, G. K. (2015). *Death beyond disavowal: The impossible politics of difference* [Kindle Fire version]. Retrieved from https://www.amazon.com/Death-beyond-Disavowal-Impossible-Incorporated-ebook/dp/B014VP6JZE

Lorde, A. (1984). *Sister outsider: Essays and speeches*. Freedom CA: Crossing Press.

Love, H. (2011). Queers ____ this. In J. Halley & A. Parker (Eds.), *After sex?: On writing since queer theory* (pp. 180–191). Durham, NC: Duke University Press.

Lugones, M. (2003). Hard-to-handle anger. In *Pilgrimages, peregrinajes: Theorizing coalition against multiple oppressions* (pp. 103–120). Lanham, MD: Rowman and Littlefield.

McClennen, S. (2008). Neoliberalism and the crisis of intellectual engagement. *Works and Days 51/52–53/54*(26 –27), 459–470.

Million, D. (2009). Felt theory: An Indigenous feminist approach to affect and history. *Wicazo Sa Review, 24*(2), 53–76.

Randolph, A. (2014). This bridge called my body: Talking race through embodying difference. In G. Yancy & M. Davidson (Eds.), *Exploring race in predominantly White classrooms: Scholars of color reflect* (pp. 31–39). New York, NY: Taylor and Francis.

Seitz, D. (2013, March 22). Interview with Lauren Berlant. *Society & Space.* Retrieved from https://societyandspace.com/2013/03/22/interview-with-lauren-berlant/

Stenberg, S. (2011). Teaching and (re)learning the rhetoric of emotion. *Pedagogy: Critical approaches to teaching literature, language, composition, and culture, 11*(2), 349–369.

Tomlinson, B., & Lipsitz, G. (2013). American studies as accompaniment. *American Quarterly, 65*(1), 1–30.

Watson, D. (2014). Staying in the conversation: Having difficult conversations about race in teaching education. In G. Yancy & M. Davidson (Eds.), *Exploring race in predominantly White classrooms: Scholars of color reflect* (pp. 40–49). New York, NY: Taylor and Francis.

Worsham, L. (1992–1993). Emotion and pedagogic violence. *Discourse, 15*(2), 119–148.

Worsham, L. (1998). Going postal: Pedagogic violence and the schooling of emotion. *Journal of Rhetoric, Culture, and Politics, 18*(2), 213–245.

Yancy, G. (2014). Introduction: White crisis and the value of *Losing one's way.* In G. Yancy & M. Davidson (Eds.), *Exploring race in predominantly White classrooms: Scholars of color reflect* [Kindle version] (pp. 1–16). New York, NY: Taylor and Francis.

7

FEELING BLACK AND BLUE IN PRESERVICE TEACHER EDUCATION

Encountering Emotion and Embodiment in Antiracist Teaching

Esther O. Ohito and Sherry L. Deckman

The term *encounter* suggests a meeting, but a meeting that involves surprise and conflict. We can ask: how does identity itself become instituted through encounters with others that surprise, that shift the boundaries of the familiar, of what we assume that we know? (Sara Ahmed, 2000, pp. 6–7)

The unwillingness to approach teaching from a standpoint that includes awareness of race, sex, and class is often rooted in the fear that classrooms will be uncontrollable, that emotions and passions will not be contained. To some extent, we all know that . . . there is always a possibility of confrontation, forceful expression of ideas, or even conflict. (bell hooks, 1994, p. 39)

O ppression is felt and lived. Racism, for example, is a somatic experience that "dislodges brains, blocks airways, rips muscle, extracts organs, breaks teeth" (Coates, 2015, p. 10). Hence, racial subjugation is *painfully* corporeal. Yet faculty and students' fears of emotional eruptions fuel the avoidance of racism and other such difficult subjects in higher education classrooms (hooks, 1994), even in equity-oriented environments. Consequently, possibilities for understanding how racial marginalization materially impacts the body dissipate as emotions or affects borne of racialized lived experiences are left un(der)-explored in the classroom, thereby positioning knowledge derived through cognitive sense-making as solely valid (Stenberg, 2002). In this chapter, we argue that the affective intensities that circulate around and attach to the body (Ahmed, 2004) must be embraced as core to antiracist teaching in higher education. In other words, we posit that pedagogies of affect and embodiment are essential to antiracist teaching. Employing such pedagogies—which are premised on the notion that *"knowledge is always grounded in bodily existence"* (emphasis in original; Shapiro, 1999/2015, p. 41)—in teaching and learning spaces is essential to cultivating antiracist identities in *both* faculty and students. Thus, we share two pedagogical practices in order to illustrate our evocation of emotion and embodiment in university-based preservice teacher education. Specifically, we expound on how these teaching strategies have allowed us, as faculty or teacher educators, to ask our students and ourselves—and attempt responses to—questions about what it means to be *a* body rather than *"no*body in a university economy designed to produce somebody individuated, assimilated and consenting to empire" (emphasis added; Gumbs, 2014, p. 237).

Once Upon a Body

To begin, we turn to our own stories as a biracial or Black/White (Sherry) and a Black (Esther) pair of pedagogues. These tales contextualize the teaching practices that we offer as counterhegemonic methods of resistance in the traditionally White, hetero/patriarchal academy in which we toil for racial justice. They are narratives of racialized, affectively charged, intercorporeal encounters in our classrooms that juxtapose feelings of vulnerability and pain displayed by our mostly White students against the vulnerability and pain of our experiences as pedagogues or teacher educators of color.

Our intent in storytelling is threefold: First, we understand that stories such as ours can be used "to explore a myriad of issues related to identity and belonging, as well as curricular matters and teaching in ways that are explicitly antiracist" (Aveling, 2006, pp. 266–267). Second, we recognize that for women of color like us, storytelling is not simply about the production of colorful tales. It is, perhaps more importantly, about the validation of our voices and experiences, which are often relegated to the margins of dominant discourses (Yosso, 2006). Third, we believe that storytelling is reparative (e.g., DeSalvo, 1999). As Christian (1988) asks rhetorically in regard to people of color, "How else have we managed to survive with such spiritedness the assault on our bodies, social institutions, countries, our very humanity?" (p. 68). Thus, we tell stories in the lineage of raconteurs who talk of racialized vulnerability and pain in order to bring healing to bruised beings. Through our storytelling, we endeavor to model not only the impact of one's own racial identity on one's engagement with antiracist pedagogies but also the importance of grappling with that identity in the context of teaching that tackles the difficulty of subjects such as racism.

Sherry's Story: Feeling Bias(ed)

"I don't understand what people mean when they talk about test bias," Katie chimed in. Our class had been revisiting the topic of racial inequality and educational outcomes and was questioning the validity of evaluating educational opportunity and success based on standardized test scores. Katie, whose facial expressions I often found difficult to read, and who tended to be less vocal than her peers, had the attention of the class. "My husband and sister are both firefighters and had to pass the city's firefighter test." Katie continued, "But now, minorities don't have to pass the test. I wouldn't want a firefighter who couldn't pass the test."

Katie's words stung my ears. She was one of two White students in a class I was teaching that took up issues of racial and class inequality in U.S. schools. She was insinuating that the tests were an objective measure of aptitude; the sentiment I heard was, "If you can't pass the test, you're not smart," ignoring both research that has shown standardized tests to be measures of cultural capital more than measures of intelligence and a court ruling that declared this specific test as discriminatory to Black applicants (see Edelman, 2016). Tanya, one of the Black women, jumped in,

> Well, I think the issue is that people say the test isn't fair to people of color because of the questions asked. I mean, you should see some of the questions on it. My boyfriend was applying to the fire department and showed me the questions. They don't make any sense or have anything to do with being a good firefighter.

I heard generosity in Tanya's attempt to respond to Katie, qualifying her statement with, "I think," maintaining space to keep the conversation going. But, Katie persisted, "There are way fewer women than minorities and my sister had to pass the test. She had to do everything the men did in order to pass. It just doesn't seem fair that minorities don't have to take the test."

At this point in the semester our class had formed a supportive and close-knit community. I felt it unraveling in this moment. I began to feel my face flush with dismay that Katie was making an argument that seemed to ignore many of the issues we had spent the semester discussing in terms of structural inequality. I grew anxious thinking about how I might respond. I felt the instinct to protect the rest of the class from the subtext of racism I heard in Katie's comments. The larger dilemma that this encounter raised for me is this: As a professor of a "diversity class" I am used to hearing some students make comments that are wounding to others in the group as part of the process of working through their ideas. It may seem necessary to allow the speakers a space to work through such thoughts (Boler, 2004; Deckman & Montilla, 2015), yet I am always unsure of how to care for other students who may be bruised by such comments, and unsettled by the fear that I may be unequipped to do so competently. It is also the case that I often deny how I *want to* respond emotionally in relationship to my personal identities for the sake of focusing on how I am *expected to* respond in my professional role as the professor.

Class was nearing the end and the conversation sat festering with tensions running high. I wasn't sure how I could help Katie work through these issues and avoid subjecting the rest of the class to what felt like the same old argument against affirmative action and other corrective policies meant to address racial inequity in U.S. society. I also wasn't sure if and how Katie could hear the points made by me, her Black professor.[1] Perhaps she even wondered if I was hired, lacking qualifications, because of my race. I felt paralyzed. In the end, I retreated to the safety of "objective data" in an attempt to urge Katie to reconsider testing bias, explaining that although I had never heard of this firefighter test before, that I had read numerous studies demonstrating bias on standardized tests for K–12 students. Reflecting on this moment left me wondering, why had I prioritized reason and "facts" over emotion and lived experience? What opportunities were left unrealized as a result? What might have happened if instead I unveiled how violated I felt as a woman of color listening to this exchange that encroached upon my anger about perceived correlations between race and (in)competence?

Esther's Story: Feeling Pain Over Peppermint Tea and Tears

On an unseasonably warm fall afternoon, tears gushed down her pale cheeks like the bursting tributaries of a furious body of water. I imagined that they were as salty as the Indian Ocean. I deeply relished that flavor during my childhood years in Kenya, which included visits to the ocean's sandy shores. I deeply craved that comforting taste at this exact moment. I reached across my desk in a clumsy effort to hand her a soft tissue, but succeeded only in knocking over my cup of lukewarm peppermint tea. Etched on the side of the ceramic utensil was the phrase, "World's Greatest Teacher!" How ironic, I thought, given that I felt utterly powerless as I witnessed this preservice teacher, my student, spiral down into an emotional dungeon. Perhaps because of that—or perhaps because I was uncertain of what to do with the intensity of the nervous energy that was being transmitted between us (Brennan, 2004)—I grunted loudly. How awkward, I sighed, feeling self-conscious.

In that moment, I desperately desired the ability to soar above the fallibility of my arms, and fly free of my skin and bones. I could not trust my Black limbs. She could not trust me. This is what she had entered my office to say. This White preservice teacher—my student—had entered my office as I sipped peppermint tea from a clay mug (mis)naming me the "World's Greatest Teacher!" to weepily announce that she trusted neither my colleagues—that is, my fellow lecturers in what was playfully called "the diversity class"—nor me. She could not avoid the course, which was a requirement for graduation from the teacher education program. What she hoped to avoid, however, was pain. She was here solely to learn about racism and other such oppressions. Baffled, I wondered, how could I teach her about such difficult subjects without triggering suffering—both hers and my own?

Stitching Together Stories of Tell-Tale Bodies

Our stories tell of tales told by bodies, both our own and those of our students, during classroom encounters. The emotional intensities described in the previous vignettes characterize many of our interactions with students during our terms at different teacher education programs. The classrooms in which we respectively engaged in antiracist teaching were emotionally fraught territories. In Sherry's case, acrimony and outrage were the more common emotive outlets, with students' angrily arguing, for example, that coursework spent focusing on antiracism is a distraction from where their focus as educators should really be—on state teaching standards. In Esther's case, crying was so common that before each class, she and her colleagues preemptively gathered boxes of soft tissue, cramming them into plastic crates overflowing with other essential materials, such as pens and scented Expo dry erase markers. Rivers of tears frequently overflowed during class—as well as afterwards—during individual meetings with students. These charged feelings flooded the earth in which our inquiry into the entanglement of emotion, embodiment, and antiracist teaching was planted.

Emotions are textured, and their expressions layered; therefore, the tears in Esther's classrooms may have stemmed from anger, and the anger in Sherry's classrooms may have been sparked by pain. Emotions are also dynamic, and therein lies the potential of pedagogies that seek to till the ground in which these feelings are rooted in order to move pedagogues and students away from safe cognitive comprehension and toward inherently risky—yet possibly more rewarding—affective and embodied meaning-making. These pedagogies are not only anti-oppressive but also anti-*repressive* in regard to the body, and as such, fertilize classrooms such that they are primed to flourish into transformative environments wherein emancipation may be emotionally felt and corporeally lived.

Feeling Emotional in Embodied Antiracist Teaching

Teaching and learning occur through, with, against, and despite our bodies (Garland-Thomson, 2003; Stenberg, 2002). This truth often goes unrecognized in the neoliberal university, which demands an allegiance to efficiency that aligns with the production of (credentialed) workers to maintain the status quo. Pedagogical practices privileged in this context tend to reify the modernist notion of the Cartesian mind/body dichotomy that pervades Western thought (e.g., Bordo, 1993/2004; de Beauvoir, 1953/2011; McLaren, 1988). In education, this has contributed to the dominant view of the classroom as "the traditional arena where supposedly disembodied minds engage" (Garland-Thomson, 2003, p. xii). Such thinking is problematic given that, as we noted previously, "oppression leaves its traces not just in people's minds, but in their muscles and skeletons as well" (Fay, 1987, p. 146). Moreover, dichotomous thinking regarding the mind/body limits what can be known about either the mind or the body, and forecloses on the possibility of learning from what results from their inherent interconnectedness (Grosz, 1994; Lesko, 2010; Shapiro, 1999/2015).

In this section, we elaborate on two teaching methods associated with our antiracist pedagogies. These are strategies that (re)claim the centrality of bodily knowledge in the corollary processes of teaching and learning by seeking to suture the mind to the body in an effort to grow students' critical (race) consciousness. We must stress that although we have primarily taught White, female students, we believe that the tools explored here transcend boundaries of difference in their usefulness. We must also state that our approaches offer different yet complementary entrances into engagement with emotionality and embodiment: Sherry's strategy accentuates the intercorporeal relationship between pedagogue and student (and among students), and Esther's method emphasizes the interdependent relationship between the pedagogue's or the student's interior emotional world and her exterior racialized body (within a sociocultural and sociohistorical frame). Bonding these approaches is our shared belief in the pedagogical pertinence of noticing *both* pedagogues' and students' particular bodies (Spellman, 1982) vis à vis antiracist teaching and learning.

Talking Circles: Bearing Witness in Racialized Encounters

The process of deeply listening to another's lived truth without judgment or the need for response has been described as "bearing witness" (see Miner, 2013).[2] Such attention to another's experience challenges the mind/body dichotomy that often stifles deep engagement with issues of racial difference in higher education and honors the inextricable link between embodiment and emotion (Lesko, 2010; Shapiro, 1999/2015). One way I (Sherry) have invited students in my teacher education classes to bear witness to one another's embodied and affective experiences with race and racism is through the practice of talking circles.

Circles offer a way for students to bear witness to the emotionality and corporeality of race and racism. I use a traditional talking circle format,[3] in which class members sit and talk in a circle. There is a keeper who frames and guides the conversation using prompts and discussion questions and a talking piece—any small object that can be easily passed around the circle, such as a small, stone-shaped piece of Venetian glass, in the case of my class—that circulates clockwise from participant to participant. Whoever has the talking piece has the attention of the group and is the speaker, while others listen and bear witness. I draw attention to corporeality and emotion by offering specific opening and closing quotes and guiding questions that make this connection as illustrated in the example that follows.

In one circle involving Katie's class—the one in which the firefighter exam debate transpired—I began with a student quote pulled from the private, weekly feedback I collect. Without attributing a name to the quote, I verbalized what this student had written: "I have still not learned to talk about race without involving emotions so for that reason I avoid those conversations. Maybe in doing so I have also become a part of the problem." The student specifically mentions her own affective response as hindering her participation, and therefore, her learning. My intention was that others in the class would be provoked to consider how their emotional reactions to issues of race might also be impacting their behavior. The circle continued. Students, using the talking piece to take turns, were then invited to respond freely in order to be fully present in their bodies, or as it were, to bear witness in the day's circle.

After a sufficient amount of time elapsed, I posed the topic for the day, which related to considering the impact of various personal identities, including race, class, gender, sexuality, and ability.[4] I gave students time to think and jot down their thoughts before I presented the first discussion question: "What is one instance where you have been disadvantaged based on your location in the social hierarchy?" Being the keeper of the circle, I had the talking piece first and was very much aware of how my tone might influence what others shared. I also felt a moment of vulnerability and concern about what it would mean or take to be open enough to model sharing for others. I was concerned about feeling too exposed as the course professor, particularly given the focus of dominant schooling spaces on the separation between mind and body; cognitive and emotional; and subsequently, personal and professional. But I shared that during this particular school year I had classes comprised primarily of male students, a first in my career as a professional educator, and that I felt like they challenged my authority in subtle ways. I pondered aloud if my gender, or my race and gender combined, caused students to question my competence. Immediately, my hands began to sweat. Had my recounting of my embodied experience alienated any of my students or made them feel uncomfortable? Would my students now view me as weak(er) because I admitted a challenge related to my own marginalization?

The talking piece was circulated and students shared their own stories of personal challenge in educational settings based on their embodied experience. Kelly, a Black woman, shared a story from a recent interview she had for a teaching position with a private organization. She was mistaken for a youth and treated very poorly by the program director with whom she was to interview. As Kelly spoke, her eyes filled with tears and the other class members and I listened with rapt attention. Here we were bearing witness. Here we were honoring the connection between the mind and body. Kelly made clear how her understandings of course materials were shaped and also influenced by this episode and the accumulation of her lived experiences in a Black woman's body. Through Kelly's example, and those of other students, we were able, as a class, in bearing witness, to make apparent how affects are "forms of embodied thinking that primarily operate nonconsciously" (Sullivan, 2013, p. 23).

Getting to a point where students could speak and hear such painful truths was a process. Under my guidance, our class worked to build community in myriad ways and learned the process of using talking circles before engaging with such "difficult subjects."[5] For instance, I required students to present the story of their names to the class. Subsequently, class members were quizzed on each other's names, the idea being that in order to consider potentially painful topics, each member of the community needed to feel known. Then, we used circles to forge agreements of how we wanted to interact as a community and so forth, until we could name our bodily privilege and oppression and still feel whole.

As the class session wrapped up, students reached out to affirm and question and appreciate one another's sharing in ways that further demonstrated the utility of corporeal teaching that honors emotionality. Their actions illuminated the contagiousness of affect. As Gibbs (2001) has remarked, "bodies can catch feelings as easily as catch fire: affect leaps from one body to another, evoking tenderness, inciting shame, igniting rage, exciting fear . . . affect can inflame nerves and muscles in a conflagration of every conceivable kind of passion" (p. 1). For instance, one student lingered to speak with Kelly. Appearing to hold back tears and with torment in her eyes, she said, "Thank you for sharing. I can't even imagine what that must have been like."

If, perhaps, all our students could learn how to "catch" each other's feelings, experience and empathize with each other's racialized pain and shame, and if we could learn how to do the same beside them, then perhaps true change would be possible. Such change would honor the understanding that "your liberation is bound up with mine,"[6] and engender community and coalition building, rather than alienation and othering. [7]

Heart Mapping: Locating the Histories of Racial Memories

Heart mapping[8] in the context of antiracist teaching is an exercise that I (Esther) have designed and employed to guide students through the excavation of racialized histories of lived experience. It involves creating a visual expression of racial memories as a launching point for a larger and longer inquiry into the nuances of race, racism, and racial identity. I use the activity to help students develop a personal stake in the generally semester-long examination of those aforementioned issues. Through my teaching, I have found that the heightened awareness that emerges as they make sense of how the racial memories of the (individual and collective/societal) past impress upon their learning and subsequent teaching in the present leads to a deepening of their critical race consciousness. Core to this activity are memory, broadly, and racial memories, particularly, both of which I expound upon next.

Remembering Racial Memories

Memory is an omniscient shadow that looms over the present—a constant companion to the here and now. It takes various forms, including the following:

> Sensory memory, of things touched and felt, sensual and alive. Physical memory, of pleasure and pain, of bodies stretched and moved in ways we had not thought possible. Spiritual memory, of knowing the energy of God/dess and seeking to find ways to ease our separation . . . from one another. Emotional memory, the feelings of sadness, happiness, envy, and hatred, to name a few. (Dillard, 2008a, p. 200)

These are the aspects of memory to which the process of heart mapping attunes but with a pointed emphasis on racial memories. Citing Oriah Mountain Dreamer (2005), Cynthia Dillard (2008b) expresses that these memories

> are intimate: they are memories that, good or bad, make you ache with desire "to find the marriage of meaning and matter in our lives, in the world.". . . And regardless of race, such intimacy is inextricably linked to racial and cultural identities. (p. 90)

Guidelines for Heart Mapping Racial Memories

The process of heart mapping offers an opportunity for concretizing, summarizing, synthesizing, and visualizing racial memories that are otherwise abstract and floating unanchored in consciousness. After gathering the necessary materials[9] and articulating a definition of *racial memories,* I typically begin this activity by modeling the crafting of my own heart map. I start with an outline of a heart. I proceed by turning to the center of the heart, and then as I reflect on my racial memories, I place at the center of the shape what feels at that exact moment like the most important person, place, or thing in regard to my racialized lived experiences. I continue by working outwards using specific words that relate to particular racial memories. Importantly, I narrate my experience of heart mapping, also in real-time, as I am modeling the activity to students. The following prompts,[10] which I encourage my students to use as they embark upon their own heart mapping, serve as guidelines:

- Which racial memories are stored at your core—that is, in your heart? Consider sensory, physical, spiritual, and emotional racial memories. (For me, for example, the smell of scented dry erase markers is an important sensory racial memory because it evokes the trauma of transitioning into a majority White high school as a newly arrived Black Kenyan immigrant.)
- What racialized lived experiences of events are etched into your memory?
- What people and places have been important to how you make meaning of race, racism, and racial identity, and why?
- What histories—individual, familial, collective, and/or societal—impress upon your racial memories?
- What secrets that rotate around race and racism—and perhaps even racial identity—do you keep in your heart? Are some of these individual secrets? Are others family secrets?
- What artifacts—items, objects, or things—are important to how you make sense of race, racism, and/or (your) racial identity?
- Which of your racial memories are steeped in intense feelings, such as happiness, sadness, frustration, joy, pain, and so on?
- What visceral reactions arise as you reflect on your racial memories of lived experiences? (Consider representing these visceral reactions visually, e.g., through your choice of colors for the heart map, or through your depictions of signs and symbols.)

I also provide my students with the following additional directives for the activity:

- Ask yourself if you want to keep some racial memories within your heart, and move others, perhaps those less important to how you make sense of race, racism, and/or racial identity to or beyond the margins of your heart.
- You may want to draw two or more hearts to represent dual sets or dueling racial memories—good and bad; happy and sad; secret and open—and then include different experiences within each heart.
- You may want to use different colors to represent different emotions, events, and relationships, and then provide a key that explains your color-coding scheme.

Heart Mapping in Action

I share an example of a heart map that I created here (Figure 7.1). In this map, I emphasize places that have been important to the evolution of my racial identity in a myriad of ways. Next, I narrate my experience of shaping one aspect of the diagram by way of illustrating the process of heart mapping.

As I was locating the state of Minnesota on this map, I was reminded of the smell of sweetly scented Expo dry erase markers. I heard the sounds of heavy chairs with skinny metal legs scraping loudly against hardwood floors. I saw neon-colored manila folders and bright yellow, graphite-filled pencils

Figure 7.1. Esther's heart map of racial memories.

peeking playfully through the zippered mouths of overstuffed backpacks. In other words, my senses were stimulated by memories of my life in a large, public high school located in a posh suburb of St. Paul, the capital city. I was an anomalous Black speck in this context—a dark-skinned, working-class Kenyan immigrant taking honors classes. My face was typically the only Black one in my classes, making me a Black dot submerged in a vast sea of Whiteness. Paradoxically, I spent my high school years feeling unseen and unknown. My teachers acknowledged my existence as a learner—after all, they graded my papers and commented on my report cards—but they did not seem to see me as an embodied human being, and did not engage with race as it was marked on bodies, theirs or mine. I was left in isolation to make sense of the stark contrast between my Black flesh and the White bodies that surrounded me, and spent those years deeply desiring the impossible—physical inconspicuousness—while navigating the dissonance that grew from my visible invisibility. This period was the genesis of my ongoing quest to detangle the knottiness of racism, teaching, and learning.

Mapping and Making Meaning of Racial Memories
Heart mapping is an embodied exercise, as evidenced by my explanation of how my racial memories of high school are reflected in the visual depiction of my heart map. (Re)engaging these and other such racial memories opens space for the mapper—be it my students, or me, the pedagogue—to oscillate between mind and body when making meaning of racialized memories of lived experiences and then making sense of those meanings in relationship to the aims of antiracism in a classroom setting. Moreover, for me, beyond the content of the heart map itself, the narration that occurs as I model the creation of a heart map allows me to place my "body-at-the-scene-of-writing" (Somerville, 2004, p. 52)—that is, to acknowledge the somatic sensations that are surging through my body in the moment as I recall racial memories. In doing so, I am able to further trouble the mind/body dualism by (expressing my) feeling of "the simultaneous connection and separation of the experiencing body in place observing itself in/through writing" (Somerville, 2004, p. 52).

Embracing Antiracist Pedagogies of Affect and Embodiment

We believe that the endeavor of higher education—as one of the few social contexts in the United States wherein individuals of diverse racial backgrounds can readily interact (Espenshade, Radford, & Chung, 2009)—should provide pedagogues and students with opportunities to build understandings of themselves in relation to the "other" that facilitate the creation of a more humane society (see Park, 2013). The best versions of socially just classrooms can be settings in which pedagogues proffer structured inquiry into the self and the other; that is, into what it means to navigate the world in different incarnations of difference or in different bodies. It is this kind of inquiry that our use of talking circles and heart mapping invite.

Talking circles and heart mapping exemplify teaching methods that speak to the pedagogical *affordances,* as opposed to the limits, of feelings of vulnerability, pain, uncertainty, and other such emotional and corporeal states. Such strategies, as reflective of pedagogies of affect and embodiment, provide pedagogues with tools to carve out space in which to (re)visit hurts accumulated in encounters with racial oppression. Equally important, they harness the unpredictable emotional intensities powering the racialized conflicts that inevitably percolate in the context of antiracist teaching (Lesko, Simmons, Quarshie, & Newton, 2008, p. 1541). Using pedagogies of affect and embodiment allows us to deploy those emotional forces in ways that move us, individually and collectively, toward antiracist teaching and learning that embraces diverse ways of knowing and being by diverting from the cerebral—and therefore, hegemonic—ways of making meaning that are heralded in the neoliberal teacher education classroom.

As equity-oriented faculty, we take to heart—that is, take seriously—Ahmed's (2000) assertion that the depths of "identity itself become instituted through encounters with others that surprise, that shift the boundaries of the familiar, of what we assume that we know" (pp. 6–7). As such, we view classroom encounters as sites of identity (de- and re-) formation: moments of learning about the ever-expanding and contracting parameters of who we believe we are as pedagogues, and who we think our students to be; moments of continual shape-shifting—that is, moments of becoming this, or transforming into that, or meeting the other, or transcending "otherness." Our hope is that the theories and practices that we have detailed in this chapter offer insights into not what to do *about* the unstructured potential embedded in the conflict that both Ahmed (2004) and hooks (1994) name as intimately tied to these encounters, but rather what to do *with* that potential—that is, how to pedagogically mobilize the emotion associated with internal and external conflict in the interest of racial justice at the level of the mind *and* the body, rather than the mind *over* the body.

Notes

1. I describe myself as "biracial or Black/White," to acknowledge some of the complexity of my identity and parentage. At the same time, I identify and present as

Black, a visibility that is perhaps magnified for me in the ultra-White context of the professorate and teacher education.

2. This is a process commonly observed by practitioners of "restorative justice," which is "a philosophical framework that shifts organizational, institutional, and social values toward healing damaged relationships and community bonds" (Ginwright, 2016, p. 30).

3. Circles are a key component of restorative justice practices. Derived from Indigenous practices, community members gather in circles to share experiences and stories (see Ginwright, 2016). Circles can have different foci, ranging from healing to responses to wrongs done to the community to curricular instruction and beyond (see Boyes-Watson & Pranis, 2014; Clifford, n. d.).

4. Adapted from Boyes-Watson & Pranis (2014), *Circle Forward: Building a Restorative School Community*, "The Impact of Social Hierarchies on Me" (pp. 172–174).

5. See Clifford (n. d.) for introductory circle exercises.

6. This commonly used quote is attributed to Lilla Watson (as cited in One Nation Indivisible, 2016, and elsewhere).

7. Silverstein (2013), for example, discusses the "racial empathy gap"—which describes the inability to understand pain across race—as being a key cause for social disparities.

8. This activity owes its genesis to Heard (1998), who discusses "heart mapping" as a brainstorming exercise. My conceptualization of heart mapping vis-à-vis racial memories asks participants to begin the process of *(un)learning* racism and racial oppression by uncovering racial memories that linger in their consciousness, and that reside at the core of their beings and bodies.

9. The basic materials essential for this activity are (preferably plain white) paper with 8 ½" × 11" dimensions at a minimum, writing utensils, and markers or colored pencils.

10. These prompts build on those suggested by Heard (1998).

References

Ahmed, S. (2000). *Strange encounters: Embodied others in post-coloniality*. New York, NY: Routledge.

Ahmed, S. (2004). *The cultural politics of emotion*. New York, NY: Routledge.

Aveling, N. (2006). "Hacking at our very roots": Rearticulating White racial identity within the context of teacher education. *Race Ethnicity and Education, 9*(3), 261–274.

Boler, M. (Ed). (2004). *Democratic dialogue in education: Troubling speech, disturbing silence*. New York, NY: Peter Lang.

Bordo, S. (2004). *Unbearable weight: Feminism, Western culture, and the body*. Berkeley, CA: University of California Press. (Original work published in 1993).

Boyes-Watson, C., & Pranis, K. (2014). *Circle forward: Building a restorative school community*. St. Paul, MN: Living Justice Press.

Brennan, T. (2004). *The transmission of affect*. Ithaca, NY: Cornell University Press.

Christian, B. (1988). The race for theory. *Feminist Studies, 14*(1), 67–70.

Clifford, A. (n. d.). *Teaching restorative practices with classroom circles*. San Francisco, CA: Center for Restorative Processes.

Coates, T. (2015). *Between the world and me*. New York, NY: Spiegel & Grau.

de Beauvoir, S. (2011). *The second sex* (C. Borde & S. Malovany-Chevalier, Trans.). New York, NY: Knopf. (Original work published 1953).

Deckman, S. L., & Montilla, B. (2015). Being tall isn't exactly the same thing as being Black. In J. Martin (Ed.), *Racial battle fatigue: Insights from the front lines of social justice advocacy*. Santa Barbara, CA: Praeger.

DeSalvo, L. (1999). *Writing as a way of healing: How telling our stories transforms our lives*. Boston, MA: Beacon Press.

Dillard, C. B. (2008a). Racializing ethics and bearing witness to memory in research. In N. K. Denzin & M. G. Giardina (Eds.), *Qualitative inquiry and social justice* (pp. 217–228). Walnut Creek, CA: Left Coast Press.

Dillard, C. B. (2008b). Re-membering culture: Bearing witness to the spirit of identity in research. *Race Ethnicity and Education, 11*(1), 87–93.

Edelman, S. (2016, March 20). FDNY's new entry exam asks about everything but firefighting. *The New York Post*. Retrieved from http://www.nypost.com

Espenshade, T. J., Radford, A. W., & Chung, C. Y. (2009). *No longer separate, not yet equal: Race and class in elite college admission and campus life*. Princeton, NJ: Princeton University Press.

Fay, B. (1987). *Critical social science*. Ithaca, NY: Cornell University Press.

Garland-Thomson, R. (2003). Foreword: Bodies enter the classroom. In R. Garland-Thomson & M. S. Holmes (Eds.), *The teacher's body: Embodiment, authority, and identity in the academy* (pp. vi–xiii). Albany, NY: State University of New York Press.

Gibbs, A. (2001). Contagious feelings: Pauline Hanson and the epidemiology of affect. *Australian Humanities Review*. Retrieved from http://www.australian humanitiesreview.org/archive/Issue-December-2001/gibbs.html

Ginwright, S. (2016). *Hope and healing in urban education: How urban activists and teachers are reclaiming matters of the heart*. New York, NY: Routledge.

Grosz, E. (1994). *Volatile bodies: Toward a corporeal feminism*. Bloomington, IN: Indiana University Press.

Gumbs, A. (2014). Nobody mean more: Black feminist pedagogy and solidarity. In P. Chatterjee & S. Maira (Eds.), *The imperial university: Academic repression and scholarly dissent* (pp. 237–260). Minneapolis, MN: University of Minnesota Press.

Heard, G. (1998). *Awakening the heart: Exploring poetry in elementary and middle school*. Portsmouth, NH: Heinemann.

hooks, b. (1994). *Teaching to transgress: Education as the practice of freedom*. New York, NY: Routledge.

Lesko, N. (2010). Feeling abstinent? Feeling comprehensive? Touching the affects of sexuality curricula. *Sex Education, 10*(3), 281–297.

Lesko, N., Simmons, J. A., Quarshie, A., & Newton, N. (2008). The pedagogy of monsters: Scary disturbances in a doctoral research preparation course. *Teachers College Record, 110*(8), 1541–1573.

McLaren, P. (1988). Schooling the postmodern body: Critical pedagogy and the politics of enfleshment. *Journal of Education, 170*(3), 53–83.

Miner, K. (2013). Restorative Justice listening . . . to bare witness. Retrieved from http://www.circle-space.org/2013/11/05/restorative-justice-listening-to-bare-witness/

Mountain Dreamer, O. (2005). *What we ache for: Creativity and the unfolding of the soul.* San Francisco, CA: Harper Collins.

One Nation Indivisible. (2016). Favorite quotes. Retrieved from http://www.one nationindivisible.org/resources/favorite-quotes/

Park, J. J. (2013). *When diversity drops: Race, religion, and affirmative action in higher education.* New Brunswick, NJ: Rutgers University Press.

Shapiro, S. (2015). *Pedagogy and the politics of the body: A critical praxis.* New York, NY: Routledge. (Original work published 1999).

Silverstein, J. (2013, June 27). I don't feel your pain: A failure of empathy perpetuates racial disparities. *Slate.* Retrieved from http://www.slate.com/articles/health_and_science/science/2013/06/racial_empathy_gap_people_don_t_perceive_pain_in_other_races.1.html

Somerville, M. (2004). Tracing bodylines: The body in feminist poststructural research. *International Journal of Qualitative Studies in Education, 17*(1), 47–63.

Spellman, E. (1982). Woman as body: Ancient and contemporary views. *Feminist Studies, 8*(1), 109–131.

Stenberg, S. J. (2002). Embodied classrooms, embodied knowledges: Re-thinking the mind/body split. *Composition Studies, 30*(2), 43–60.

Sullivan, S. (2013). On the need for a new *ethos* of White antiracism. *philoSOPHIA, 2*(1), 21–38.

Yosso, T. J. (2006). *Critical race counterstories along the Chicana/Chicano educational pipeline.* New York, NY: Taylor & Francis.

8

TRANSFORMATIONAL PEDAGOGIES OF THE ABJECT BODY

An Argument for Radical Fat Pedagogies

Breanne Fahs

eminist pedagogies have long championed tools that allow for critical inquiry and a reshaping of the social and political world. For example, standard feminist curricula in women and gender studies include content about the importance of personal transformation (e.g., seeing course material as relevant to one's own life) and engaging critically with oppressive structures that shape and govern our access to power and choice (Boxer, 2001; Shircliffe, 2000). Similarly, feminist praxis, the fusion between theory and practice, has informed women and gender studies courses as they work within both the humanities and the social sciences, and as they help students imagine the "real world" applicability of their course material (Naples, 2002; Sheridan, 2012). Helping students to develop a critical feminist consciousness within the classroom, particularly related to their own bodies, has been a central goal of feminist pedagogy since the emergence of women and gender studies as a field in the early 1970s (Boxer, 2001; Stake, 2007).

Surprisingly, then, little work has yet examined the teaching of fat studies within the feminist classroom. Whereas one new edited collection has started to think about "fat pedagogies" (Cameron & Russell, 2016), fat studies is still not routinely incorporated into introductory women and gender studies courses, for example, or introductory humanities courses more broadly (Cooper, 2010). As a field still in its infancy, fat studies has emerged as a forceful rebuttal against cultural norms of body shame and all-too-narrow views of "healthy size" (Rothblum & Solovay, 2009; van Amsterdam, 2013), although its relationship to the broader curriculum is still tenuous. Key tenets of fat studies include the following: an emphasis on "health at any size," a focus on fat acceptance and lessening of fat shame, fat activisms (particularly within public health), critical attention to the moralizing qualities of fat shaming behavior, overlaps between fat identities and other social identities like race and disability, and reduction of stigma for fat bodies (Cooper, 2010; Hebl & Heatherton, 1998; Perez-Lopez, Lewis, & Cash, 2001; Rothblum & Solovay, 2009; van Amsterdam, 2013). Applying these priorities to the classroom poses a serious challenge to those doing work both in fat studies and in related disciplines; this chapter takes up the question of how to apply (radical) fat studies thinking to our pedagogical work as teachers.

Missing in these fat studies pedagogies, however, is the portrait of fatness as something *permanently* (and proudly?) on the margins and unwilling to assimilate into mainstream notions of "appropriate" bodies. We might call this, within the fat studies realm, the *missing discourse of refusal.* What would it mean, for example, if fatness were framed not as something that is "just as good/acceptable" as thinness, but as its own sort of queering of bodies and size altogether? How can we better teach about fat bodies that refuse to embrace discourses of thinness (and its attendant notions of "health" and "wellness" and "perfection")? Might greater attention to fat refusal to assimilate lead to some interesting and productive inroads and move fat studies beyond a framework that maintains thinness as relatively unchallenged, particularly pedagogically? Who might advocate for, and align with, the goals of an anti-assimilationist fat studies? Still more, how can those outside of fat studies begin to incorporate radical fat studies thinking into their own pedagogical work?

This chapter examines fat studies—or, possibly, *radical* fat studies—as an interdisciplinary collaborator with disability studies, trans studies, queer studies, and "freak" studies in order to examine how radical fat studies might situate fatness (and other abject bodies) as embracing the margins and the fringes (and thus reshape cultural norms of bodies). Given that the word *radical* stems from the task of "going to the root" of something, I argue that fat studies at its core is staunchly anti-assimilationist and that, much like its intellectual allies mentioned earlier, could benefit from recognizing this resistant identity more fully, particularly on the ground with students in different critical classrooms. In this chapter I look at pedagogical practices of teaching fat studies alongside queer anti-assimilationist work, trans writing about embracing the "freak" body, and queer crip theories of working within abjection (rather than outside of it). I then trace my pedagogical work with students in my course Abject Bodies and the Politics of Trash (formerly known by its less respectable name, Trash, Freaks, and SCUM) to imagine a space for fatness as an outlaw/outsider status. By looking at fat bodies without the need to contain, confirm, shape, alter, confine, or shame them (e.g., refusing to discuss the reductive notions of "but it's healthier!" and "fatness is bad for you!"), radical fat pedagogies examine fatness (and the intellectual allies of fat bodies) as a threat to assumptions about gender, size, respectability, and marginalization. I conclude the chapter with some concrete recommendations for classroom pedagogies that could more directly account for radical fat studies perspectives.

The Emergence of Fat Pedagogies

As more and more signs point to the seriousness, longevity, and impact of the emerging field of fat studies—the publication of the *Fat Studies Reader* (Rothblum & Solovay, 2009) followed by the 2012 debut of *Fat Studies* journal—the discipline has moved from community activism toward more institutional recognition in the last five years. An array of recent journal articles and books have examined fat studies as a field with wide implications for public health, social sciences, and feminist theories of the body (Fikkan & Rothblum, 2012; Probyn, 2008; Rothblum & Solovay, 2009). In tandem with this shift in attention on body size, popular news media has begun to cover fat studies courses as a new twist on diversity and inclusiveness (Osler, 2016); an extension of college conversations about body norms (North, 2010); as college's "hot new course" (Binder, 2010); and, in right-wing reactionary publications, as the latest avenue for liberals to feel victimized and complain about discrimination (Bokhari, 2016).

While the news media debates the merits of fat studies, scholars within fat studies have recently started to think together about what it means to move fat studies into the classroom (Cameron & Russell, 2016; Hetrick & Attig, 2009). Research about prejudices and biases directed toward fat professors and fat students (Escalera, 2009; Fisanick, 2014; Koppelman, 2009) and the importance of moving fatness from a state of invisibility to visibility (Cooper, 2010; Watkins, Farrell, & Doyle-Hugmeyer, 2012) constituted some of the early goals of fat pedagogy work. Within the last year, attention to the affective practices of fat studies (e.g., using empathy and mindfulness; Farrell, 2016), recognizing thin privilege (Bacon, O'Reilly, & Aphramor, 2016), examining fat hatred within the classroom (Royce, 2016), fighting against neoliberal rhetoric of individual responsibility for weight loss and health (Rothblum, 2016), reimagining how to talk about fatness with studies in health courses (Ward, Beausoleil, & Heath, 2016), critical analyses of bullying and weight bias (McNinch, 2016; Pringle & Powell, 2016), and imagining fat pedagogy as a "public pedagogy" (Rich, 2016) have represented some of the most recent iterations fat pedagogies work has taken. Most of this pedagogical work has explored the conditions and consequences of fat phobia (both internalized and externalized) with students, but most have not offered methods for constructing fat identities as shamelessly rebellious or "trouble-making" on purpose.

The portrait here of fat pedagogy—which is confidently arguing for the necessity of fat acceptance, inclusion of different bodies, and retraining/ rethinking about fatness as not disgusting or wrong—notably overlooks the more radical position of imagining fatness as a *refusal* to gain the approval of others by emulating or striving for thinness. Even the Fat Pedagogy Manifesto (Russell & Cameron, 2016)—evoking the genre and language of radical social change—instead largely frames fat pedagogies as needing to shift away from one-size-fits-all, thus reinforcing many of the original goals of fat studies as working toward fat acceptance rather than fat refusals. I want to ask: What would fat pedagogies look like if fatness was constructed as defiantly subversive, not looking for approval, not aspiring toward acceptance, and instead, operating as a rambunctious and rebellious identity that mocks, defies, and smashes notions of "appropriate" bodies? How can feminist professors move classroom discussions away from reductive conversations about "health" and more toward the defiant potential of bodies that refuse smallness? How can students and professors work to call out their assumptions about fat bodies in meaningful ways?

Freaks and Geeks: Linking Arms With Other Anti-Assimilationist Allies

As an interdisciplinary scholar and professor, working among and between fields like women and gender studies, psychology, sociology, sexuality studies, queer studies, history, and cultural studies, I have learned to take great pleasure in the practice of "thinking together" and creating, as Lois Weis and Michelle Fine (2001) call it, *disruptive pedagogies* based on counter-hegemonic moments. That is, working with colleagues within and outside my fields, teaching students from across multiple cross-listed areas, and bringing together varied perspectives in my own writing, the process of thinking together, of purposefully seeking out contrasting disciplinary viewpoints in service of a common scholarly goal, has been of enormous value intellectually throughout my career. Women's studies—a field that is always interdisciplinary and one that moves wildly between humanities and social science perspectives—requires attention to scholarly alliances and overlaps just as it values the processes and outcomes of thinking together. When imagining radical fat studies, I argue that thinking together about such ideas alongside queer anti-assimilationist work, trans writing about embracing the "freak" body, and queer crip theories of working within (rather than outside of) abjection—each outlined later—have all proven useful in tracing precise links and overlaps among seemingly incongruent fields.

A crucial overlap between radical fat studies and queer anti-assimilationism gives insight into the toxicity of striving for assimilation. For example, Mattilda Sycamore's *That's Revolting!* (2008) or *Why Are Faggots So Afraid of Faggots* (2012) argues for *defiant faggotry*, a flagrant disregard for assimilationist goals like marriage and the "nuclear" family, and a refusal to engage in straight-acting cultural norms like joining the military and mind-less consumerism. This work, which argues instead for sexual flamboyance, gender liberation, and queer refusals, situates queer identities as purpose-fully on the margins and as an identity that can (and should) defy norms of so-called straight culture. Along these lines, Kate Bornstein's (2010) *Gender Outlaws* argues for the radical anti-assimilationist potential of trans bodies, whereas Ryan Conrad's (2014) *Against Equality* argues against gay marriage on the grounds that it links basic human rights to an inherently conserva-tive tradition, just as hate crime legislation strengthens anti-queer institu-tions like police and prisons rather than dismantling them. These works frame queer identity not as seeking approval from straight culture but as flagrantly disobeying the rules and norms of straight culture, suggesting that radical fat studies might also imagine what the fat body can *do* when it refuses to become smaller, more likeable, or more attractively thin.

Trans writings about freak culture and the embrace of the freak body also have important implications for radical fat studies, as the freak purposefully rebels against norms that enforce the similarity of bodies. From Gwendolyn Ann Smith's (2010) claim that "we're all someone's freak" to Susan Stryker's (1994) famous embrace of transgender rage and celebration of her freak trans body, trans scholars have situated the freak body as something to celebrate rather than conceal. Stryker (1994) deploys the specter of the "monster" to talk about how her body forces others to confront things they find uncom-fortable about themselves:

> To encounter the transsexual body, to apprehend a transgendered con-sciousness articulating itself, is to risk a revelation of the constructedness of the natural order. Confronting the implications of this constructedness can summon up all the violation, loss, and separation inflicted by the gender-ing process that sustains the illusion of naturalness. My transsexual body literalizes this abstract violence. (p. 254)

Radical fat studies might also ask: What does the fat body invoke in others, and how does this confrontation serve a necessary and important role in upending ideas about "appropriate" body size?

Finally, queer crip theories—or radical disability studies—also teach radical fat studies about the importance of working within and embracing abjection rather than rejecting it. Alison Kafer (2013) argued that disability should not leave "non-disability" in place as the normal, but should instead argue for a radical vision of disability as itself a rejection of compulsory able-bodiedness. Similarly, other works in queer crip theory have argued for a revolutionary new view of sexuality (McRuer & Mollow, 2012), the importance of new narratives of gay men's disabled lives (Guter & Killacky, 2003), and the recognition of disability not as "fixed" but as fluid and subject to projections of others (Samuels, 2014). Each of these texts has reframed disability away from its reference point of "able-bodiedness" and has instead worked to undermine the "normality" of able-bodiedness (and challenge what able-bodiedness even is). These frameworks provide crucial implications for (radical) fat studies as they trace its identity in relation to thinness, "obesity," and other cultural depictions of body size. I also argue that fat studies pedagogies cannot adequately account for the radical work of fat studies without these other complementary perspectives.

Teaching Trash, Freaks, and SCUM

To illustrate concretely how I have worked to forge territory for radical fat studies in the classroom, I developed an upper-division women and gender studies course (cross-listed with American studies, ethnic studies, and a master's program in social justice and human rights) called Trash, Freaks, and SCUM. This course was recently retitled, at the urging of the university administration to have a more respectable and, ironically, less trashy name, as Abject Bodies and the Politics of Trash; this shift occurred because the provost's office felt that the original title, with "freaks" and "scum" in it, was coded as too nonacademic, confrontational, difficult, and low-brow. This course is offered at Arizona State University, where students come from a range of race, class, and sexual identity backgrounds, and many students are outside of the traditional student age range (18- to 22-years-old). I typically teach approximately one-third male students and two-thirds female students in each course, along with at least one transgender or gender queer student each semester. Students are typically left-leaning but have most often grown up in the (very) conservative environment of central Arizona. During the semesters that I teach fat studies content, I typically introduce this material no sooner than four weeks into the course, after students have been introduced to the theoretical foundations of the course.

Radical fat studies material fits well with this course, as the philosophical premise of the course is that knowledge should be produced and gleaned from the gutter, and that trash serves a role in how we understand the world. Working through texts like Valerie Solanas's (1968) *SCUM Manifesto*, Edward Humes's (2013) *Garbology*, Rachel Adams's (2001) *Sideshow U.S.A.*, and Julia Kristeva's (1982) *Powers of Horror*, students consider trash both literally (e.g., how much trash do we produce and how can we reduce this amount?), and metaphorically (whose bodies acquire the label of "trashy"?). Together with content on freak studies, disability studies, and critical race studies, the fat studies work students read looks at extreme fatness and extreme Otherness to undermine and unwork contemporary ideologies of fatness as morally "sinful" and ultimately abject. We move beyond discourses of stigma and shame and instead look at the cultural hatred of fatness but also the potential for resistance inherent in the fat body (particularly as it aligns with other fields like queer crip studies).

Together, we focus specifically on the production of the fat body as freak, alongside discussions of early anthropological efforts to imprison African men in New York zoos (Adams, 2001), Susan Stryker's (1994) compelling work on the plight of trans people as virtual Frankensteins, and Rachel Adams's (2001) analysis of Diane Arbus's freak photography. We read JuliaGrace Jester's (2009) analysis of fat burlesque and Amy Farrell's (2009) work on fat women in tourist postcards. In this way, the fat "freak" becomes clearly aligned (politically and historically) with freaks of color, trans freaks, queer freaks, and other freaky women. The cartoon-like caricatures of fat women—still prominent today—link up with the overtly hateful and racist portrayals of native Africans as "backward" and "primitive," trans people as living through conditions of self-loathing and fear, and the overwhelming difficulty of circus performers with extreme or abject bodies. As I wrote in my 2016 essay, "A Tale of Three Classrooms," "Ultimately, these links work to situate fatness as one of many identities subjected to 'freak' status by dominant (White, male, middle and upper-class, heterosexual, thin, able-bodied) culture" (Fahs, 2016, p. 226).

Fatness as Outlaw Status: A Vision for Radical Fat Studies in the Classroom

My teaching of fat identity and fat bodies also pushes students to consider a vision of fatness as being outlaw or outsider rather than something mired in discourses of health, beauty, wellness, and individual "efforts" (or not) to lose weight. Building on the important previous work done in fat studies and fat pedagogies (particularly Cameron & Russell, 2016, and Rothblum & Solovay, 2009), my goals in situating fatness in this way are multiple. Along these lines, I offer the following concrete recommendations for how professors can incorporate radical fat studies thinking into their pedagogical work:

1. Strip away the typical discourses of fatness that emphasize the subject as singularly responsible for her body. This might include readings and discussions in the classroom that emphasize the sociocultural framings around fatness and the various institutions that willingly produce fatness, such as the food industry; workplace politics that rarely allow for movement and freedom; and the links among social class, access to healthy foods, exercise culture, and fatness. Teaching that the body *is produced* by culture and not the individual is a crucial first step in teaching radical fat studies work.

2. Discuss fat hatred and fat shaming as historically relevant and connected to other kinds of historical hatred that we now find less "in vogue." Professors could work with students to identify different behaviors in which they engage that reinforce the links between thinness and morality, fatness and immorality. Classroom exercises could include setting groundrules for "calling out" fat-phobic behavior and practices in the classroom, as well as analyzing the treatment of fatness by using other identity categories as a basis for exposing the absurdity or bizarreness of fat phobia. For example, much like the ways that the marriage equality movement relied upon the absurdity of anti-interracial-marriage rhetoric, fat studies must now draw from other forms of oppression—sexism, racism, and so on—to illustrate the absurdity of continuing to allow fat phobic rhetoric in the culture at large.

3. Fuse together rebellion against the medical model of fatness and direct activist tactics and interventions. Classroom interventions could include assigning an activist project for small groups of students to engage in fat activism, organizing a public event on campus that questions the medical framing of fatness, having a fat "speak-out" to give voice to the problems of fat phobia, and brainstorming about radical fat activist tactics. Professors should emphasize that activism is not limited to group protesting but can include a variety of other activities: sabotage, clowning, direct confrontation, letter writing, online activism, sit-ins, personal refusals, and beyond.

4. Imagine some kind of space for the non-self-loathing and empowered fat person (particularly, fat woman). Professors could work with students to

question their assumptions about the fat body and "fat people," particularly by looking at the problems of assimilation across identity groups. In some cases, embodying this identity of a non-self-loathing fat person may in and of itself be a classroom intervention. Professors could also get creative about this and have students invent a fat superhero or engage in dialogue about fat people they admire (e.g., Melissa McCarthy, etc.), ideally weaving in anti-assimilationist rhetoric into this conversation.

5. Connect fat identities to other identities that have, thus far, successfully created radical spaces for anti-assimilation and celebration of Otherness (particularly trans studies, freak studies, and queer crip studies). Fat studies classrooms should always prioritize seeing the struggles of fat activism as deeply connected to the struggles of other groups and movements. Syllabi should include readings across these areas and assignments and exams could work to require students to outline these links more fully. Students should never be allowed to engaged in the "oppression Olympics," where they compare oppressions, but rather, should look for more links and overlaps between different identities and movements.

6. Push students to imagine a more radical fat identity without the need to contain, confirm, shape, alter, confine, or shame fatness. Helping students to imagine an anti-assimilationist fat perspective via changes in language, dress, and expectations for fat people could be useful. Similarly, having students purposefully break "fat rules" might also be interesting. (I had a student who designed her own extra credit assignment about breaking "fat girl rules" and it was profoundly interesting and quite radical.)

My own vision for fat studies imagines fatness as a body that invites critical examinations of wider categories like respectability, marginalization, refusal, and power. I want fat studies to more often "go to the roots" and look at some of the stories that inform the production of the fat body, as those same stories impact the very foundations of fat studies as a field. For example, how can we imagine radical fat studies if the field of fat studies is worrying about respectability and not being marginalized academically? How can fat studies become more radical if many of the core assumptions (and much of the corresponding research) situates fatness as something that should/can assimilate to, and get approval from, the world of thinness and thin bodies (much like queerness gets funneled and assimilated toward discussions of gay marriage)? Whereas fat acceptance and fat empowerment are excellent first steps, I argue that fat studies and fat pedagogies have far more potential if they embrace their more radical edges. What can fat refusal—or the unwillingness to strive for thinness—teach us about body politics? How can a Foucauldian view of biopolitics and the intricacies of power *imposed on* the body inform an emerging vision for radical fat studies?

Moving the budding field of fat studies in a more radical direction rather than an assimilative one could deeply impact the activist leanings of the field. For example, a more radical fat studies could result in better mental health for fat people (particularly women) when they stop trying to emulate thin (or patriarchal) culture (Bondi & Burman, 2001; Caplan, 1992), just as social movement theories teach us that a more radical flank of fat studies might help fat activists mobilize for broader social change in laws and policies (Fitzgerald & Rodgers, 2000; McCammon, Bergner, & Arch, 2015; Robnett, Glasser, & Trammwell, 2015). We must not ignore the militant, angry, performative, outrageous, trouble-making side of fat studies; rather, we must nurture it as transformative and full of possibilities.

Susan Stryker (1994) said in her call to other freaks: "May you discover the enlivening power of darkness within yourself. May it nourish your rage. May your rage inform your actions, and your actions transform you as you struggle to transform your world" (p. 254). I close this chapter with a plea for scholars and activists who work on issues of embodiment, power, social identity, and feminism to imagine fat studies differently, to purposefully embrace its difficult and defiant potential, and to see fat identity as affectively infused with rage, power, and flagrant disregard for discourses that contain (literally and metaphorically) the female body.

References

Adams, R. (2001). *Sideshow U.S.A.: Freaks and the cultural imagination.* Chicago, IL: University of Chicago Press.

Bacon, L., O'Reilly, C., & Aphramor, L. (2016). Reflections on thin privilege and responsibility. In E. Cameron & C. Russell (Eds.), *The fat pedagogy reader: Challenging weight-based oppression through critical education* (pp. 41–52). New York, NY: Peter Lang.

Binder, E. (2010). "Fat studies" go to college. *The Daily Beast.* Retrieved from http://www.thedailybeast.com/articles/2010/11/03/fat-studies-colleges-hot-new-course.html

Bokhari, A. (2016). "Fat studies": The latest grievance course for campus crazies. *Breitbart.* Retrieved from http://www.breitbart.com/tech/2016/01/12/fat-studies-the-latest-course-tailored-for-campus-crazies/

Bondi, L., & Burman, E. (2001). Women and mental health: A feminist review. *Feminist Review, 68*(1), 6–33.

Bornstein, K. (2010). *Gender outlaws: The next generation.* Berkeley, CA: Seal Press.

Boxer, M. J. (2000). *When women ask the questions: Creating women's studies in America.* Baltimore, MD: Johns Hopkins University Press.

Cameron, E. (2014). Toward a fat pedagogy: A study of pedagogical approaches aimed at challenging obesity discourse in post-secondary education. *Fat Studies,* *4*(1), 28–45.

Cameron, E., & Russell, C. (2016). *The fat pedagogy reader: Challenging weight-based oppression.* New York, NY: Peter Lang.

Caplan, P. J. (1992). Driving us crazy: How oppression damages women's mental health and what we can do about it. *Women & Therapy, 12*(3), 5–28.

Conrad, R. (2014). *Against equality: Queer revolution, not mere inclusion.* San Francisco, CA: AK Press.

Cooper, C. (2010). Fat studies: Mapping the field. *Sociology Compass, 4*(12), 1020–1034.

Escalera, E. A. (2009). Stigma threat and the fat professor: Reducing student prejudice in the classroom. In E. Rothblum & S. Solovay (Eds.), *The fat studies reader* (pp. 205–212). New York, NY: New York University Press.

Fahs, B. (2016). A tale of three classrooms: Fat studies and its intellectual allies. In E. Cameron & C. Russell (Eds.), *The fat pedagogy reader: Challenging weight-based oppression through critical education* (pp. 221–229). New York, NY: Peter Lang.

Farrell, A. E. (2009). "The White man's burden": Female sexuality, tourist postcards, and the place of the fat woman in early 20th-century U.S. culture. In E. Rothblum & S. Solovay (Eds.), *The fat studies reader* (pp. 256–262). New York, NY: New York University Press.

Farrell, A. E. (2016). Teaching fat studies in a liberal arts college: The centrality of mindfulness, deep listening, and empathic interpretation as pedagogic methods. In E. Cameron & C. Russell (Eds.), *The fat pedagogy reader: Challenging weight-based oppression through critical education* (pp. 61–70). New York, NY: Peter Lang.

Fikkan, J. L., & Rothblum, E. D. (2012). Is fat a feminist issue? Exploring the gendered nature of weight bias. *Sex Roles, 66*(9–10), 575–592.

Fisanick, C. (2014). Fat professors feel compelled to overperform. *The Chronicle of Higher Education.* Retrieved from https://chroniclevitae.com/news/425-christina-fisanick-fat-professors-feel-compelled-to-overperform#sthash.EQn4lThq.dpuf

Fitzgerald, K. J., & Rodgers, D. M. (2000). Radical social movement organization: A theoretical model. *The Sociological Quarterly, 41*(4), 573–592.

Guter, B., & Killacky, J. R. (2003). *Queer crips: Disabled gay men and their stories.* New York, NY: Routledge.

Hebl, M. R., & Heatherton, T. F. (1998). The stigma of obesity in women: The difference in Black and White. *Personality and Social Psychology Bulletin, 24*(4), 417–426.

Hetrick, A., & Attig, D. (2009). Sitting pretty: Fat bodies, classroom desks, and academic excess. In E. Rothblum & S. Solovay (Eds.), *The fat studies reader* (pp. 197–204). New York, NY: New York University Press.

Humes, E. (2013). *Garbology: Our dirty love affair with trash.* New York, NY: Penguin.

Jester, J. (2009). Placing fat women on center stage. In E. Rothblum & S. Solovay (Eds.), *The fat studies reader* (pp. 249–253). New York, NY: New York University Press.

Kafer, A. (2013). *Feminist, queer, crip.* Bloomington, IN: Indiana University Press.

Koppelman, S. (2009). Fat stories in the classroom: What and how are they teaching about us? In E. Rothblum & S. Solovay (Eds.), *The fat studies reader* (pp. 213–222). New York, NY: New York University Press.

Kristeva, J. (1982). *Powers of horror: An essay on abjection.* New York, NY: Columbia University Press.

McCammon, H. J., Bergner, E. M., & Arch, S. C. (2015). "Are you one of those women?": Within-movement conflict, radical flank effects, and social movement political outcomes. *Mobilization, 20*(2), 157–178.

McNinch, H. (2016). Fat bullying of girls in elementary and secondary schools: Implications for teacher education. In E. Cameron & C. Russell (Eds.), *The fat pedagogy reader: Challenging weight-based oppression through critical education* (pp. 113–122). New York, NY: Peter Lang.

McRuer, R., & Mollow, A. (2012). *Sex and disability.* Durham, NC: Duke University Press.

Naples, N. A. (2002). The challenges and possibilities of transnational feminist praxis. In N. A. Naples & M. Desai (Eds.), *Women's activism and globalization: Linking local struggles and global politics* (pp. 267–281). New York, NY: Routledge.

North, A. (2010). Should "fat studies" be taught in school? *Jezebel.* Retrieved from http://jezebel.com/5681887/should-fat-studies-be-taught-in-school

Osler, C. (2016). "Fat studies" embrace diversity and take on the biases of being overweight. *USA Today College.* Retrieved from http://college.usatoday .com/2016/02/22/fat-studies-embrace-diversity-and-take-on-the-biases-of-being-overweight/

Perez-Lopez, M. S., Lewis, R. J., & Cash, T. F. (2001). The relationship of anti-fat attitudes to other prejudicial and gender-related attitudes. *Journal of Applied Social Psychology, 31*(4), 683–697.

Pringle, R., & Powell, D. (2016). Critical pedagogical strategies to disrupt weight bias in school. In E. Cameron & C. Russell (Eds.), *The fat pedagogy reader: Challenging weight-based oppression through critical education* (pp. 123–132). New York, NY: Peter Lang.

Probyn, E. (2008). IV. Silences behind the mantra: Critiquing feminist fat. *Feminism & Psychology, 18*(3), 401–404.

Rich, E. (2016). A public pedagogy approach to fat pedagogy. In E. Cameron & C. Russell (Eds.), *The fat pedagogy reader: Challenging weight-based oppression through critical education* (pp. 231–240). New York, NY: Peter Lang.

Robnett, B., Glasser, C. L., & Trammwell, R. (2015). Waves of contention: Relation among radical, moderate, and conservative movement organization. *Research in Social Movements, Conflicts, and Change, 38,* 69–101.

Rothblum, E. D. (2016). Weapons of mass distraction in fat studies: "But aren't they unhealthy? And why can't they just lose weight?" In E. Cameron & C. Russell

(Eds.), *The fat pedagogy reader: Challenging weight-based oppression through critical education* (pp. 71–80). New York, NY: Peter Lang.

Rothblum, E., & Solovay, S. (2009). *The fat studies reader.* New York, NY: New York University Press.

Royce, T. (2016). Fat invisibility, fat hate: Towards a progressive pedagogy of size. In E. Cameron & C. Russell (Eds.), *The fat pedagogy reader: Challenging weight-based oppression through critical education* (pp. 21–30). New York, NY: Peter Lang.

Russell, C., & Cameron, E. (2016). A fat pedagogy manifesto. In E. Cameron & C. Russell (Eds.), *The fat pedagogy reader: Challenging weight-based oppression through critical education,* (pp. 251–256). New York, NY: Peter Lang.

Samuels, E. (2014). *Fantasies of identification: Disability, gender, race.* New York, NY: New York University Press.

Sheridan, S. (2012). Feminist knowledge, women's liberation, and Women's Studies. In S. Gunew (Ed.), *Feminist knowledge: Critique and construct* (pp. 36–55). New York, NY: Routledge.

Shircliffe, B. J. (2000). Feminist reflections on university activism through women's studies at a state university: Narrative of promise, compromise, and powerlessness. *Frontiers, 21*(3), 38–60.

Smith, G. A. (2010). We're all someone's freak. In K. Bornstein (Ed.), *Gender outlaws: The next generation* (pp. 26–31). Berkeley, CA: Seal Press.

Solanas, V. (1968). *SCUM Manifesto.* New York, NY: Olympia Press.

Stake, J. E. (2007). Predictors of change in feminist activism through women's and gender studies. *Sex Roles, 57*(1–2), 43–54.

Stryker, S. (1994). My words to Victor Frankenstein above the village of Chamounix: Performing transgender rage. *GLQ, 1*(3), 227–254.

Sycamore, M. B. (2008). *That's revolting! Queer strategies for resisting assimilation.* Berkeley, CA: Soft Skull Press.

Sycamore, M. B. (2012). *Why are faggots so afraid of faggots? Flaming challenges to masculinity, objectification, and the desire to conform.* San Francisco, CA: AK Press.

van Amsterdam, N. (2013). Big fat inequalities, thin privilege: An intersectional perspective on "body size." *European Journal of Women's Studies, 20*(2), 155–169.

Ward, P., Beausoleil, N., & Heath, O. (2016). Creating space for a critical examination of weight-centered approaches in health pedagogy and health professions. In E. Cameron & C. Russell (Eds.), *The fat pedagogy reader: Challenging weight-based oppression through critical education* (pp. 81–90). New York, NY: Peter Lang.

Watkins, P. L., Farrell, A., & Doyle-Hugmeyer, A. (2012). Teaching fat studies: From conception to reception. *Fat Studies, 1*(2), 180–194.

Weis, L., & Fine, M. (2001). Extraordinary conversations in public schools. *International Journal of Qualitative Studies in Education, 14*(4), 497–523.

9

"THE LEAST WE CAN DO"

Gender-Affirming Pedagogy Starting on Day One

Erica Chu

*I*t's the first day of class. I rush to get to my classroom and find a seat. I'm a little nervous, but everything will be fine. The teacher starts taking roll. Shoot. Maybe I should have e-mailed ahead of time to ask them not to use my birth name. My heart is racing. I try to sound normal as I say "here" nonchalantly, leaning over my desk, hand up to my face trying to hide the heat that's risen there, the look of panic and disgust. I hate that this is so hard. Why do I have to be this way? It'd be so much easier if I wasn't. I hope no one noticed. I'll e-mail the teacher later. It'll be fine. But what if they forget and use the wrong name or pronoun? They always seem to forget. A person a few seats away keeps looking at me. Typical. There's always some jerk who doesn't get it. I'm trans! So what? They just don't get it. Still. I hate this so much. I'll just look down and try to wait it out. It's okay. It'll be okay. What was that the teacher just said? Oh well, it'll be fine. I'll just try to make it through the class. Okay, introductions. I can do this. Just don't flinch. Ugh. I flinched. I bet I looked like such an idiot. That person is now leaning out of their chair to stare at me to figure me out. But of course they won't. No one gets me. What do I expect? But why is this so difficult!? I just want class to be over. Can it please be over? I'll just stare at the paper in front of me. Maybe it'll be easier next class. Okay. Let me just get out of here.

As the previous narration shows, what happens on the first day of a class affects how one student navigates feelings of anxiety, alienation, shame, frustration, and anger as well as others' ignorance about gender. These feelings in turn affect their ability to concentrate on course content. In this narration, the student is gender variant and identifies as trans. *Gender variant*, like the terms *transgender* and *trans*, refers to those who identify as a gender other than what they were assigned at birth. But unlike *transgender* or *trans*, which are sometimes contested, gender variant includes intersex people and those who identify with a gender form not considered normal by Western-based gender standards. Examples of this latter group could include *nadleeh* (Navajo), *māhū* (Hawai'i), *fa'afine* (Samoa), *hijra* (India), and *kathoey* (Thailand), among many other forms of gender variance in the Americas, Pacific, Africa, and Asia with or without specific names. *Intersex* refers to "people who are born with any of a range of characteristics that may not fit traditional conceptions about male or female bodies" (InterACT, 2017). Though not often in the spotlight, intersex is relatively common.

This particular student has chosen a name and pronouns that affirm their *gender identity* (the gender they identify as, which may or may not be the same as the gender they were assigned at birth), but other students will not have as clear of an understanding about their own gender—let alone their gender's relationship to gendered language in and outside the classroom. The procedures related to names and pronouns that instructors choose to follow on the first day of class set a vital precedent for how gender is defined and negotiated in the classroom for the remainder of a course and in turn how each of the students who are a part of that course will continue to think about their own gender and the genders of others long after the term has ended.

Those of us who teach college classes generally have an awareness that what we teach may have a lasting impact on the lives of our students, but seldom do we consider how seemingly small choices, such as how to call roll, might affect the health and well-being of students who are gender variant. Our pedagogical choices also play an active role in how easy it is for other students to explore and accept their own variant gender identities now and in the future. It is important we don't fall into the trap of developing a gender-inclusive pedagogy that is only triggered when a student comes out to us as gender variant. This type of strategy puts an unrealistic burden on students to disclose their gender identities. The truth is, students will not always come out to you. Some will, but many others will not for a variety of reasons such as their lack of trust in faculty and institutions, their reliance on identifying differently in different kinds of contexts, their political beliefs about who has the right to know about their gender, or the knowledge that coming out to you has little bearing on how they will interact with you.

Another danger instructors can have is assuming we will be able to initiate a gender-inclusive pedagogy when we recognize gender variant students, but this can lead to alienating such students and to leaving out a good many other types of students. Instead of assuming everyone is cisgender until we're able to identify them as something else, we would be wise to assume gender variance is always already in the room. The statistical probability of a student being born with intersex traits (1.7%) is about the same as those born with red hair (InterACT, 2017). The current rate of adults identifying as transgender is estimated at 0.6% of the U.S. population (Flores, Herman, Gates, & Brown 2016), yet people begin identifying their gender variance at different times of their lives. Some college students may be fully comfortable identifying as some kind of gender variant as college students, and some may only begin questioning their gender during college or long after. And importantly, gender variance is not always visible. Human bodies are diverse, and gender is expressed diversely. A scarf may be a sign of femininity among women or men or a sign of masculinity among women or men, or it may just be a piece of cloth worn without gendered association. In the same way, hips, broad shoulders, breasts, or a beard can mean any number of things. What is more, over one-third of gender variant people are *nonbinary* (James et. al, 2016), meaning they may or may not identify as a woman or a man, they may or may not have mixed masculine and feminine identities or pronouns you have never heard of, and they may or may not look like any cisgender student in your class. Gender is complex, and even when you are trained to understand it, you cannot necessarily see it because is not self-evident. Gender-affirming pedagogy doesn't require you understand the intricacies of every gender identity, but it does require you make space for the multiple kinds of gender identities that exist in your classroom.

We might ask ourselves how our pedagogical choices will affect students who are and will remain cisgender and what role those students will play in making life easier or harder for gender variant people. These aren't questions most educators have been trained to consider, but the consequences of not considering them are dire given the incredible violence facing gender variant people today and the incredible opportunity instructors across disciplines have to discourage that violence with seemingly small changes to their pedagogy. Indeed, developing an intentionally gender-affirming pedagogy allows for gender variant and cisgender students to engage in the process of unlearning some of the oppressive practices that mark gender variance as impossible. And this unlearning benefits gender variant people inside and outside our classrooms. In what follows, I will first explain why gender-affirming pedagogy is so desperately needed in college classrooms across disciplines. I will then offer strategies for college instructors to begin developing their own gender-affirming pedagogies by sharing my experience with mediating gendered language with a specific focus on first-day procedures. I end with some recommendations for instructors as they begin to enact gender-affirming pedagogy in their own classes.

What's at Stake

In most cultural contexts, *heterosexism* (the assumption that heterosexuality is the only normal sexuality) and *cissexism* (the assumption that identifying as the gender a person is assigned at birth is the only normal gender identity) work together to stigmatize gendered expression and desire that is not in keeping with a very rigid set of behaviors and ways of thinking of oneself. I say "in most cultural contexts" because Western-based assumptions about normative gender and sexual identities have become most common due to colonization; however, in many regions of the world, Indigenous communities have traditions of gender and sexual identities and roles that are not as narrow as Western forms. The result of colonially enforced heterosexist and cissexist assumptions is that gender variance is marked as worthy of contempt, rejection, ridicule, or pity; therefore, the vast majority of people are conditioned to accept without question the assumption that gender is innate and based on the extremely limited criteria doctors, parents, and government entities use to assign a person's gender. Because recognition of the viability of gender variant lives is not widespread, relatively few are aware enough to stop engaging in behaviors that further stigmatize gender variance, and it is even rarer for folks to consider their own gender identities beyond what they were assigned at birth. The continuation of this cissexist conditioning results directly in violence against gender variant people, especially those who are consistently *misgendered* (having one's gender identified incorrectly by others).

Although race, ethnicity, or sexuality are definitely not subjects of conversation with everyone you meet in a given day, gender is referred to constantly because *gender attribution* (the process of identifying the gender of others) is embedded in everyday linguistic interactions. Those who want to see how frequently gender is referred to should count the number of times they use the following words in a day: she, her, he, him, his, ma'am, sir, Mr., or Ms. As you might imagine, these words are incredibly common, and misgendering is unfortunately part of the everyday violence of language. Some may ask why the tendency to refer to gender is necessarily violent—isn't that a little extreme? My response is no, it's not. Whereas gendered words in and of themselves are not violent, their persistent use for people who do not identify with those words is violence. If you're a woman, just use yourself as an example in the following thought exercise (if you aren't a woman, imagine that you are).

You wake up tomorrow, leave your home, and are greeted by your neighbor with "Hey brother, how's it going?" Your reaction might be surprise or annoyance, but you'll either ignore it or correct it. Let's say you reply, "I'm not actually a brother, but I'm great, thanks." Your neighbor furrows their brow, looks annoyed, and says "Okay . . ." patronizingly. You decide to stop for a cup of coffee. The cashier says, "What can I get for you, sir?" and after giving your order, they ask for your name and then look at you strangely, ask you to repeat the name and spell the name. They then uncomfortably interact with you, all the while examining your face and body for signs that your name might actually belong to someone like you. The barista finishes your drink and calls your name. You immediately walk forward to pick it up, and everyone stares at your face and body once more trying to discover what it is you are.

How would you react? Many of us would laugh it off and go on with our morning, others of us would do a thorough inventory of what we were wearing, how we acted, what we "did" to warrant this kind of attention. If this happens to you every day and sometimes multiple times a day, you may get used to it, but you may also work very hard to minimize your exposure to that kind of treatment. You may even feel ashamed of who you are or who you want to be because of what keeps happening to you.

These are examples of just one type of misgendering. Other types may be different in their forms, meanings, and consequences, but all misgendering is damaging. Misgendering accompanied by the curiosity, rejection, hate, and ignorance of others is not a healthy environment for anyone, and it is directly responsible for challenges facing gender variant people when it comes to their physical, mental, and economic well-being because when the widespread cultural practice of misgendering is accepted as normal, so is the cissexism that manifests itself in other violent ways. Gender variant people are subject to harassment and violence in public spaces and also face high rates of assault by medical practitioners, police, and while incarcerated (James et al., 2016). Hate crimes and violence from police continue to be a major concern for gender variant people and transgender women of color in particular (Ahmed & Jindasurat, 2014, pp. 8–9). According to the U.S. Transgender Survey, the largest survey of gender variant people in the United States, transgender people experience triple the rate of unemployment and twice the rate of poverty compared to the national average with significantly higher rates among Middle Eastern, American Indian, Multiracial, Latino/a, and Black respondents (James et al., 2016). Reflecting on the past year alone, 48% of respondents reported being denied equal treatment or service, verbally harassed, and/or physically attacked because of being transgender (James et al., 2016). Given these consequences to being misgendered or rejected because

of assumptions about gender, it seems reasonable that gender variant people face difficulties with poverty, health, and mental health. A startling 40%
of gender variant respondents had attempted suicide in their lifetime (James
et al., 2016, p. 3) compared to the 10% to 20% lifetime suicide rate among
gay, lesbian, and bisexual adults and the 4.6% rate among the general population (Haas, Rodgers, & Herman, 2014, p. 2). And 48% of respondents had
serious thoughts of killing themselves during the past year. So gender variant
people are subjected to the violence of others in the world, and the violence
they face often leaves them no room to imagine themselves living in this world.

The violent rejection of gender variance begins with language—and usually the very small pieces of it: he, she, his, hers. When we as teachers, with
power over the small systems that are our classrooms, make assumptions
about what gendered words to use for someone based on our own perceptions
about what is and is not acceptable for men, women, or folks who are something else, we participate in the cultural support of more pernicious forms of
violence. Even something as simple as opening the class with, "Good morning, ladies and gentlemen," is a rejection of the presence—and even the possibility—of those who do not fit the category of either. Or when I use "she"
to refer to a student who is in fact a man, I reject their self-determination. In
fact, when I use "she" to refer to any student from whom I have not heard
what pronouns they use, I publicly endorse the cultural practice of enforcing
gender on others. Such a gender attribution system is an institutional mode
of control, which leads directly to violence against gender variant people
because it sends the message that their self-determination is meaningless.
Failing to disrupt cissexism supports a system that enforces cissexism through
violence against gender variant people or through perpetuating the belief that
gender variant lives are not worth living. Though the intention is often vastly
different, refusing to make space for gender variance has a similar effect as
forcefully eliminating it.

I realize this all might seem a little heavy, but the truth is that it really is
that easy to inadvertently support violent systems of control that endanger
the lives of gender variant and potentially gender variant people. Our cultural
conditioning to reject gender variance begins at birth and is reinforced every-
where from medical facilities and government institutions to public restrooms,
kitchen tables, and bathroom mirrors. Unlearning that conditioning takes
knowledge, practice, and intentionality. And it often means butting up against
cultural norms and being willing to modify our processes as we learn more
about what does and doesn't work in which contexts. The good news is we
don't have to fix everything all at once. Even just making some small changes
in how we gender others in the classroom is a huge step toward affirming
gender variance because interrupting linguistic systems of control opens up

the cultural and institutional possibility of gender variance. Making linguistic space for gender variance normalizes a new set of rules for how gender is assigned—not based on oppressive systems reliant on narrow definitions of "normal" bodies or even on stereotypes about gendered clothing or behavior—but on the basis of self-determination. For instance, normalizing the question "What pronouns do you use?" radically alters the psychic space for what one is allowed to be and for what one is expected to affirm.

The Least We Can Do

In the remainder of this chapter, I will present a few strategies for college teachers across disciplines who want to begin to develop gender-affirming pedagogical practices. Because learning about gender variance is often a life-long process, the chances of any of us dealing with gender in a perfect way are minuscule. But doing anything to disrupt the accepted gender attribution system is a much needed first step. Doing nothing only supports violence being committed against gender variant people. And, of course, we ought to strive for more than just the bare minimum. José Esteban Muñoz (1999) writes about the utopian possibility of making queer worlds, which speaks to imagining presents and futures full of possibility beyond the restrictions of heterosexist and cissexist modes of control. Imagine what could be possible if questioning one's gender assigned at birth was a simple and easy task. Stopping to imagine a world where gender variant people are free from the policing of their identities and bodies and lives is well worth the effort. What would gender variant people be able to do, to be, to create? When we engage in queer worldmaking, we prioritize that kind of future. In our classrooms, we have the opportunity to create communities that can serve as models for what the larger world can become. What's more, we have direct influence on what our students will be able to anticipate as acceptable and what they will be able to begin to imagine as possible.

I would like to emphasize that the strategies I discuss are based on my experiences, and other gender variant people may have a diversity of opinions on these topics. Yet these strategies are a beginning for the development of your own gender-affirming pedagogy. The process of creating queer worlds is not an easy task, and it requires a commitment to LGBTQ, intersex, and decolonizing work (Driskill, Finley, Gilley, & Morgensen, 2011) and the evolving theory and language that correspond with them. There is much teachers can do to create the types of spaces and communities capable of imagining gender-affirming presents and futures. There are units and readings, projects and activities, presentations, performances, and collaborations, but I will focus mainly on first-day procedures that can begin the process of disrupting the linguistic system that requires gender attribution based on the assumptions of the speaker—usually faulty assumptions about bodies or gendered stereotypes. Instead I recommend introducing students to a gender attribution system based on the self-determination of the person being spoken about. In one sense, this is a small and simple change, but it requires an awareness of the violence other gender attribution systems cause. Once armed with that knowledge, we'll find that adding a couple procedures on the first day of the course is just a first step, but a necessary one. And it is just the least we can do.

Come Out to Your Students

Anticipating the presence of sexual and gender variant students in your class (regardless of whether or not anyone ever comes out to you as such) is something easier said than done, but it can begin with something that is relatively easy to understand, recognize, and add to your list of first-day procedures. What I'm talking about is developing an intentional method for dealing with names and pronouns. It's important, however, to keep things as simple as possible because when gender is presented as a complex and convoluted system of specialized knowledge only accessible to some, gender variant people can be further stigmatized, and those learning about it for the first time may reject it. In "Stick Figures and Little Bits: Toward a Nonbinary Pedagogy," A. Finn Enke (2016) notes that "a transpedagogical approach seeks to invite everyone into the process of linguistic creativity and agency while minimizing the stresses that accompany privileged trans feminist knowledge as well as widespread ignorance of trans and gender variation" (p. 216). Without alienating those who have not yet had the opportunity to learn about and appreciate gender variance, we must, therefore, find a way to address and dismantle the privilege that allows that kind of ignorance. So on the first day of class, it makes sense for you, as the instructor, to introduce yourself. Introductions are simple and one of the best opportunities for normalizing the process of sharing one's name and pronouns.

I have gotten into a habit that makes broaching the topic of pronouns very easy. I list my pronouns and title quite clearly on the first page of my syllabus. On the first day of the course, I verbally tell the class that I expect them to address me by the title and pronouns I specify. This semester, I told them they could call me "Professor Chu" or "Erica" and that they should use the pronouns "they/them/their/theirs/themself" when speaking about me, and I gave example sentences of how to use my pronouns. Personally, I can't help but talk about gender on the first day of class because if I don't, I'll be uncomfortable all semester and will have to deal with being misgendered and called all variety of titles I'd prefer not to have to hear. Cisgender instructors and some binary transgender folks don't seem to have the problem of being misgendered because the pronouns and titles they prefer are more likely to be assumed on the part of the students. Although it might seem that I'm the one at the disadvantage, my situation gives me persistent personal motivation to help my students understand gender attribution, and it gives me an easy opportunity to teach them about pronouns they might not be used to using. In fighting for my own ability to survive my working environment, I am able to serve as a pretty big object lesson for my students about why never assuming gender is so important. This is a skill they can use to affirm or expand their view of themselves, and it's also a skill they need in their workplaces, social spheres, and homes.

Coming out to your students is only one possibility for beginning to disrupt students' reliance on gender attribution systems rooted in oppression, but it is a significant one. Even if you are not gender variant, or not able or willing to come out as such to your students, coming out with the name and pronouns you want students to use is a significant step. Even if you don't have a preference for pronouns, addressing this to your students prepares them for situations when someone does feel strongly about what pronouns should be used for them. It is becoming more common for those in spaces where folks are attuned to some of the needs of gender variant people to introduce themselves with their names and pronouns, and it is even becoming fairly common to see pronouns included in written biographies, in the signatures of e-mails, on business cards, and on name tags at events. For many gender variant people (especially those who do not use the pronouns "he" or "she"), this is a necessity, but the more common the practice of stating one's pronouns becomes, the more natural it will become for people to unlearn oppressive gender attribution systems.

I should also caution those beginning the process of self-identifying their pronouns—especially cisgender folks—to pick and choose which situations are appropriate. The first day of class is a wonderful opportunity to introduce yourself and your pronouns, but doing so on some other occasions can give the impression that a cisgender person wants to be recognized as an ally rather than as someone who wants to actually work to change how gender is inaccurately attributed.

Collect Names From Students to Replace Those on the Roster

In addition to introducing myself with my name, title, and pronouns, I also require students to introduce themselves to me by filling out a first-day questionnaire that asks for each student's name as it appears on the roster along with the name they will be using in the course. Asking students to write a response on the first day of the course gives students a semi-private time to consider how they want to present themselves to me, and by extension, the rest of the class. Unless the class is small, and already a congenial environment for gender variant people (i.e., gender studies class), I highly recommend not asking students to share their pronouns orally as an opening activity. Sharing pronouns can be an anxiety-producing ordeal, and it's better to give students a heads-up that something like that will happen—either the class period before or several minutes before. This also gives them an opportunity to assess if they can trust that you have actually created a space where they won't be stigmatized. Having students write their pronouns normalizes the process for all students, but requiring that they be shared orally first, or only, can stigmatize those whose pronouns others find incongruent with the student's physical appearance. Keeping track of pronouns so they can be referred to by you or others in the class is also something that is incredibly useful, and not something conducive to being recorded based on hearing others speak. It is the name they write on the questionnaire—not the school-generated roster—that I use as a basis for the sign in-sheet and any other materials requiring student names. I find it vital to never read names from the roster without revising it based on students' input. Refusing to take such precautions when calling roll or passing around an attendance sheet welcomes the alienation and potential stigmatization of any student whose name does not match what is on the roster. Even if you never read the name aloud, the presence of a birth name on a sign in sheet can be enough to potentially damage their learning experience not to mention their self-acceptance.

These practices are in line with studies that focus on the experiences and needs of trans students in college such as Singh, Meng, and Hansen's (2013) study of 17 trans students, and Jonathan T. Pryor's (2015) analysis of 5 transgender students' experiences. Both reveal a persistent need for trans-affirming language practices in the classroom and across campus (Pryor, 2015; Singh et al., 2013). Pryor (2015) also states that faculty can "be proactive by placing supportive statements in their syllabi, establishing the classroom as a safe space for all students" (p. 453). Such statements in syllabi are useful, but instructors must be willing to remain committed to understanding ideologies that can present themselves in the class and do harm to students—especially those who may have taken certain risks because of the presence of such statements. For example, a student could disclose to the class they are intersex in part because of the affirming statement on the syllabus about accepting all kinds of identities only to meet the instructor's ignorance on the topic or their inability to stop dismissive or aggressive comments from other students. In such a case, the instructor has actually put the student at greater risk because of a statement they were not prepared to live up to. Similar problems could arise related to pronouns, so instructors should take care to consider whether making student names and pronouns available to others in the class makes sense given the class size, need of other students to ever use pronouns, and your own ability to control the culture of the classroom. We must be cautious about advertising our classes as safe spaces if they aren't in fact safe. That being said, we should work diligently to make them as affirming as we can.

I've heard instructors claim that if a student is made uncomfortable by the name on the roster being used in class, they can have it changed by the time they enroll in the course. There are all manner of barriers to having one's name changed on a roster, not the least of which is that schools often have inadequate policies for allowing students to change their names. Although no data exists about name changes specifically, in one study less than half (46%) of respondents had changed their school records to match their gender identity (Grant et al., 2011). Most colleges require a legal name change such as a court order or new state ID to change the name on student records, and the process of legally changing one's name is a long, difficult, and often expensive process. Even figuring out how to navigate a name change in one's state can be a taxing experience. At times a student may even have succeeded in obtaining a legal name change and then filed a name change with the college, yet the name that appears on a class roster may still be inaccurate. Faculty should also realize that it is a long and stressful process even to arrive at the decision to change one's name (VanderSchans, 2015)— let alone finalize which name, establish that name among friends and family, and file all the paperwork with various government and school offices that will result in the correct name appearing on a class roster. Some gender variant students may need affirming opportunities to test out names before committing to a legal name change; others may never wish to change their legal documents. Providing an opportunity every semester for all students to establish their name in each new social space is an important method for creating space for human diversity—and not just in terms of gender identity. One's name is often also an indicator of dynamic relationships to kinship structures, ethnicity, religion, and gendered understandings of self. Some students will contact instructors before the first day of class to inform them of their name, roster name, and their pronouns, but it is unreasonable to expect students to do this when they may know little about how faculty would react or whether or not their e-mail would even be read before the first day. In addition, students often have a hard time attending or being on time on the first day of class. Adding another task for a marginalized person is not an adequate solution.

Equally important to collecting students' names is narrating to the class how names will be dealt with in the course and what your rationale is for making those policies. There may be semesters when no one's name will differ from the roster name, but disrupting oppressive gender-attribution systems requires making space for not only gender variant people currently in your classroom but also those students who may come out as gender variant later on. In addition, cisgender students also need to learn that gender variance is a possibility they may encounter and be expected to accommodate and affirm. Voicing the rationale for your pedagogical decisions is an important lesson that students desperately need so they can begin to imagine gender-affirming queer worlds rather than merely conform to a required policy.

Normalize the Need to Ask for Pronouns

Because other students will typically use whatever names and pronouns are used by the instructor, it is important teachers use the correct name and pronouns in class every time—especially during those crucial moments when students are becoming introduced to each other for the first time. The instructor using incorrect pronouns will negatively affect whether or not students will use the correct pronouns after that point. In "Trans* Disruptions: Pedagogical Practices and Pronoun Recognition," Tre Wentling (2015) reports that only 63.4% of binary trans students in his survey reported that their instructors consistently used their correct pronouns, and only 15% of nonbinary students reported the same. Gender variant students have learned that college classrooms are not safe spaces, and if we intend to make our classrooms more gender-affirming, we must account for our own use of pronouns. This means we need to divorce "looks" from pronouns. Gender is not self-evident; it is self-determined. And the only way to know which pronouns to use is to ask. For addressing gender variant folks who use binary pronouns, using "he" and "she" correctly may or may not take some work, but you can and must get them right. Making excuses or turning it into a big deal is not ideal for anyone. Practice outside of class, and be prepared. In moments of doubt, simply avoid any pronoun. Restate the person's name. But consistently relying on such tactics defeats the purpose of gender-affirming pedagogy, because it avoids gender rather than affirming it.

For addressing gender variant folks who use nonbinary pronouns, many of us may be more challenged. Doing so requires practicing gender neutral and nonbinary pronouns before we even encounter students in our classes who use them (two of the most common examples of nonbinary pronouns include they/them and ze/hir). I've heard of families, roommates, and groups of friends practicing gender neutral or nonbinary pronouns with each other, on pets, or as a replacement for all gendered pronouns for a period of time. Finding creative ways to train yourself certainly makes it more fun, but in front of the class, accuracy is vital because you are the model the class is look-ing to. This isn't to say you must now become perfect. Mistakes are bound to happen, and in my classes, I encourage students to politely call out pronouns if I or another student makes a mistake with someone's pronouns. I try to normalize mistakes and prepare students for appropriate ways to react to being corrected. For instance, "Sorry. What are the correct pronouns? I'll get it right next time" is acceptable, because it allows the speaker to acknowledge the mistake and apologize for it, and it provides the information they need to do better next time. On the other hand, "That was really just awful. But this is really hard" or "I just really should have known because look at you!" are inappropriate, because they center the experience of the speaker, attempt to solicit comfort, and call attention to stereotypes that give no indication of what someone's pronouns are. How you respond to making a mistake is as important of a lesson as you getting it right.

All this being said, you must have a system of accountability in place for you and for the other students in the class. Asking students to be vulnerable by sharing their pronouns means you must create an environment where students will be respected and not ostracized even when mistakes may hap-pen. This means not letting misgendering go unnoticed. Normalizing the fact that mistakes take place only makes sense when everyone is on board to respect each other. So for classes that are too large for very much account-ability, you may want to consider how or if you ask students to share their names and pronouns with the class.

Persistent misgendering can have a very negative impact on students' experience and performance in the class. Enke (2016) states, "Educational equity demands we pay attention to the ways that misgendering . . . cre-ates significant educational barriers" (p. 218) that disrupt students' learning and ability to proceed in school. Similar to race, language, ability, and class, gender variance can complicate a student's experiences and their ability to reach their educational goals because of stigma, fear, harassment, discomfort, and complications with motivation, concentration, anxiety, depression, and other mental health concerns. What is more, misgendering can stifle or delay students' gender expression, exploration, and creativity. Given the violence that results from assumptions based on accepted gender attribution systems, it is surprising that something as simple as a questionnaire can begin the process of denaturalizing those systems.

In lieu of a questionnaire, some faculty use notecards, introductory e-mails, or another written method for collecting students' information. These are great options, but I prefer a printed questionnaire that allows you

to provide multiple choice options for pronouns, which is especially important for those students who have never been asked their pronouns before. It
can be quite eye-opening and even an emotional experience to see a question
like this for the first time:

> What pronouns do you want me to use when I speak about you? (Check all
> that you feel comfortable with being used to describe you.)
>
> ☐ She/her/her/hers/herself
>
> ☐ He/him/his/his/himself
>
> ☐ They/them/their/theirs/themself
>
> ☐ Ze/ze/hir/hirs/hirself
>
> ☐ Other(s). Please specify:

The last option gives students the freedom and creativity to include pronouns not listed. For students—especially those who've never encountered
a diversity of pronouns—seeing their own pronouns alongside others helps
normalize the process of not assuming a person's pronouns "match" some
set of cues other than their own self-selection. Enke (2016) reminds us that
"as long as trans and genderqueer embodiments are stigmatized or unimagi-
nable, and as long as gender-neutral pronouns are unappreciated in the vast
majority of contexts, using them may feel like aggressively speaking a foreign
(queer) language in otherwise polite company" (p. 220). You may indeed
have to work at learning a new language and new gender attribution system,
but such is this work. Becoming familiar with varied pronouns and rejecting
the notion of gender attribution based on stereotypes about gendered bodies
and behaviors and instead affirming gender self-determination lessens the
stigma of gender variance by providing students with some tools for imagining lives gendered otherwise. Such imagination can lead to a way out of
being the victims and enforcers of compulsory (cisgender) heterosexuality
and compulsory adherence to gender assigned at birth, as well as all of the
socially prescribed requirements for that gender.

Information-Gathering Considerations

On my first-day questionnaire, I also have other questions I find useful,
such as year in school, prerequisites taken, whether they've taken the course
before, as well as at least one open-ended question like, "Is there anything
else you want me to know?" This question serves many purposes. Some students choose to disclose issues related to gender, sexuality, documentation

status, disability, jobs, schedules, family, and so on. Such questions are important in terms of anticipating the presence of gender variant students in a class, but more significantly, they create an opportunity to lay aside the assumption that each student enters a classroom with the same identities, backgrounds, and challenges. In *Teaching to Transgress*, bell hooks (1994) complains about professors who refuse to see their students as "whole human beings with complex lives and experiences rather than simply as seekers after compartmentalized bits of knowledge" (p. 15). She goes on to say, "Progressive, holistic education, 'engaged pedagogy' is more demanding than conventional critical or feminist pedagogy. For, unlike these two teaching practices, it emphasizes well-being" (p. 15). Ignoring the well-being of our students reduces them to mere vessels of knowledge, but actively caring for students' well-being allows us to foster the spiritual and intellectual growth of our students. A student's self-actualization as a result of your caring for their well-being could result in them identifying as gender variant, dedicating themself to social justice work, or passing your course while managing all that's going on their life. We can't even know the possibilities unless there is some kind of mechanism for understanding students' challenges to well-being and ultimately to the self-actualization we will be attempting to empower them to reach. Having a sense of the challenges our students are experiencing means we must make listening a practice embedded into the structures of our classes. Too often, we assume this means picking up on what our students disclose to us, which is of course true, but we must also create mechanisms that invite reflection and relevant disclosure. We cannot listen if we've provided students with few opportunities to speak to us. Of course, holistic educational practices are relevant for all of our students, but in terms of gender-affirming practices, it's important to recognize that due to the violence gender variant people face, gender variance is often accompanied by other significant problems such as poverty, housing instability, family problems, and physical and mental health concerns. Although I'm focusing mainly on gender attribution in this chapter, this is one first-day procedure that's worth considering as well.

A first-day questionnaire in a printed medium also provides a formality and even a bureaucratic blandness to the process of disclosing personal information that may affect a student's performance in a course. Normalizing the process of assuming nothing about students' names, pronouns, and gender is one such mechanism of gender-affirming systemic change. By asking questions when we meet our students, we remove the unstated assumption that all students come into a classroom the same, which usually means cisgender among other things.

Now, of course it is not our right (and in some cases not legal) to ask questions about students' sexuality, gender identity, race, ethnicity, disability, household income, or the number of children they have. Students have a right to privacy, but asking for a student's name and pronouns on the first day of class is one small act that signals that we are prepared to create a community that affirms all genders. Creating such a community means fostering mutual respect and support for all kinds of people, which leads to transformative classroom communities that imagine futures for themselves, the people they are becoming, and the communities they care about—in all their gendered possibilities. Although being intentional about pronouns is a seemingly minor pedagogical decision, it is gender-affirming pedagogy in action.

Conclusion

It takes some preparation and a commitment to creating a world that affirms all kinds of gender identities to achieve what I suggest in this chapter. This may seem like a lot of work, especially given the fact that there will likely be many semesters—and potentially most or even all semesters—when you will not see or hear about any students who are gender variant benefitting from your first-day procedures. But gender-affirming pedagogy is not about student praise or ticking something off a list of trendy practices that will make you look like a progressive instructor. It is about creating space for transformative possibility in and outside your class. When we allow oppressive assumptions about gender attribution to remain the default in our classrooms, we create worlds that extend violence against gender variant people within the walls of our classroom as well as the communities our students inhabit. Doing so presents gender identity as a supposedly self-evident system based on stereotypes steeped in cissexism, heterosexism, and colonialism. But each new semester we have the opportunity to intentionally engage in the labor of queer worldmaking, an endeavor that requires our renewed commitment and our openness to gender possibilities.

Recommendations

As you work to create or strengthen your own gender-affirming pedagogy beyond the first day, I offer a few suggestions to consider.

- Organize a group of fellow instructors who also want to work on being more gender-affirming. Meet before the semester begins to share your ideas and rationales. Check in with each other during the semester, and meet up before the next term begins to discuss what went well and what you want to do differently.

- Gender attribution is just one facet of gender-affirming pedagogy. As you work to more fully develop your own pedagogy, commit to learning more about transgender (including nonbinary), intersex, and Indigenous and non-western forms of gender variance. Commit also to understanding colonialism and how to engage in decolonial work. The widespread acceptance of heterosexism and cissexism is a colonial imposition after all, and if you teach on occupied land (i.e., the United States), this is even more important (Morgensen, 2011). Learning more by catching up on the latest scholarship is a great idea, but don't underestimate the usefulness of building literacy and solidarity though groups, events, and social media.

- Consider how you address groups of students. If you aren't already doing so, utilize gender neutral forms of address instead of gendered terms such as *ladies* and *guys*. Try scholars, folks, friends, or simply y'all. If you're addressing a large group, avoid limited binary forms like "ladies and gentlemen." Either use a gender-neutral form like "honored guests" or add a third category. It can even be lighthearted such as "ladies, gentlemen, and otherwise fancy friends," or "guys, gals, and everybody else." Keep in mind, though, that some of these inclusive third categories can cause people to laugh, which, in the absence of other forms of gender affirmation, can have an effect opposite of what is intended.

- Foster community. Acknowledge your own limitations and engage the class in decision-making about protocols related to gender affirming practices. For instance, toward the beginning of the semester, check in with the class about how names and pronouns are made available to each other, or discuss what would be useful to help hold each other accountable for using the correct pronouns. Building a gender-affirming space requires everyone in the space to buy into the process. This will not always be possible, but doing what we can matters.

- Refer students. Once gender-variant and questioning students feel comfortable around you, they may share a lot with you. Be prepared to gather information about services and information hubs on and off campus so you can refer students as needed.

- Hold your institution responsible for resources and services that are lacking. Organize other faculty and staff to put pressure on institutional bodies that can aid in providing resources for gender variant and questioning students. You may find that advocating for these resources will also help other marginalized students, so work collectively with other interested parties such as those advocating for sexual assault survivors, people with disabilities, people of color, first year students, international students, and undocumented students.

- Complicate discussions of biological sex. Recognize the social construction of biological sex (see Fausto-Sterling's [2000] *Sexing the Body* for an introduction to this topic) and adjust how you speak about sex and gender in your class. Whereas some make a distinction between *male* and *man* to indicate the difference between sex (as a biological category) and gender (as a social category), sex and gender are both constructed by societal belief in two discreet gender categories. Language around sex may attempt to reference material aspects of bodies, but societal beliefs shape how that materiality is interpreted. The biomedical categories of male and female are not stable. Intersex folks and transgender people utilizing medical intervention make this stability impossible—not to mention children, those experiencing puberty or menopause, those with conditions affecting hormone production, and some cancer survivors, among many other folks. Despite the social construction of the discreet biological categories of male and female, most academic disciplines rely exclusively on this interpretation of biological difference. Acknowledging that all language related to gender or sex is fraught territory is useful even if you must still use fraught categories, and acknowledging the instability of gendered categories you use when you teach makes space for gender variance and prepares students to encounter multiple audiences when they use gendered language. For these reasons, consider relying less on terms like *men* or *male* when you're talking about biological categories and try adopting terminology such as *those assigned male at birth* in those instances. In addition, talk about intersex people as another category of biological variation when appropriate, but take care not to stigmatize intersex bodies or positionalities. (Learn more about the US intersex movement in Georgiann Davis's [2015] *Contesting Intersex*).
- Interrupt oppressive ideology. Redirecting oppressive ideology need not be alienating for students. You can always affirm the student displaying the ideology by talking about how and why their view is common, but point out what's wrong with it and provide alternative ways of thinking and speaking about gender. In atmospheres that are hostile, appeal to *accuracy, course concepts,* and *professionalism,* rather than *justice, kindness,* and *decency.* In some states and municipalities, consistently using the wrong pronouns or otherwise disrespecting

gender identities can be grounds for suit or fine. Self-protection is not an ideal motivator for respecting others, but helping students get used to using the correct pronouns does prepare them for the expectations of the workplace.

- Solicit feedback. An e-mailed survey link addressing the strategies you are trying can help you consider what is and is not working—even if you receive only a handful of responses. Make sure the survey allows anonymous responses. Survey Monkey or Google Forms are good options.

- Be accountable. You are not going to do everything the way every gender variant person would like. That's okay. Definitely apologize to a gender variant student who is unhappy with how you've handled something in class, listen to the feedback they want to give, and take it into consideration as you move forward. Even if the student has some views that you consider theoretically flawed, their experience can be important for you to understand. If your identity is different from theirs, you might be tempted to concede your point right away to prove your allyship. I recommend giving yourself more time to consider their comments. Doubting yourself is a necessary and productive experience that can't always be done in the length of a short conversation. Check in with yourself, talk to knowledgeable people who can help, refer to the resources at your disposal, do some more research, and allow your views to evolve. Take responsibility when you fail or could have done things better, and even when you don't agree with a student about how gender is handled in class, demonstrate your commitment to being accountable. It will go a long way in building gender-affirming pedagogy that students can trust.

References

Ahmed, O., & Jindasurat, C. (2014). *Lesbian, gay, bisexual, transgender, queer, and HIV-affected hate violence 2013*. National Coalition of Anti-Violence Programs, New York City Gay and Lesbian Anti-Violence Project. Retrieved from https://avp.org/wp-content/uploads/2017/04/2013_ncavp_hvreport_final.pdf

Davis, Georgiann. (2015). *Contesting intersex: The dubious diagnosis*. New York, NY: New York University Press.

Driskill, Q.-L., Finley, C., Gilley, B. J., & Morgensen, S. L. (Eds.). (2011). *Queer Indigenous studies: Critical interventions in theory, politics, and literature*. Tucson, AZ: University of Arizona Press.

Enke, A. F. (2016). Stick figures and little bits: Toward a nonbinary pedagogy. In Y. Martínez-San Miguel & S. Tobias, (Eds.), *Trans studies: The challenge to hetero/ homo normativity* (pp. 215–229). New Brunswick, NJ: Rutgers University Press.

Fausto-Sterling, A. (2000). *Sexing the body: Gender politics and the construction of sexuality*. New York, NY: Basic.

Flores, A. R., Herman, J. L., Gates, G. J., & Brown, T. N. T. (2016). How many adults identify as transgender in the United States? Los Angeles, CA: The Williams Institute. Retrieved from https://williamsinstitute.law.ucla.edu/wp-content/ uploads/How-Many-Adults-Identify-as-Transgender-in-the-United-States.pdf

Grant, J. M., Mottet, L. A., Tanis, J., Harrison, J., Herman, J. L., & Keisling, M. (2011). *Injustice at every turn: A report of the national transgender discrimination survey*. National Center for Transgender Equality and National Gay and Lesbian Task Force. Retrieved from http://www.thetaskforce.org/static_html/downloads/ reports/reports/ntds_full.pdf

Haas, A. P., Rodgers, P. L., & Herman, J. L. (2014, January). *Suicide attempts among transgender and gender non-conforming adults*. American Foundation for Suicide Prevention and the Williams Institute. Retrieved from https://williamsinstitute .law.ucla.edu/wp-content/uploads/AFSP-Williams-Suicide-Report-Final.pdf

hooks, b. (1994). *Teaching to transgress: Education as the practice of freedom*. New York, NY: Routledge.

InterACT. (2017). Intersex 101: Everything you want to know! InterACT: Advocates for intersex youth. Retrieved from https://interactadvocates.org/wp-content/ uploads/2017/03/INTERSEX101.pdf

James, S. E., Herman, J. L., Rankin, S., Keisling, M., Mottet, L., & Anafi, M. (2016). *The report of the 2015 U.S. transgender survey*. Washington, DC: National Center for Transgender Equality. Retrieved from http://www.transequality.org/ sites/default/files/docs/usts/USTS%20Full%20Report%20-%20FINAL%20 1.6.17.pdf

Muñoz, J. E. (1999). *Disidentifications: Queers of color and the performance of politics*. Minneapolis, MN: University of Minnesota Press.

Pryor, J. T. (2015). Out in the classroom: Transgender student experiences at a large public university. *Journal of College Student Development, 56*(5), 440–455.

Singh, A. A., Meng, S., & Hansen, A. (2013). "It's already hard enough being a student": Developing affirming college environments for trans youth. *Journal of LGBT Youth, 10*(3), 208–223.

VanderSchans, A. (2015). The role of name choice in the construction of transgender identities. *Western Papers in Linguistics/Cahiers linguistiques de Western, 1*(2), 1–21.

Wentling, T. (2015). Trans* disruptions: Pedagogical practices and pronoun recognition. *Transgender Studies Quarterly, 2*(3), 469–476.

10

CREATING INCLUSIVE CLASSROOMS

Toward Collective and Diverse Intersectional Success

Dian D. Squire, Azura Booth, and Brandon Arnold

The corporate culture within which higher education is now situated "suggests a hazardous turn in U.S. society, one that both threatens our understanding of democracy as fundamental to our freedom and the ways in which we address the meaning and purpose of public and higher education" (Giroux, 2002, p. 430). This corporate culture, as encompassed by neoliberalism, as a theory, political philosophy, and its resultant actions, dictates how the university should be structured and reproduced in order to minimize personal liberties and participatory democracy, and increase market freedoms at the expense of those most marginalized (Carr & Pluim, 2015; Hamer & Lang, 2015). One way these restrictions manifest is through classroom dynamics. Normative understandings of classroom learning suggest that students enter the classroom as empty vessels ready to receive whatever information is fed to them, with teachers depositing knowledge into their students' brains (Freire, 2008). A neoliberal classroom reinforces this "banking model" of education, an oppressive educational model that is inequitable, dehumanizing, and unsafe for the "other" (Kumashiro, 2000).

The challenge remains: How do we, as educators and facilitators of learning, ensure that the classroom is inclusive and affirming of all students at the intersections of their multiple identities especially on predominantly White campuses? Designing a more radical classroom is essential to this liberatory formation of the classroom. Radical classrooms force students to look at the problematic behaviors of others, larger society, and government, as well as ourselves. Radical classrooms provide an equitable opportunity for all students to engage, learn, share, and begin imagining solutions to reconstructing a more just world. The goal of our class was not to find solutions that address the symptoms of the problems, such as affirmative action as a solution to increase racial diversity in higher education, but to look deeper and discover the root causes of identified problems. We used the university as a site for study, and the student experience as evidence of the ways the university oppressed us; universities were built for and by White people, and although students of color and nontraditional students do participate in higher education, they are still not designed for them to succeed (Hamer & Lang, 2015; Patel, 2015). In order to address this problem, we would have to reimagine the entire university system, especially the admission process. We used this course to try to completely reimagine the system of higher education to be one that is more inclusive and beneficial to all. This project was especially important because addressing deep-seated structural inequality is the only way to create equitable outcomes for all students.

One reality remained though: When one wishes to address issues of structural oppression, they may also face barriers to engaging in those discussions. The work of deconstructing oppression is no easy task, as neoliberal universities at their essence enact structural violence against communities of color and other marginalized populations (Hamer & Lang, 2015). Essentially, conservative institutional policies reinforce a noncritical, liberal mentality, stripping away all social supports and reinforcing a hegemonic understanding of society as equal for all, despite a history of oppression; it is now well-recognized that universities were quite literally built on the back of Black and Native/Indigenous peoples and continue to reproduce structures of White supremacy to this day (Patel, 2015; Wilder, 2013). Current working philosophies of diversity subvert legal protections for minoritized groups on college campuses through liberal rhetoric, silencing oppression, community wealth destruction, gentrification, and defunding of support services (Hamer & Lang, 2015). These oppressions also extend into the classroom through pedagogy and curriculum, which often reproduce Whiteness as normative.

A system of perpetuating Whiteness reinforces racial inequalities and neoliberalism accrues various forms of capital for White elites (Harris, 1993; Lipsitz, 2006), thereby reinforcing the privileges and benefits of Whiteness. This accumulation can continue in the college classroom without deep analysis of both curriculum and pedagogy. Bourdieu (1986) wrote "education ignores the contribution which the educational system makes to the reproduction of the social structure by sanctioning the hereditary transmission of cultural capital" (para. 6). Leaving unjust systems untouched allows for a continuing decline of democratic ideals, dehumanization of students (and teachers), and a perpetuation of social divides among a variety of social groups (Freire, 2008; Giroux, 2015; Kumashiro, 2000).

Critical pedagogy has the radical power to deconstruct these systems; and a critical race pedagogy and curriculum (Yosso, 2002) in particular allows a centering of the most marginalized voices. At the intersections of race and gender in particular, critical pedagogy can actualize and affirm students' "experiences and identities both inside and outside the classroom. . . . [It allows students to] expose and deconstruct the normative values of the academy as well as work toward a more inclusive environment that supports success for marginalized students" (Harris, 2016, p. 163). There is potential for radical self-change that provides critical hope (Preskill & Brookfield, 2008) to students that they can survive, thrive, and change their universities. Additionally, a liberatory education has the potential for students to engage in radical revolution and social change (Freire, 2008).

To demonstrate values and goals of a liberatory and critical pedagogy, this chapter describes how one course aimed to serve as a space of resistance for challenging a racist, patriarchal, corporate university system. The multimodal pedagogical exercises highlighted in this chapter center student narratives and a deep exploration of power and privilege in an intermediate level undergraduate course that utilized various critical social theories as lenses of analysis. The goal was to create a space of equitable learning for all students that affirmed and supported students in their identities and at their varying developmental levels around engaging with these topics while at the same time providing theoretical tools for deconstructing the university system.

Additionally, this chapter centers narratives from the instructor who identifies as a cisgender gay man of color, and two students, a second-year, able-bodied, cisgender, heterosexual biracial woman, and a fourth-year, ablebodied, cisgender, heterosexual White man. The instructor provides insight into the creation of this course and the students explore their identities and related experience in the course. We engaged in conversation, in the form of a group interview, to come to final consensus of the efficacy of the pedagogical technique and the classroom experience. Finally, we provide discussion and implications for instructors.

University Context

The University of Denver (DU) is a private, predominantly White, nonreligious institution that enrolls approximately 5,700 undergraduate students, and 6,000 graduate students, 79% of whom are White (University of Denver, 2015). The university is well known for its international programs and enrolls 9% international students. The approximate cost of attendance for one year is $60,000 for undergraduate students (University of Denver, 2016).

DU is located at many interesting intersections. The university is very successful in hockey and lacrosse, two sports known for being traditionally White and wealthy. The main graduate programs are in business, engineering, and law, fields that are typically very male-dominated. These are just a few examples of the units of engagement within the university that appear to actively promote dominant sex and racial paradigms. However, when juxtaposed to its geographical location, an interesting quandary appears. Denver is a rapidly growing economic, political, and social hub. Denver was ranked highly by *Forbes* in a number of different economic categories and has a housing market that is quickly on the rise (Badenhausen, 2015). Politically, Colorado is a purple state, being hotly contested in both the 2008 and 2012 elections and going Democratic in the 2016 presidential election. However, Denver itself is a very diverse and progressive-minded area of the state. Denver was the host site of the 2008 Democratic party convention, was one of the first states to consider a form of the DREAM Act (Leber, 2013), and also was the first state to pass legislation legalizing recreational marijuana use. Socially, Denver's culture is generally accepting of the LGBTQIA+ community and it has also seen many vibrant, multicultural demonstrations. Yet DU, nestled right in the middle of the city, is fairly antithetical to Denver. Tuition is very expensive, so the student population is predominantly wealthy. In addition, there is a very strong conservative political presence.

Introduction to Critical Social Theories

Although the university is known for being predominantly White and wealthy, this was not reflected in our Introduction to Critical Social Theories class. It was a relatively racially diverse classroom. In total, 17 students enrolled. Ten students identified as White, one as Asian American, one as Latina, one as Middle Eastern, three as Black, and one as biracial. Fifteen students were cisgender women, and two were cisgender men. The classroom comprised students that ranged from first years to graduating seniors. Students identified as queer, lesbian, students with mental and/or emotional disabilities, various socioeconomic classes, and various college-attending generational statuses.

This course provided a vibrant canvas from which we could explore both identity and the contexts within which one exists. Throughout the term, students engaged at the intersections of their identities. As Nicolazzo (2016) stated, intersectionality "seeks a connection between one's identities and lived experiences on the one hand, and the historical, geographic, legal, political, and social contexts in which one lives" (p. 5).

For some people in the class, it was their first class learning about such critical ideas, but some of the students were already fluent in these theories due to previous coursework. We covered critical race theory, Whiteness as property, feminist theories, spatial justice, neoliberalism, third spaces, critical pedagogy, and critical hope. A large part of our discussions were dedicated to seeing how these various social theories manifested themselves on campus. The underlying outcome of the course required that students view all systems through a critical lens and question normative assumptions.

Pedagogical Examples

This section outlines a few pedagogical tools used to set the tone of the course and to explore students' identities, allowing them to get to know each other, and providing a venue for them to talk about power and privilege. Students entered the class from a variety of worldviews, experiences, number of years in college, majors, and social identities. At some level, it was important to situate the purpose of the class within their university experience, as the course would use the university as an incubator of study. Additionally, with the understanding that the classroom organizes university life in particular ways (Giroux, 2002, 2015), these activities began to break down normative understandings of how a classroom operates.

The first classes were spent allowing students to get to know each other, providing time for class members to acknowledge and dismiss conscious and implicit preconceived notions of each other, and to recognize that each of us held privileges and experienced marginalization because of our various identities. To that end, we watched the video *The danger of a single story* by writer Chimamada Adichie (2009), the students and instructor wrote and shared *I Am From* poems, and the students participated in an exploration of their own power and privilege through a fishbowl activity. Before any of these activities took place, a brave space (see Arao & Clemens, 2013) discussion was used to set expectations for engagement in the classroom.

The Danger of a Single Story

In *The danger of a single story*, a TED Talk presentation, Chimamanda Ngozi Adichie (2009) explores the danger of stereotyping people and only understanding a group of people as a monolith. These monolithic understandings are a part of everyday culture including in television and in children's literature. After watching the video, students were asked to engage in a two-minute freewrite reflection. All students then shared their initial thoughts about the video including how their perspectives may have changed since the last time they watched it, if applicable. The freewrite share was followed by multiple large-group questions. Some questions included: What stories did you grow up reading or listening to? When Adichie said, "our lives, our cultures, are composed of many overlapping stories," what do you think this means? How do you project single stories on others? How do our emotions shift when we realize there is more than a single story? This discussion allowed each person to begin to share their stories and the ways they have been stereotyped in order to begin breaking down barriers. Concurrently, the students began to shift their own paradigms about each other and how they view the world by realizing that groups of people do not exist as a monolith and by learning about a person's culture that they may have had limited engagement with prior to the class. Additionally, this activity began to shift the sole onus of teaching away from the teacher and onto the students as cocreators of knowledge (Freire, 2008).

I Am From *Poems*

In the second session, occurring two days later, the students were asked to create an *I Am From* poem. First published by George Ella Lyon (n.d.), *I Am From* poems allow people to explore and share multiple aspects of their lives, starting from their upbringings, to important mentors in their lives, to foods and smells they remember. The basic format of the *I Am From* poem is that each line starts with "I am from . . ." and then is followed by a list of words or phrases that explore a prompt. Following is the basic outline used for this activity:

> I am from [description of home, sensory details, things found around the home]
> I am from [traditions, family traits, names, values, ancestry]
> I am from [phrases or sayings you often heard as a child]
> I am from [foods you ate, things you did as a kid, an object you held, neighborhood details]
> I am from [incidences that affected you]
> I am from [people who have supported you, changed you, helped you, raised you]

It is important for the instructor to share their own *I Am From* poem before asking students to share their own. This allows an additional barrier to be broken down, for the students to learn more about the instructor, and it also provides an example of the finished poem. At the end of the share, students then identified commonalities and differences from their peers. This allowed another point of connection across seemingly different student bodies. Additionally, there was a realization about the complexities of the human experience, the nuances of identity, and what each student found salient.

Fishbowl

The final activity was a fishbowl activity. Fishbowls can occur in many ways, but ultimately, they allow intense conversation among a small group of people who sit in an inner circle while the remainder of the class sits in an outer circle and makes silent observations. Within the fishbowl, five to six students were asked questions about the spaces they inhabit and how they are privileged/marginalized in those spaces. Students of color discussed what it meant to be a person of color in the university. White students explored the privileges they had in the classroom setting, and all students engaged in discussions that allowed them to begin to identify the various privileges they had because of their able-bodiedness, race, sex, gender, or opportunities. Students on the outside took notes about the inner circle's discussion and about nonverbal language, who was talking and how much they spoke, and any other interesting observations. As students on the outside felt comfortable, they would raise their hands to enter the circle and somebody from the inside would step out. Ultimately, each person ended up in the middle. At the end, general observations were made by the students and notes shared.

In the next section, we discuss our experience of being in this class, our perspectives on these activities and how it shaped our time in the class, how the students perceived it as differing from other courses, and the ways they viewed their university afterwards. We spent multiple meetings constructing the protocol and spent two hours interviewing each other. The interview was transcribed and posted to a document-sharing site (i.e., Google Docs) where each person continued to edit the transcripts and respond to each other's thoughts and comments over a one-month period. In the first round of interviews, Azura and Brandon interviewed Dian. In the second set of interviews, Azura and Brandon interviewed each other. Then all of the authors finetuned and expanded on their answers in order to engage in a member-check and employ higher levels of trustworthiness. Additionally, this interviewing technique allowed the students to be full participants in the writing of this chapter, in line with the broad philosophical underpinnings of the course.

Findings

In this section, we present the findings of the interviews. The first segment relates to the organization of the class in relation to supporting students with multiple marginalized identities. The second segment reflects the students' thoughts about the space they held in the class and how the pedagogy influenced their experience and learning.

Organizational Philosophy

The organization and preparation of the course was an important consideration for Dian. Part of the reasoning for creating this type of course lay in the fact that he was hired by DU to enact significant campus change, mainly around racial justice. He noted:

> I think that my role was to come into DU and analyze it for all its inequities and do what I can to promote more equitable culture and this is one way that I could do that and was given the opportunity to do that and I knew how to do that work.

One of the general problems many instructors face is an inability to know who is enrolled in the class, what background they were coming in with, and how they would react to the curriculum. This was revealed in his answer regarding why he chose to run this course. He stated that he "didn't know what that [promoting equity] would look like though coming into the actual classroom. I didn't know what students were going to enroll."

Due to this uneasiness, Dian believed that planning the course activities outlined earlier in this chapter were important to be his "full self in the classroom" and to see "growth from a lot of different students in different ways." Part of the importance of these activities derives from a broader socialization project that paints individuals as representative of broader groups and those groups as having a single experience. For minoritized communities, those experiences are often portrayed as negative. When thinking about the first day of class, Dian remarked that there is always the "initial opportunity" to stereotype people before you know them. However, engaging in a fishbowl activity

> illuminates true intentions and value systems and experiences that allow people to come to conversations with different viewpoints. . . . [It's] really important especially in a discussion-based class that you know who's sitting next to you. You may eventually talk about [an experience] with somebody you barely know, especially when there's a power dynamic, and you have to do that [work].

Ultimately, engaging in a critical pedagogy was important to Dian not only because it helped to break down power dynamics in the classroom but also because he believed that it taught students how to engage in similar work outside of the classroom. He noted that "we can . . . equalize differences of power . . . and allow people to bring the experiences that they bring to that room without completely erasing them." Critical pedagogical principles, for Dian, led to critical praxis where students could ask themselves, How do we use that knowledge as power to revolutionize a system?

Experiencing the Class

In this section, we share the experiences of Azura and Brandon. As noted previously, Azura identifies as a biracial, cisgender woman, and Brandon identifies as a White, cisgender man. Their experiences are revealing of the ways that these pedagogical tools can support the learning and inclusion of students of color, and also help White students to better understand and support their peers of color. Their narratives also highlight how they each experienced the class in different ways.

For Brandon, who was an advanced philosophy major and had previously read some of the texts, the differences in students were examined through developmental levels. He stated that he "thought the people in class were going to be a lot more animated on the things that they wanted to say. . . . But I think I started to realize that a lot of people in class were still forming those opinions." Unlike Brandon, Azura's preconceptions about the class related to the racial composition of the class. Azura explained,

> I expected the class to have less people of color simply because the University of Denver does not have that many people of color, and the demographics of my class usually reflect this. With that being said, I was pleasantly surprised to see so many people of color in this class who were all ready to share their own experiences and I was also excited to learn about social theories from a Person of Color [POC], because I felt that I would not have been as comfortable sharing my experiences as a POC with an all-white class to a white professor.

In these two instances, it is apparent that identity played a role in the way that Azura and Brandon reflected on the course and who was in attendance, with Azura focusing on the race of her peers and Brandon reflecting on the intellectual readiness of his peers to engage in deeper conversations. Racial identity was central to Azura's learning experience but did not seem as salient to Brandon. This does not mean that Brandon entered the class in a color-blind manner, but because of his privileged identities, he did not enter the room thinking about race first. He did however try to "be proactive" in letting his peers know that he is not a "very stereotypical straight white male" and that he entered the class with a critical worldview.

Upon reflecting on the activities described in the previous sections, Brandon did believe that there was a positive effect on his relationship with his peers as a result of his engagement, which allowed him to broach differences in identity. He noted that the fishbowl

> was super helpful for me because I was trying to be very honest with it. My same assumption was that everyone else was doing the same thing. I think that creates a strong level of trust and bond within the class that is super helpful. . . . I approached the activity trying my best to leave any assumptions out, [and] I was able to just expand my knowledge about the students.

Azura also found similar benefit in engaging in the activity. Despite noting that she interacted with people across difference regularly, she still recognized that she entered spaces holding stereotypes about people and the origin of those stereotypes. She noted:

> I thought the fishbowl and *I Am From* poems helped create an environment of honesty and trust. The expectation was that everyone would be as honest and open as they could be, and I think everyone lived up to that expectation. In a class like this, where people are sharing their personal and maybe painful experiences, it's important to trust that the people you are sharing with aren't going to judge or try to negate your experiences. Sharing the *I Am From* poems challenged any assumptions based on stereotypes we may have attached to our peers before they could fully form, which is especially important in a class designed not only to challenge assumptions based on stereotypes, but also to challenge the stereotypes themselves. . . . We have more room to actually consider what they said and why they may have said it.

Engaging in these class activities ultimately allowed both students to feel that they could share their full lived-experiences. As Azura stated: "I can say that I did feel more willing to contribute my experiences to the class."

Due to that ability to engage across difference and trust their peers as a result of engaging in the activities, Azura and Brandon recognized positive outcomes of the course despite the neoliberal organization of the university that caused Azura to see classes as "a business transaction" and Brandon to view them as a "credit-debt cycle" or market-driven model of education. Both students noted that they preferred seminar courses because faculty were more flexible in their teaching, centered teaching and student voice, had more quality learning opportunities, were less transactional, and could allow instructors to "engage in a lot of different levels of discussion," as Brandon reflected.

Because this course was seminar style, Brandon felt that the course changed his worldview and helped him to "isolate the specific issues, and also see the structures that [he] would either have to work within in order to create some change, or [to decide whether] these structures [prevent] change and [cause] oppression." He also noted that the activities allowed him to view the teacher–student relationship in a new way, to break it down so that he could see the instructor as "a friend and an ally who is working on this [deconstruction of oppressive systems] with us."

Azura expanded on Brandon's comments about the relationship between student and teacher, stating that

> the student is usually expected to believe everything the teacher says with-out question, and we are never asked to question how the university as a whole functions. So the fact that we were invited and even encouraged to question DU and the way we are normally taught was very different.

In the end, both students were able to engage with different others and come to new conclusions about the way that a neoliberal structuring of the university can be limiting to the educational experience of students and enter the space as their full selves and learn across difference. Brandon concluded by saying that

> this has helped me to see how the barriers to neoliberalism, especially in the classroom, can be challenged and can be broken down. . . . Being exposed to a classroom that challenged neoliberalism will really help me in my reflection piece as I continue to think about it and engage it.

Discussion and Implications

Our analysis revealed a few themes regarding how we viewed the course, lessons learned, and how the course worked to battle neoliberal classroom culture by centering student voice. First, course organization is important to student learning. Instructors should be cognizant of student development levels and the ways that students learn. This includes understanding others and constructing spaces for dialogue. Second, instructors should set up a course that uses students' lived experiences as an incubator for study. Third, the curriculum is important to centering a study of power, privilege, and oppression that can lead to lasting outcomes after the course ends.

Related to the course setup, Dian noted that "learning has to be some-what normative" in a neoliberal university. Fortunately, the curriculum in this course was able to be shaped in ways that supported learning of "the other" (Kumashiro, 2000) through the centering of student experience and voice. Azura also spoke about how she often views class as transactional, noting that "I do think that the neoliberal university causes me to see my classes as a business transaction instead of a place to gain knowledge." This transaction is the result of a university that frames education through market principles, where instructors deposit knowledge into passive students, whose diverse forms of knowledge and perspective are dismissed (Giroux, 2015). In response to this prevailing culture, instructor and student set out to coconstruct their classes as spaces of resistance; Dian through curricular and pedagogical design, and Azura through course selection, hoping to find classes with students with shared identities.

Interestingly, Brandon reflected that he thought the course would be more "animated," or as he stated in another part of his interview, "combative," which was a cultural norm he experienced in his philosophy and political science classrooms. However, Brandon's expectation could also stem from a normative individualistic and competitive culture that results when resources are limited and students are grappling to be at the top of their class. According to Giroux (2015), "neoliberalism legitimates a culture of cruelty and harsh competitiveness" (p. 102). In this business model, competition is valued. However, in our course, we attempted to remove that competitiveness by exploring individual life experiences, goals, and worldviews. We also began with an assumption that each person entered the class with the same level of opportunity to succeed as humans rather than products of the university. This is certainly important for elevating the voices of students of color, who are often silenced in class.

The course description stated the following:

> It is the hope that participants will be better suited to analyzing the world broadly, and their spheres of influences specifically with an eye toward engaging in critical thought and praxis toward equity. As a microcosm of broader society, we will utilize DU and Denver as an incubator of study.

Therefore, each lesson was intended to turn a collective analytical eye toward the campus environment and relatedly, the students' experiences on campus. Freire (2008) called this method *problem-posing education*, where students can bring their lived experiences into the classroom and learn from them. Giroux (2015) noted that higher education must be "a space in which education enables students to develop a keen sense of prophetic justice, claim their moral and political agency, utilize critical analytical skills, and cultivate an ethical sensibility" (p. 110). Gottesman (2016) expanded on that notion, writing "that critical education should be the central feature of revolution-ary movement building" (p. 10). Azura spoke to her political agency, stating that she would have to work toward changing systems in order to create more problem-posing education. These opportunities provide a space for students to deconstruct their normative assumptions of the university and to reconstruct more equitable systems (Harris, 2016). Both Brandon and Azura reflected on the ways that they would extend their learning beyond the scope of the course.

Finally, Brandon and Azura spoke about the role of faculty in the "reproduction of the social structure by sanctioning the hereditary trans-mission of cultural capital" (Bourdieu, 1986, para. 6). Expanding on his comment about the credit–debt cycle, Brandon noted that this may be because in the neoliberal university there is still an "obligation of the credit–debt cycle . . . because you need a little bit of that obligation piece in order for students to be incentivized to actually do the readings," an unfortunate observation of the current state of higher learning. Despite this obligation, both Azura and Brandon reflected on the types of instruc-tors that they best learn from. Brandon identified that person as "someone who is a friend and an ally who is working on this together with us" and Azura noted that the instructor should be somebody who helps students to realize "that it's ok to question the way we are being taught, and that the professors don't necessarily know everything." The lecture style of teach-ing reinforces a banking model of education when not supplemented with additional discussion, problem-posing education, and reflection on lived-experiences. Brandon reflected on enjoying courses where he could connect more personally with instructors.

Universities can be reflective on the types of learning spaces offered, how they incentivize faculty to teach in student-centered ways and build relation-ships with students, particularly those who are students of color. Additionally, faculty must be helped in using pedagogical tools that help keep students engaged in the literature, as well as change the culture of learning so that students are personally invested in their learning and do not engage in learn-ing simply to receive credit. As Brandon questioned: "Am I going to get a professor who is caring about the teaching and has thought about the dif-ferent ways that kids learn and the different styles?" For a student to ask this question is disheartening. An instructor who is not cognizant of the various backgrounds, identities, and viewpoints that students bring into the class-room and who does not shape an equitable classroom environment remains a problematic instructor.

Conclusion

Competition, self-centered education, and a lack of attention to students of color have quickly deteriorated the transformative learning opportunities of all students (Giroux, 2002, 2015). Particularly for the most marginalized communities, specifically communities of color, this effect is exponential (Hamer & Lang, 2015). However, pedagogical projects of critical teaching and learning exist that aim to reignite a political and social resistance to this destructive economic, political, and social regime. This chapter explored various aspects of one such space of resistance and highlighted how the instructor conceptualized the course, and how two students experienced the course. Through active consideration of student development, learning, faculty role, and course construction, students can engage in ways that lead to more critical considerations of systems and a collective diverse and intersectional success for all. It was our intention to highlight a few ways that spaces of resistance can be coconstructed by students and teachers, providing language and strategies that may ultimately subvert oppressive structures. As Azura positively reflected, "In the future, I will be less afraid to change things and question the way things are done." This is how we hope all students will leave the classroom—and that they will have the tools and critical hope to do so.

References

Adichie, C. N. (2009, July). Chimamanda Ngozi Adichie: The danger of a single story [Video file]. Retrieved from https://www.ted.com/talks/chimamanda_adichie_the_danger_of_a_single_story

Arao, B., & Clemens, K. (2013). From safe spaces to brave spaces: A new way to frame dialogue around diversity and social justice. In L. Landreman (Ed.), *The art of effective facilitation: Reflections from social justice educator* (pp. 135–150). Sterling, VA: Stylus.

Badenhausen, K. (2015, July 29). Denver leads Forbes' 2015 list of best places for business and careers. *Forbes.* Retrieved from http://www.forbes.com/sites/kurt-badenhausen/2015/07/29/denver-leads-the-2015-best-places-for-business-and-careers/#64cf2b3763ad

Bourdieu, P. (1986). The forms of capital. In J. Richardson (Ed.), *Handbook of theory and research for the sociology of education* (pp. 241–258). New York, NY: Greenwood.

Carr, P. R., & Pluim, G. W. J. (2015). Education for democracy, and the specter of neoliberalism jamming the classroom. In M. Abendroth & B. J. Porfilio (Eds.), *Understanding neoliberal rule in higher education: Educational fronts for local and global justice* (pp. 289–310). Charlotte, NC: Information Age Publishing.

Freire, P. (2008). *Pedagogy of the oppressed.* New York, NY: Bloomsbury Publishing.

Giroux, H. (2002). Neoliberalism, corporate culture, and the promise of higher education: The university as a democratic public sphere. *Harvard Educational Review, 72*(4), 425–464.

Giroux, H. A. (2015). Democracy in crisis, the specter of authoritarianism, and the future of higher education. *Journal of Critical Scholarship on Higher Education and Student Affairs, 1*(1), 7.

Gottesman, I. (2016) *The critical turn in education: From Marxist critique to post-structuralist feminism to critical theories of race.* New York, NY: Routledge.

Hamer, J. F., & Lang, C. (2015). Race, structural violence, and the neoliberal university: The challenges of inhabitation. *Critical Sociology, 41*(6), 897–912.

Harris, C. I. (1993). Whiteness as property. *Harvard Law Review, 106*(8), 1707–1791.

Harris, J. C. (2016). Liberatory graduate education: (Re)Building the Ivory Tower through critical race pedagogy. In N. N. Croom & T. E. Marsh (Eds.), *Envisioning critical race praxis in higher education through counter-storytelling* (pp. 147–164). Charlotte, NC: Information Age Publishing.

Kumashiro, K. K. (2000). Toward a theory of anti-oppressive education. *Review of Educational Research, 70*(1), 25–53.

Leber, R. (2013, March 8). Colorado approves in-state tuition for undocumented immigrants. Retrieved from http://thinkprogress.org/immigration/2013/03/08/1693461/colorado-approves-in-state-tuition-for-undocumented-immigrants/

Lipsitz, G. (2006). *The possessive investment in Whiteness: How White people profit from identity politics.* Philadelphia, PA: Temple University Press.

Nicolazzo, Z. (2016). "It's a hard line to walk": Black non-binary trans* collegians' perspectives on passing, realness, and trans*-normativity. *International Journal of Qualitative Studies in Education. 29*(9), 1173–1188. doi:10.1080/09518398.2016.1201612

Patel, L. (2015). Desiring diversity and backlash: White property rights in higher education. *The Urban Review, 47*(4), 657–675.

Preskill, S., & Brookfield, S. D. (2008). *Learning as a way of leading: Lessons from the struggle for social justice.* San Francisco, CA: Jossey-Bass.

University of Denver. (2015). Homepage. Retrieved from www.du.edu

University of Denver. (2016). *2015–2016 Cost of Attendance.* Retrieved from http://www.du.edu/financialaid/undergraduate/cost/

Wilder, C. S. (2013). *Ebony and ivy: Race, slavery, and the troubled history of America's universities.* New York, NY: Bloomsbury Publishing.

Yosso, T. J. (2002). Toward a critical race curriculum. *Equity &Excellence in Education, 35*(2), 93–107.

PART THREE

RADICAL PEDAGOGY IN "NEUTRAL" PLACES

It is often assumed that transformative pedagogy and praxis are limited to the social sciences and humanities classrooms. However, teaching difficult subjects is also necessary in STEM fields and other disciplines where such conversations would seem irrelevant and/or unnecessary. Moreover, engaging in radical teaching efforts in unexpected ways can transcend imposed and arbitrary expectations of teaching and learning. The chapters in this part offer strategies for including discussions of diversity within curricula that is often regarded as objective and thus, politically neutral.

During the Supreme Court case, *Fisher v. University of Texas*, Chief Justice Roberts posed the following question, "What unique perspective does a minority student bring to a physics class?" With this question, Chief Justice Roberts interprets the sciences as neutral spaces in which there exists only objective forms of knowledge. Two chapters in this section, Thomas Poon's "A Call for Difficult Conversations Around Diversity in STEM Courses" and Jennifer S. Fang's "Diversity Matters in the STEM Classroom," challenge such perceptions, arguing that the persistence of views like Chief Justice Roberts's is one of the many reasons that students of color and women are woefully underrepresented in STEM fields at the college level and beyond. Poon approaches this issue from the vantage point of a university administrator and a professor of chemistry, noting that the STEM disciplines are conspicuously absent from broader campus conversations regarding diversifying college curricula. Poon offers best practices for ways that faculty (with varying levels of "comfort") in the hard sciences might engage in critical conversations around race, sexuality, and gender. Jennifer S. Fang's chapter "Diversity Matters in the STEM Classroom" takes on Chief Justice Roberts's question more directly by offering evidence that learning environments that "take affirmative steps to enhance the quality of interactions between diverse students—often addressing disparities in the educational experiences of underrepresented students—are rewarded with better student outcomes" (p. 228, this volume).

In "Between Critique and Professional Ambition," Akhila L. Ananth contemplates the dilemma of teaching in the field of criminal justice, which has historically not offered students, especially students with marginalized identities and backgrounds, the opportunity to question often invisible structures and systems that produce the inequalities they experience. The chapter provides powerful examples of pedagogical strategies to nurture critical consciousness among students as they consider their career paths.

Jasmine L. Harris's chapter, "Uncomfortable Learning: Teaching Race Through Discomfort in Higher Education," brings the collection full circle. While most of the chapters in this collection have focused on ways that faculty can make the classroom and the campus environment amenable to difficult conversations about race, Harris argues that pedagogies focused on *safe spaces* and *brave spaces* do not adequately address how faculty can productively make use of discomfort. Through the use of case studies and various theoretical frameworks, Harris suggests that negative emotions can be powerful tools in advancing a socially just pedagogy.

11

A CALL FOR DIFFICULT CONVERSATIONS AROUND DIVERSITY IN STEM COURSES

Thomas Poon

The 2015–2016 academic year was a particularly turbulent year for U.S. higher education (Hartocollis & Bidgood, 2015), especially for students of color, women, and the LGBTQ community. Prominent media attention on sexual assault on college campuses (Gala & Gross-Schaefer, 2016), incidents of violence against people of color (Chuck, 2014; Lightblau, 2016; Smith, 2015), and political issues raised during the run-up to the Republican and Democratic primaries (Brown, 2016) created swift and passionate responses from college students and faculty across the country (Brown, Mangan, & McMurtrie, 2016). As an interim president at a small liberal arts college during this time, I experienced the difficulties of addressing these challenges as well as the privilege of getting to know the constituencies who sought substantive change and who demanded better of their institutions. I was struck by the multifaceted experiences and range of backgrounds from those involved. They were first-generation students, undocumented students, students on financial aid, and students who identified with one or more affinity groups. They were also students majoring in STEM[1] fields, and these STEM students faced many of the same issues that their classmates in the humanities and social sciences were facing, including microaggressions in the classroom, challenges with schoolwork, feeling a sense of isolation in their courses or major programs, and the impression that their instructors were not aware of the challenges they faced. I thought back a few years to a semester when I taught a course titled The Science of Identity, a first-year seminar course that discussed controversial topics around diversity through a scientific lens. Several students in that course indicated to me that they appreciated the issues that we discussed and the opportunity we had to approach them from different viewpoints, including scientific viewpoints. I lamented that the course was not currently being offered at a time when the subject was so relevant. I thought about the STEM courses that were being offered that year and wondered whether the instructors in those courses were discussing these subjects in the context of their scientific disciplines. I soon learned from students that there was little to no incorporation of such topics in their STEM courses.

A study conducted by Angela C. Johnson found that the practice of decontextualizing science in STEM curricula and the promulgation of the myth that science is a meritocracy negatively impacts women STEM majors of color (Johnson, 2007). Would the inclusion of issues around diversity within STEM courses be beneficial to students' learning or to other aspects of their lives? The effect of such discussions on students enrolled in many non-STEM courses was abundantly apparent on campus that year. This was evident in town hall meetings, in public e-mails, and at rallies and demonstrations where students spoke passionately and convincingly about injustices both at the local and national level. It was obvious in their language that students were informed by concepts and ideas learned in political science, history, sociology, ethnic studies, feminist studies, and gender studies courses. However, a STEM-based narrative[2] was notably absent from the discourse. Were the issues at hand devoid of any relevance to the STEM fields? Are we, as STEM educators, doing enough to equip our students with the skills and confidence to engage in difficult conversations about diversity from a disciplinary perspective? Could the lack of such discussions in STEM curricula be turning women and students of color away from the STEM fields?

Since the turn of the twenty-first century, higher education has seen noticeable gains in U.S. degree attainment at the bachelor's level. Between 2000 and 2014, there has been a 51% increase in the number of bachelor's degrees conferred, with every diversity demographic seeing significant increases as shown in Table 11.1. Increases are also seen in the number of STEM degrees conferred during the same time period for all demographics.

A closer look at the demographic data, however, reveals some troubling statistics in the area of diversity in STEM education. In terms of absolute numbers, the Asian American/Pacific Islander and Black affinity groups have not kept pace in their STEM degree attainment with their cohort's overall increase in bachelor's degree attainment. For example, the number of STEM degrees conferred to Black students in 2013–2014 increased by 42.4% since 1999–2000, compared to an overall increase of 77.1% in the number of

TABLE 11.1

Comparison of Bachelor's Degrees Awarded in 1999–2000 and in 2013–14

	Bachelor's degrees		% Increase	STEM degrees		% Increase
	1999–2000	2013–14		1999–2000	2013–14	
All	1,237,875	1,869,814	51.1	203,961	319,253	56.5
Male	530,367	801,692	51.2	128,811	206,987	60.7
Female	707,508	1,068,122	51.0	73,670	111,680	51.6
American Indian or Alaskan Native	8,717	10,786	23.7	1,192	1,491	25.1
Asian American or Pacific Islander	77,909	131,680	69.0	24,228	39,372	62.5
Black	108,018	191,298	77.1	15,175	21,605	42.4
Hispanic	75,063	202,412	169.7	10,422	28,685	175.2
White	929,102	1,218,792	31.2	141,202	201,594	42.8

Note. Data from National Center for Education Statistics (2017)

bachelor's degrees conferred to Black students over the same time frame. A comparison of STEM degrees by race shows that Hispanic students, with a 4.1% increase relative to other groups, are the only affinity group to post substantial gains in STEM degree attainment since the turn of the twenty-first century.

The same is true for women in STEM. In 1999–2000, 36.4% of STEM degrees were conferred to women, compared to 35.0% in 2013–2014 (Snyder, de Brey, and Dillow, 2016; Snyder and Hoffman, 2003). This slight decrease cannot be attributed to a decrease in women seeking college degrees as the percentage of women earning bachelor's degrees has remained flat at 57% between 1999–2000 and 2013–2014. These static trends in the distribution of STEM degrees for women and most students of color, even while more students are earning college degrees, is frequently blamed for the disproportionate number of underrepresented minorities in postdegree STEM careers and is often referred to as the "pipeline leak" (Allen-Ramdial & Campbell, 2014, p. 613). It is particularly surprising because of the litany of efforts that have been adopted and studied since 2000 to improve STEM education in higher education through new pedagogical approaches and programs (Fairweather, 2008). With the United States projected to become a majority-minority nation by 2044 (Colby & Ortman, 2015) and the availability of STEM jobs predicted to grow on top of the 20% increase it has already experienced since 2000 (Neuhauser & Cook, 2016), we need new approaches to attract people from underrepresented affinity groups to the STEM disciplines and to retain them.

This chapter represents a call for difficult conversations around diversity in STEM curricula, especially in introductory college courses, as a way to be more culturally responsive to underrepresented students in the STEM fields and in order to better prepare future STEM professionals to participate at all levels of discourse in society. It will propose a framework for incorporating difficult conversations and provide strategies that are based on recent best practices for facilitating difficult discussions on college campuses and established scholarship on teaching and learning in STEM.

The Need for Cultural Competency in STEM Education

Over the past 20 years, a body of research has developed that examines the effects of introducing *culture*, broadly defined, into STEM courses and curricula, and it almost universally suggests the need for greater cultural competence in STEM education (Phuntsog, 1999; Tanner & Allen, 2007). *Cultural competency* is a term originally applied in healthcare education and practice to describe strategies for providing high-quality care to patients irrespective of race, ethnicity, culture, and language (Betancourt, Green, Carillo, & Park, 2005). The term has since been adopted by the education sector (Ladson-Billings, 2001) to describe frameworks for eliminating racial, cultural, and gender disparities in teaching, with the goal of improving learning and increasing retention. Although research on cultural competency in postsecondary education is increasing, much of the education literature in this area focuses on strategies and approaches for K–12. Nonetheless, the best practices identified in these studies are generally applicable to higher education and specifically to STEM education. For example, in *Culturally Responsive Teaching: A Guide to Evidence-Based Practices for Teaching All Students Equitably*, Basha Krasnoff (2016) identifies the following activities as "culturally responsive best practices for teaching racially, ethnically, culturally, and linguistically diverse students:

1. Acknowledge students' differences as well as their commonalities.
2. Validate students' cultural identity in classroom practices and instructional materials.
3. Educate students about the diversity of the world around them.
4. Promote equity and mutual respect among students.
5. Assess students' ability and achievement validly.
6. Foster a positive interrelationship among students, their families, the community, and school.
7. Motivate students to become active participants in their learning.

8. Encourage students to think critically.
9. Challenge students to strive for excellence as defined by their potential. (Krasnoff, 2016, pp. 18–20)

It is difficult to deny that modern collegiate-level STEM education has benefited from greater assessment and systematic research on student learning (Fairweather, 2008), the development of innovative active modes of learning (Bonwell, 1991; Freeman et al., 2014), a focus on critical thinking (Bissell & Lemons, 2006), and the maintenance of rigor in the curriculum (Gasiewski, Eagan, Garcia, Hurtado, & Chang, 2012). However, this represents only half of the best practices identified by Krasnoff (2016) as necessary for responsive teaching to diverse students. The STEM disciplines are only just beginning to recognize the need to help students acknowledge their differences and commonalities, validate student cultural identity, educate students about the diversity in the world, and promote mutual respect among students in the classroom (Krasnoff, 2016). It is these additional practices that will make STEM education more accessible to students from diverse backgrounds.

One example of the impact that the integration of cultural content in courses may have on the growth of student diversity is in the teaching of psychology. When compared with the corresponding trends for STEM degree attainment (Figure 11.1), psychology shows much larger increases (Figure 11.2) over the same 14-year period for all students of color. Although several factors

Figure 11.1. Distribution of STEM bachelor's degrees in 1999–2000 and 2013–14.

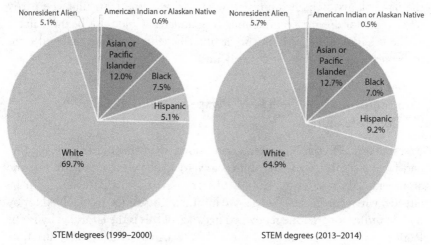

STEM degrees (1999–2000)   STEM degrees (2013–2014)

Source. NCES, 2016.

Figure 11.2. Distribution of psychology bachelor's degrees in 1999–2000 and 2013–14.

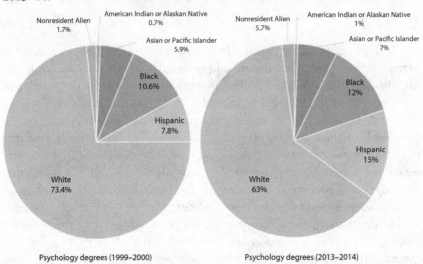

Source. NCES, 2016.

could be responsible for this growth in diversity, it can be noted that a study by Fuentes and Shannon (2016) found that 68% of the 200 undergraduate psychology programs studied offered diversity courses as electives for the major. The authors also reported that among the psychology courses that did not explicitly focus on diversity, 28% contained at least one diversity topic in the title or course description. Both of these findings suggest that the psychology curriculum is replete with content related to diversity topics and issues. Could the psychology discipline's infusion of diversity in the curriculum be partly responsible for diversity gains among its graduates? Could this be translatable to the teaching of STEM, and what other benefits could be achieved from incorporating discussions of diversity into STEM curricula?

The Importance of the STEM Perspective and Activism by STEM Professionals

Research on effective argumentation shows that the more peer support and factual information contributed toward a cause, the more effective the argument (Andrews et al., 2006). History has shown that change can be effected when controversial issues are informed by science and lobbied for by STEM professionals. One renowned instance of this is the effort led by Linus Pauling and other scientists in the 1950s to halt nuclear testing, an effort vehemently opposed and impeded by the U.S. State Department and other entities. Through their activism and their use of research data, such as the baby tooth survey findings from St. Louis, Missouri (Logan, 1964), Pauling and more than 11,000 scientists from around the world became a collective voice that garnered public support and political influence. The result was the treaty banning nuclear weapon tests in the atmosphere, in outer space, and under water signed by the Soviet Union, the United Kingdom, and the United States in 1963 (Schwelb, 1964).

Conversely, when STEM-informed viewpoints are absent or not effective in influencing public debate, equally important and arguably detrimental decisions are made that effect policy and shape history. One such example is the debate over research with human embryonic stem cells, cells from the early stages of fetal development. The discovery of embryonic stem cells in mice in 1981 (Evans & Kaufman, 1981) heralded a promising new era of research and potential medical breakthroughs. It also set off warning bells for groups concerned with a myriad of issues. Those with religious interests, for example, were very concerned. The viewpoints of these groups effected legislation that restricted federal research funding for embryonic stem cell research in the United States. It is claimed that this legislation hampered embryonic stem cell research for several years (Cook, 2004), even though private companies and states such as California, Missouri, and New Jersey provided avenues for such research to continue. We will never know how much further along in clinical studies U.S.-based researchers would now be if the debate had favored the other side. We also do not know if enough voices could have been cultivated to shift this debate. For example, would greater emphasis on scientific argumentation and rhetoric in STEM education have produced more effective voices on this controversial issue?

We do know that there are ample controversies, closer to home and to our turbulent times, centered around imbalances in employment, education, and enforcement of the law, inequities that can be attributed to human biases and socioeconomic factors. Do the STEM fields have something to say about these inequities? Mathematician Cathy O'Neil believes so. In her book *Weapons of Math Destruction*, O'Neil (2016) posits that mathematical algorithms contribute to pervasive inequality in many sectors of society. O'Neil's book has garnered attention from the STEM community as well as from the mainstream media (McGinty, 2016). Through her public advocacy and her book's call for greater scrutiny on the misuse of mathematics, O'Neil has expanded the narrative around race, inequality, and other issues.

There are many other examples where the narrative of a debate informed by the STEM fields stands to be usurped by more vocal or more compelling viewpoints. The environment, food production, overpopulation, and education policy, to name a few, have all been the subject of controversies enlightened by STEM at one point or another and that have any combination of interests from political, social, ethical, or religious devotees. We live in an age where such topics are frequently and openly debated in spaces that can rapidly influence policy. Our STEM students need to be exposed not just to disciplinary content, but also to situations where they can practice applying their disciplinary knowledge to multidisciplinary situations and be equipped and encouraged to speak up. It is up to STEM educators to assure that the voice of future STEM professionals remains relevant in an ever-changing society. Neglecting to do so would endanger the standing of science in the public sphere, a standing some claim has already been diminished in modern times (Watts, 2014).

Framework for Incorporating Discussions Around Diversity in STEM Courses

Incorporating difficult discussions around diversity in the classroom will be a new approach and a significant change for most STEM instructors. It is likely to be questioned by students and faculty alike, but it will be entirely worthwhile if, as posited earlier, it provides a means for instructors to become more culturally responsive to marginalized students in their courses, validates students of color, women, or students from the LGBTQ community, encourages critical and multidisciplinary thinking among STEM students, and provides students with much-needed experience in debate from a scientific standpoint. In order to more easily facilitate such change, the following five steps are offered as a framework and basis for embarking on this endeavor:

1. Determine the level of engagement and types of activities to be undertaken.
2. Have a plan for maintaining rigor and breadth while increasing depth.
3. Communicate your goals.
4. Establish the classroom and activity as a "brave space."
5. Assess the effectiveness of your activities.

Determine the Level of Engagement and Types of Activities

In any teaching endeavor, there is a broad spectrum of ways to engage with the subject matter, and each is tailored toward particular goals. For example, one instructor may wish to simply explore the receptivity of the class to controversial subjects, whereas another may wish to have students explore a topic with great depth and rigor. The effectiveness of an approach will depend on several factors, including the level of engagement and the approach chosen to address the subject matter. This section identifies three levels of engagement and several different approaches for introducing difficult conversations in the classroom around diversity.

Figure 11.3 symbolically represents the options instructors have for bringing diversity topics into their courses. It suggests that the pedagogical tools, or approaches, used will greatly impact the level of engagement. The three levels presented here are meant only as starting points for consideration as instructors decide how to effect change in their courses. The first is a *contextual level* of engagement. As its name implies, this level of engagement introduces difficult topics as a way to provide context or relevance to scientific subject matter. A biology instructor might, for instance, presage phenotypical differences between males and females in the animal kingdom by asking students to think about controversial statements made by past public figures regarding differences between the innate abilities of men and women (Bombardieri, 2005; Madhavan, 2015). Although this level of introduction of controversial material may seem superficial or even sensationalistic, studies have shown that orienting questions and calls for student prior knowledge can increase learning of new material (Osman & Hannafin, 1994). A second, and greater, level of interaction with diversity topics can be achieved through an *applied level* of engagement. Here, a diversity topic would be used to support or refute a disciplinary theory or conjecture, although the extent of the discussion would be mostly limited to one or more STEM fields. For example, students might be asked to consider the often difficult topic of racial profiling and other forms of racial discrimination by first exploring the genetic basis, or more accurately, the lack of a genetic link between race and human DNA (Adelman, 2003; Rogow, 2003; Winant, 2004). A third kind of engagement, the *integrative level*, uses both STEM-based and non-STEM narratives to discuss diversity issues. This level of engagement with the material recognizes that a STEM-based approach to a difficult topic can be informed by theories, practices, and viewpoints outside of the STEM fields and vice versa. An example of this level

Figure 11.3. Illustration representing three levels of engagement and possible processes for achieving integration of diversity topics in STEM courses.

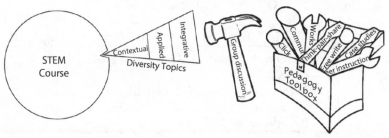

of engagement would be to take the race and genetics example mentioned earlier and ask students to consider social constructs for the concept of race and to suggest how this juxtaposes with biological definitions of race.

Achieving the desired level of engagement will be facilitated by the appropriate choice of methodology. In the past 25 years, higher education has benefited from an array of innovations in pedagogy, all supported by educational research on their effectiveness (Brower & Inkelas, 2007; Kuh, Kinzie, Schuh, & Whitt, 2010; Pascarella & Terenzini, 2005). As a result, a STEM instructor's toolbox is deep and varied, and far too expansive to fully cover here. However, Table 11.2 presents a selection of active learning methodologies grouped into one of three types of approaches. *Individual* approaches allow students to engage the material privately, potentially sharing one's thoughts only with the instructor. They are ideal for probing the receptivity of the class to diversity topics as well as for determining if students are making the desired connections between the diversity topic and STEM concepts. *Cooperative* approaches require students to share their thoughts with one or more fellow students. A methodology from this category is ideal for providing students with experience in debate from a scientific standpoint. *Immersive* approaches are the most time-consuming and experiential, and

TABLE 11.2
Possible Teaching Techniques for Engaging Students on Topics Around Diversity in STEM

Type of Approach	*Methodology*
Individual	One-minute paper (Almer, Jones, & Moeckel, 1998) Free-write (Drabick, Weisberg, Paul & Bubier, 2007; Elbow, 1973) Clickers (Wolter, Lundeberg, Kang, & Herreid, 2011)
Cooperative	Peer instruction (Crouch & Mazur, 2001) Think-Pair-Share (Azlina, 2010) Group discussions/seminaring (DeMarois, 2002; Helterbran, 2011; O'Connor & Michaels, 1996) Case studies (Crowe et al., 2011; McDade, 1995) Debate (Bell, 2004; Gervey, O'Connor Drout, & Wang, 2009)
Immersive	Community-based inquiry (Quitadamo, Faiola, Johnson, & Kurtz, 2008) Field trips (Jakubowski, 2003; Orion, 1993) Workshop-based learning (Udovic, Morris, Dickman, Postlethwait, & Wetherwax, 2002)

have great potential to impact student thought and learning. The dedication of significant class time required for an immersive approach also signals to the student the integral nature and importance of diversity conversations in STEM and vice versa.

These levels of engagement, types of approaches, and classroom methodologies are just some examples of the many options available to instructors who wish to incorporate diversity topics into their courses. No one combination is ideal for every instructor or class. For example, an instructor who wants to incorporate diversity topics for the first time might choose a contextual level of engagement as a goal and seek to achieve this goal through an individual approach such as the use of clickers to get students to think about the connections between STEM and diversity. Another instructor who might have the same engagement goal but who may also wish to provide students with practice in formulating an argument and expressing their viewpoints, might choose a more cooperative approach that involves a think-pair-share activity. An instructor may wish to achieve an applied level of engagement and feel that the cooperative approach of using case studies could be effective for the subjects she seeks to cover.

Maintain Rigor and Breadth, While Increasing Depth

Krasnoff's (2016) list of best practices for teaching racially, ethnically, culturally, and linguistically diverse students includes "challenging students to strive for excellence" (p. 20) in the course. Most educators would agree that student excellence in a course entails developing a complete understanding of the material and concepts of that course as determined by the faculty members in the discipline. Thus, it will be important to maintain rigor and breadth of coverage in any course that incorporates difficult discussions around diversity. Any STEM instructor who sacrifices these features at the expense of engaging in diversity topics is likely to be criticized by colleagues and students alike. But is this a fair criticism? An early paper in the development of active learning by Grabiner and Dunlap (1995) sets forth theoretical and practical criteria for establishing rich environments for active learning in the classroom. One passage from their paper especially rings true in the context of this discussion:

> We must move from emphasizing decontextualized reading and computational skills to developing independent thinkers and learners who engage in life-long learning. This does not mean that we abandon the important skills of reading and computation; it means instead that we should be teaching reading and computation within more situated contexts that demonstrate the value of those skills. (p. 9)

This passage suggests that if we choose relevant diversity topics to incorporate into our classrooms and situate these topics effectively within the content of the course, students will learn the concepts and more effectively develop the skills that we seek. Spending *less* time lecturing on a given topic or on doing problems without context, for example, will actually improve student mastery of the subject if these activities are replaced with poignant and meaningful applications of the subject matter to diversity issues. Instructors who have already infused active learning pedagogy throughout their courses, have likely seen gains in learning by their students as a result of their approaches. For those who are new to active learning and who wish to incorporate diversity topics in their class, this author recommends the following:

- Read the literature and consult with colleagues who have adopted the active learning methodology that you wish to utilize.
- Familiarize oneself with the diversity topic(s) you plan to present/discuss, especially from a multidisciplinary perspective. A search of the *Chronicle for Higher Education* (chronicle.com), *Inside Higher Ed* (insidehighered.com), and *Diverse: Issues In Higher Education* (diverseeducation.com) will likely yield up-to-date articles and information on the chosen diversity topic(s).
- Seek guidance on facilitating difficult dialogs around diversity (see later discussion).

Communicate Your Goals

One of the most effective ways to gain receptivity from students and peers when implementing change in course instruction is to clearly communicate your goals. Students need to know that culturally inclusive pedagogy helps all students become affirmed in their cultural connections (Tanner & Allen, 2007) and increases retention and learning (Sleeter, 2012). They will benefit from knowing that active pedagogies have been shown to result in greater learning (Freeman et al., 2014) and will help them become better at defending their positions using scientific principles, even when engaging in topics outside of STEM. It is also advantageous to gain allyship from fellow colleagues, as they can advocate for you in many circumstances and also champion your efforts and intentions. Discuss your plans and goals with other faculty, with your department chair, and with support personnel who may have a significant role in assisting you (e.g., lab coordinators, IT personnel, community engagement center personnel). Some institutions offer course development funding to faculty who incorporate technology or active learning into their classes, or who otherwise modify their courses for a particular goal or mission of the college. For faculty who apply for such funds, their approved proposal is a possible document to share with those being sought as allies. Sharing key papers that support one's intended goal is another way to help colleagues understand your pedagogy. It would also be advantageous to have a short, 10- to 20-second description of what you are trying to accomplish in your course, something akin to an elevator speech that will convey that you are knowledgeable and passionate about student learning. This description could additionally form the basis for a description of your efforts in faculty annual reports and self-statements for promotional milestones.

Establish the Classroom and Activity as a "Brave Space"

One prominent concern for educators in the wake of the student activism that occurred in higher education throughout 2015 and 2016 is the ability to engage their students in the free exchange of ideas in an environment that encourages participation and that is free from psychological harm (Saul, 2016). Such environments are known as *safe spaces* and have been the subject of research and reflection since the early 1990s (Barrett, 2010; Peters, 2003; Rom, 1998). Student activism has placed the spotlight back on safe spaces (Gitlin, 2015), and it is important to consider the student perspective on what constitutes a safe space in the classroom. Holley and Steiner (2005) obtained student feedback on several factors in learning environments that contribute to their perceptions of safe spaces. They found that 84% of students in their study reported that their learning in a course was affected by being in a safe classroom environment. Table 11.3 lists the variables surveyed in the study and the top three characteristics students cited as contributing to safe or unsafe spaces.

Many of the items in Table 11.3 reinforce suggestions from the literature on creating safe spaces, and they are also relevant in a new movement that is emerging in higher education, the creation of *brave spaces*. Arao and Clemens (2013) propose a reframing of dialogue around social justice issues and argue that authentic learning often requires communication that is incompatible with the definition of safety. They suggest that conducting difficult conversations within a framework of safety may place students from privileged groups on the defensive, while subjecting target group students to expectations that reinforce historically oppressive societal practices. Neither scenario is an effective learning environment for students, which is why Arao and Clemens propose a framework that cultivates brave spaces in the classroom when controversial topics around race and diversity are necessary. The signature steps in the framework are to (a) talk about brave spaces with students at the outset

TABLE 11.3
Variables and Top Three Characteristics That
Contribute to Safe or Unsafe Spaces

Variable	Characteristics of Safe Spaces	Characteristics of Unsafe Spaces
Instructor	Not biased, nonjudgmental, open Modeled participation, set ground rules Comfortable with conflict	Critical toward students Biased, opinionated, judgmental Did not consider others' perspectives
Peers	Good discussion skills Honestly shared ideas, opinions, and facts Nonjudgmental, open to perspectives	Afraid to or did not speak Biased, judgmental, or close-minded Apathetic about the course
Self	Tried to be open-minded Honestly shared ideas, views, and values Actively participated, spoke up	Did not participate Was fearful or felt vulnerable Did not invest in the course
Physical Environment	Seating allowed seeing everyone Appropriate room size Good lighting	Seating not conducive to discussion Small or cramped room Uncomfortable temperature

Source. Holley & Steiner (2005).

of the course or the activity and make this discussion a valuable part of the learning experience, and (b) establish ground rules for engaging in discussions within the course or activity. Ground rules can be accomplished in one of the following ways:

- Via a predetermined list of ground rules generated by the instructor
- By allowing the class to develop its own set of ground rules
- By using a hybrid of the previous two approaches, where the instructor presents a list followed by additions and edits to the list from the class (Arao & Clemens, 2013)

The following ground rules may offer a good starting point for faculty seeking to establish their STEM class or activity as a brave space. Each is a call for participants to do the following:

- Honor different viewpoints and strive to understand sources of disagreements (Arao & Clemens, 2013).
- Own the intentions of what one says as well as the impact of what one says (Arao & Clemens, 2013).
- Challenge oneself to step back when dominating a conversation and to step forward when one has yet to contribute (Pendakur, 2016). If one is unable to step forward, strive to understand the reasons preventing one's participation (Arao & Clemens, 2013).
- Refrain from attacking others by not speaking for others, not making accusations, and not labeling another person or another's arguments with derogatory adjectives.
- Keep what is said within the classroom, while taking what is learned outside of the classroom (Pendakur, 2016).
- Let others know when they have impacted you negatively and use this as a teachable moment. Some brave space advocates refer to this as "calling someone in" rather than as "calling someone out," and the reinforcement of this vernacular is crucial for open conversation (Pendakur, 2016).
- Strive to apply scientific or mathematical models to one's arguments and to the issues at hand.

The last bulleted point is, of course, what binds the controversial topic to most STEM course learning objectives, and instructors may need to direct the conversation in this direction if it strays too far. Effective faculty facilitation of the brave spaces framework has great potential to enhance student learning and to create an environment conducive to open and honest debate.

Assess the Effectiveness of Your Activities

Much has been written about both the advantages (Reynolds, Livingston, & Willson, 2010) and disadvantages (Torrance, 2007) of assessing postsecondary student learning. The faculty members who introduce diversity topics and concomitant activities into their courses will most likely want to know their impact on student learning and skill development. Although the methodology for doing so is beyond the scope of this chapter, one should seek both quantitative and qualitative approaches to determine if goals are being met. Sources of data will include numerical ratings and written comments on teaching evaluations, longitudinal data on retention numbers for STEM students in one's program, improvement in writing and oral presentation as determined by rubric-based assessments, and metrics designed to evaluate student knowledge of concepts from the diversity-based activities. Such metrics could, for example, be exam questions either on the STEM topic alone or questions that integrate the STEM topic with the diversity issue. The results of the assessment activity will be helpful in refining the activity and planning other activities for future courses. In this author's experience, positive outcomes of a new approach can also be used to reinforce the effectiveness of the pedagogy to students. In such instances, instructors should always seek to do the following:

- Point out when more depth or breadth of coverage has been achieved in class as a result of the activity.
- Remind students of the benefits gained through the approach.
- Take opportunities to compare the approach to prior approaches used in the course, especially when a benefit has been derived such as better performance on relevant exam questions. (Poon & Rivera, 2015)

Positive outcomes could also be added to a faculty's set of teaching narratives such as those found in annual reports, promotion dossiers, and elevator speeches.

Conclusion

In the same year that the U.S. Supreme Court made its landmark ruling on same-sex marriage, a wave of anti-LGBT bills and laws surfaced that allowed states and other entities to discriminate against the LGBT community (Bendery & Signorile, 2016; Mason, Williams, & Elliott, 2016). Prominent examples of such legislation are laws that restrict bathroom usage. These laws are rooted in fears or beliefs that arise from cisgender dominant classifications of human beings. Religious freedom and public safety are often passionate arguments used in these debates. Seldom called upon is the increasing evidence in biology (Bagemihl, 1999; Mustanski et al., 2005) and neuroscience (Kranz et al., 2014; Rametti et al., 2011) that gender exists on a broad spectrum, evidence that is building as scientific research progresses and technology advances. One day, the evidence might be incontrovertible, allowing one side to be validated in this highly polarized dispute. As STEM educators, we will prepare the next generation of STEM professionals to make exciting new discoveries. However, if students are not also equipped with the skills, confidence, and competency needed to become fully active participants in the aftermath of these discoveries, their potential to effect societal change may never be reached. Who is responsible for providing future STEM professionals with these abilities? Barack Obama provided the answer in his February 5, 2008, speech to supporters during his campaign for the Democratic presidential nomination when he said, "Change will not come if we wait for some other person or if we wait for some other time. We are the ones we've been waiting for. We are the change that we seek."

Notes

1. Although some agencies, such as the National Science Foundation, include the social sciences in its definition of *STEM* (Gonzalez & Kuenzi, 2012, p. 1), this author's use of the acronym will herein refer to the natural and physical sciences (S), technology (T), engineering (E), and mathematics (M).

2. Throughout this chapter, the phrase *STEM-based narrative* or *STEM-based approach* will be used to describe any treatment of a question or issue using scientifically sound analyses, evidence, or facts supported by known theories and practices in the STEM disciplines, including the mathematical and statistical disciplines. It is not to be confused with the phrase *scientific method*, which is a popularized term that does not do justice to the varied processes that STEM professionals use in their work.

References

Adelman, L. (Executive Producer). (2003). *RACE: The power of an illusion* (Executive Producer). [Video]. San Francisco: California Newsreel.

Adichie, C. N. (2009). The danger of a single story. Retrieved from www.ted.com/talks/chimamanda_adichie_the_danger_of_a_single_story.html.

Allen-Ramdial, S.-A. A., & Campbell, A. G. (2014). Reimagining the pipeline: Advancing STEM diversity, persistence, and success. *BioScience, 64*(7), 612–618.

Almer, E. D., Jones, K., & Moeckel, C. L. (1998). The impact of one-minute papers on learning in an introductory accounting course. *Issues in Accounting Education, 13*(3), 485–495.

Andrews, R., Bilbro, R., Mitchell, S., Peake, K., Prior, P., Robinson, A., See, B. H., & Torgerson, C. (2006). *Argumentative skills in first year undergraduates: A pilot study*. York, U.K.: The Higher Education Academy.

Arao, B., & Clemens, K. (2013). From safe spaces to brave spaces. In L.M. Landreman (Ed.), *The art of effective facilitation: Reflections from social justice educators* (pp. 135–150). Sterling, VA: Stylus.

Azlina, N. A. N. (2010). CETLs: Supporting collaborative activities among students and teachers through the use of think-pair-share techniques. *International Journal of Computer Science Issues, 7*(5), 18–29.

Bagemihl, B. (1999). *Biological exuberance: Animal homosexuality and natural diversity*. New York, NY: St. Martin's Press.

Barrett, B. J. (2010). Is "safety" dangerous? A critical examination of the classroom as safe space. *Canadian Journal for the Scholarship of Teaching and Learning, 1*(1), 1–12.

Bell, P. (2004). Promoting students' argument construction and collaborative debate in the science classroom. In M. C. Linn, E. A. Davis, and P. Bell (Eds.), *Internet environments for science education,* (pp. 115–143). Mahwah, NJ: Lawrence Eribaum Associates, Inc.

Bendery, J., & Signorile, M. (2016) Everything you need to know about the wave of 100+ anti-LGBT bills pending in states. *Huffington Post.* Retrieved from http://www.huffingtonpost.com/entry/lgbt-state-bills-discrimination_us_570ff4f2e4b0060ccda2a7a9

Betancourt, J. R., Green, A. R., Carrillo, J. E., & Park, E. R. (2005). Cultural competence and health care disparities: Key perspectives and trends. *Health Affairs, 24*(2), 499–505.

Bissell, A. N., & Lemons, P. P. (2006). A new method for assessing critical thinking in the classroom. *BioScience, 56*(1), 66–72.

Bombardieri, M. (2005, January 17). Summers' remarks on women draw fire. *Boston Globe,* p. 17. Retrieved from http://archive.boston.com/news/education/higher/articles/2005/01/17/summers_remarks_on_women_draw_fire/

Bonwell, C. C., & Eison, J. A. (1991). *Active learning: Creating excitement in the classroom.* Retrieved from https://www.ydae.purdue.edu/lct/hbcu/documents/Active_Learning_Creating_Excitement_in_the_Classroom.pdf

Brower, A., & Inkelas, K. K. (2007). Assessing learning community programs and partnerships. In B. L. Smith and L. B. Williams (Eds.), *Learning communities and student affairs: Partnering for powerful learning.* Retrieved from http://www.evergreen.edu/washingtoncenter/docs/monographs/lcsa/lcsa8assessing.pdf

Brown, S. (2016). "Trump" chalkings open new debate over speech and sensitivity. *The Chronicle of Higher Education.* Retrieved from http://chronicle.com/article/Trump-Chalkings-Trigger/235984

Brown, S., Mangan, K., & McMurtrie, B. (2016). At the end of a watershed year, can student activists sustain momentum? *The Chronicle of Higher Education.* Retrieved from http://www.chronicle.com/article/At-the-End-of-a-Watershed/236577

Chuck, E. (2014, August 13). The killing of an unarmed teen: What we know about Brown's death. *NBC News.* Retrieved from http://www.nbcnews.com/storyline/michael-brown-shooting/killing-unarmed-teen-what-we-know-about-browns-death-n178696

Colby, S. L., & Ortman, J. M. (2015). Projections of the size and composition of the U.S. population: 2014 to 2060. *Current Population Reports* (pp. 25–1143). Washington, DC: U.S. Census Bureau.

Cook, G. (2004, May 23). U.S. stem cell research lagging without aid, work moving overseas. *Boston Globe.* Retrieved from http://ccl.idm.oclc.org/login?url=http://search.proquest.com/docview/404904694?accountid=10141

Crouch, C. H., & Mazur, E. (2001). Peer instruction: Ten years of experience and results. *American Journal of Physics, 69*(9), 970–977.

Crowe, S., Cresswell, K., Robertson, A., Huby, G., Avery, A., & Sheikh, A. (2011). The case study approach. *BMC Medical Research Methodology, 11*(1), 1–9.

DeMarois, P. (2002). Using "seminaring" to actively engage students in a calculus class. In M. H. Ahmadi (Ed.), *Readings in innovative ideas in teaching collegiate mathematics,* (pp. 107–117). Lanham, MD: University Press of America.

Drabick, D. A. G., Weisberg, R., Paul, L., & Bubier, J. L. (2007). Keeping it short and sweet: Brief, ungraded writing assignments facilitate learning. *Teaching of Psychology, 34*(3), 172–176.

Elbow, P. (1973). *Writing without teachers.* Oxford, England: Oxford University Press.

Evans, M. J., & Kaufman, M. H. (1981). Establishment in culture of pluripotential cells from mouse embryos. *Nature, 292*(5819), 154–156.

Fairweather, J. (2008). *Linking evidence and promising practices in science, technology, engineering, and mathematics (STEM) undergraduate education.* Washington, DC: Board of Science Education, National Research Council, The National Academies.

Freeman, S., Eddy, S. L., McDonough, M., Smith, M. K., Okoroafor, N., Jordt, H., & Wenderoth, M. P. (2014). Active learning increases student performance in science, engineering, and mathematics. *Proceedings of the National Academy of Sciences, 111*(23), 8410–8415.

Fuentes, M. A., & Shannon, C. R. (2016). The state of multiculturalism and diversity in undergraduate psychology training. *Teaching of Psychology, 43*(3), 197–203.

Gala, S., & Gross-Schaefer, A. (2016). Sexual assault: The crisis that blindsided higher education. *International Journal of Social Science Studies, 4*(8), 23–41.

Gasiewski, J. A., Eagan, M. K., Garcia, G. A., Hurtado, S., & Chang, M. J. (2012). From gatekeeping to engagement: A multicontextual, mixed method study of student academic engagement in introductory STEM courses. *Research in Higher Education, 53*(2), 229–261.

Gervey, R., Drout, M. O'Connor., & Wang, C. C. (2009). Debate in the classroom: An evaluation of a critical thinking teaching technique within a rehabilitation counseling course. *Rehabilitation Education, 23*(1), 61–73.

Gitlin, T. (2015, November 22). Why are student protesters so fearful? *New York Times.* Retrieved from https://www.nytimes.com/2015/11/22/opinion/sunday/why-are-student-protesters-so-fearful.html

Gonzalez, H. B., & Kuenzi, J. J. (2012). *Science, technology, engineering, and mathematics (STEM) education: A primer.* Washington, DC: Congressional Research Service.

Grabinger, R. S., & Dunlap, J. C. (1995). Rich environments for active learning: A definition. *Research in learning technology, 3*(2), 5–34.

Hartocollis, A., & Bidgood, J. (2015, November 12). Racial discrimination demonstrations spread at universities across the U.S. *New York Times.* Retrieved from https://www.nytimes.com/2015/11/12/us/racial-discrimination-protests-ignite-at-colleges-across-the-us.html

Helterbran, V. R. (2011). Promoting critical thinking through discussion. *Journal of College Teaching & Learning (TLC), 4*(6), 1–6.

Holley, L. C., & Steiner, S. (2005). Safe space: Student perspectives on classroom environment. *Journal of Social Work Education, 41*(1), 49–64.

Jakubowski, L. M. (2003). Beyond book learning: Cultivating the pedagogy of experience through field trips. *Journal of Experiential Education, 26*(1), 24–33.

Johnson, A. C. (2007). Unintended consequences: How science professors discourage women of color. *Science Education, 91*(5), 805–821.

Kranz, G. S., Hahn, A., Kaufmann, U., Küblböck, M., Hummer, A., Ganger, S., ... & Lanzenberger, R. (2014). White matter microstructure in transsexuals and controls investigated by diffusion tensor imaging. *The Journal of Neuroscience, 34*(46), 15466–15475.

Krasnoff, B. (2016). Culturally responsive teaching: A guide to evidence-based practices for teaching all students equitably. Region X Equity Assistance Center at Education Northwest. Retrieved from http://educationnorthwest.org/sites/default/files/resources/culturally-responsive-teaching.pdf

Kuh, G. D., Kinzie, J., Schuh, J. H., & Whitt, E. J. (2010). *Student success in college: Creating conditions that matter.* San Francisco, CA: Jossey-Bass.

Ladson-Billings, G. (2001). *Crossing over to Canaan: The journey of new teachers in diverse classrooms. The Jossey-Bass education series.* San Francisco, CA: Jossey-Bass.

Lightblau, E. (2016, November 15). Attacks against Muslim Americans fueled rise in hate crime, F.B.I. says. *New York Times.* Retrieved from https://www.nytimes.com/2016/11/15/us/politics/fbi-hate-crimes-muslims.html

Logan, Y. (1964). The story of the baby tooth survey. *Scientist and Citizen, 6*(9–10), 38–39.

Lyon, G. E. (n.d.). Where I'm from. Retrieved from http://www.georgeellalyon.com/where.html.

Madhavan, D. (2015, November 29). Sunni cleric says women are only fit to deliver children, calls gender equality un-Islamic. *India Times.* Retrieved from http://www.indiatimes.com/news/india/sunni-cleric-kanthapuram-ap-aboobacker-musliar-says-women-are-only-fit-to-deliver-children-calls-gender-equality-an-un-islamic-farce-247827.html

Mason, E., Williams, A., & Elliott, K. (2016, July 1). The dramatic rise in state efforts to limit LGBT rights. *Washington Post.* Retrieved from https://www.washingtonpost.com/graphics/national/lgbt-legislation/?tid=sm_tu

McDade, S. A. (1995). Case study pedagogy to advance critical thinking. *Teaching of Psychology, 22*(1), 9–10.

McGinty, J. C. (2016, October 14). Algorithms aren't biased, but the people who write them may be. *Wall Street Journal.* Retrieved from http://www.wsj.com/articles/algorithms-arent-biased-but-the-people-who-write-them-may-be-1476466555

Mustanski, B. S., DuPree, M. G., Nievergelt, C. M., Bocklandt, S., Schork, N. J., & Hamer, D. H. (2005). A genomewide scan of male sexual orientation. *Human Genetics, 116*(4), 272–278.

National Center for Education Statistics (2018, February 1). Digest of Education Statistics. Retrieved from https://nces.ed.gov/programs/digest/

Neuhauser, A., & Cook, L. (2016, May 17). 2016 U.S. News/Raytheon STEM index shows uptick in hiring, education. *U.S. News and World Report.* Retrieved from http://www.usnews.com/news/articles/2016-05-17/the-new-stem-index-2016

Obama, B. (2008, February 5). Super Tuesday speech in Chicago, IL. Retrieved from http://obamaspeeches.com/E02-Barack-Obama-Super-Tuesday-Chicago-IL-February-5-2008.htm

O'Connor, M. C., & Michaels, S. (1996). Shifting participant frameworks: Orchestrating thinking practices in group discussion. In D. Hicks, (Ed.), *Discourse, learning, and schooling* (pp. 63–103). New York, NY: Cambridge University Press.

O'Neil, C. (2016). *Weapons of math destruction: How big data increases inequality and threatens democracy.* New York, NY: Crown Publishing Group.

Orion, N. (1993). A model for the development and implementation of field trips as an integral part of the science curriculum. *School Science and Mathematics, 93*(6), 325–331.

Osman, M. E., & Hannafin, M. J. (1994). Effects of advance questioning and prior knowledge on science learning. *The Journal of Educational Research, 88*(1), 5–13.

Pascarella, E. T., & Terenzini, P. T. (2005). *How college affects students: A third decade of research* (Vol. 2). San Francisco, CA: Jossey-Bass.

Pendakur, S. (2016, September 15). *Facilitating discussion on challenging topics.* Presentation at Claremont McKenna College, Claremont, CA.

Peters, A. (2003). Isolation or inclusion: Creating safe spaces for lesbian and gay youth. *Families in Society: The Journal of Contemporary Social Services, 84*(3), 331–337.

Phuntsog, N. (1999). The magic of culturally responsive pedagogy: In search of the genie's lamp in multicultural education. *Teacher Education Quarterly, 26*(3), 97–111.

Poon, T., & Rivera, J. (2015). The flipped classroom as an approach for enhancing student and instructor experiences in organic chemistry. In K. Daus & R. Rigsby (Eds.), *The promise of chemical education: Addressing our students' needs* (pp. 29–42). Washington, DC: American Chemical Society Symposium Series.

Quitadamo, I. J., Faiola, C. L., Johnson, J. E., & Kurtz, M. J. (2008). Community-based inquiry improves critical thinking in general education biology. *CBE-Life Sciences Education, 7*(3), 327–337.

Rametti, G., Carrillo, B., Gómez-Gil, E., Junque, C., Segovia, S., Gomez, Á., & Guillamon, A. (2011). White matter microstructure in female to male transsexuals before cross-sex hormonal treatment: A diffusion tensor imaging study. *Journal of Psychiatric Research, 45*(2), 199–204.

Reynolds, C. R., Livingston, R. B., & Willson, V. L. (2010). *Measurement and assessment in education.* San Francisco, CA: Pearson.

Rogow, F. (2003). *Discussion guide for RACE: The power of an illusion.* San Francisco, CA: California Newsreel. Retrieved from http://www-tc.pbs.org/race/images/race-guide-lores.pdf

Rom, R. B. (1998). "Safe spaces": Reflections on an educational metaphor. *Journal of Curriculum Studies, 30*(4), 397–408.

Saul, S. (2016, September 7). Campus 101: Learning how not to offend. *New York Times*. Retrieved from https://www.nytimes.com/2016/09/07/us/campuses-cautiously-train-freshmen-against-subtle-insults.html

Schwelb, E. (1964). The nuclear test ban treaty and international law. *The American Journal of International Law, 58*(3), 642–670.

Sleeter, C. E. (2012). Confronting the marginalization of culturally responsive pedagogy. *Urban Education, 47*(3), 562–584.

Smith, A. (2015, March 19). UVA student Martese Johnson's bloody arrest sparks probe, protest. *NBC News*. Retrieved from https://www.nbcnews.com/news/us-news/bloody-arrest-university-virginia-student-prompts-police-review-n326226

Snyder, T. D., de Brey, C., & Dillow, S. A. (2016). *Digest of education statistics 2015* (NCES 2016-014). Washington, DC: National Center for Education Statistics, Institute of Education Sciences, U.S. Department of Education.

Snyder, T. D., & Hoffman, C. M. (2003). *Digest of education statistics 2002* (NCES 2003-060). Washington, DC: National Center for Education Statistics, Institute of Education Sciences, U.S. Department of Education.

Tanner, K., & Allen, D. (2007). Cultural competence in the college biology classroom. *CBE–Life Sciences Education, 6*(4), 251–258.

Torrance, H. (2007). Assessment as learning? How the use of explicit learning objectives, assessment criteria and feedback in post-secondary education and training can come to dominate learning. 1. *Assessment in Education, 14*(3), 281–294.

Udovic, D., Morris, D., Dickman, A., Postlethwait, J., & Wetherwax, P. (2002). Workshop biology: Demonstrating the effectiveness of active learning in an introductory biology course. *Bioscience, 52*(3), 272–281.

Watts, S. (2014). Society needs more than wonder to respect science. *Nature, 508*(7495), 151.

Winant, H. (2004). Race: The power of an illusion. *The Journal of American History, 91*(2), 733–734.

Wolter, B. H. K, Lundeberg, M. A., Kang, H., & Herreid, C. F. (2011). Students' perceptions of using personal response systems ("clickers") with cases in science. *Journal of College Science Teaching, 40*(4), 14–19.

12

DIVERSITY MATTERS IN THE STEM CLASSROOM

Jennifer S. Fang

Amerca's science and engineering classrooms have a diversity problem. Whereas U.S. higher education suffers from racial disparities in student enrollments, the gap is even wider in classrooms devoted to the teaching of science, technology, engineering, and mathematics (STEM). Black, Hispanic, and Native students are significantly underrepresented among recipients of associate's or bachelor's degrees in STEM compared to their distribution in the general 18- to24-year-old population, and this racial gap grows only wider among recipients of advanced degrees in STEM (Figure 12.1). In other words, as a STEM student progresses through the study of STEM fields, the classroom becomes increasingly racially homogenous. By the time the average student graduates with an advanced degree in STEM, he or she will emerge having pursued the studies in an academic environment that completely fails to reflect the diversity of the United States at large.

Whereas White students obtain STEM and non-STEM bachelor's degrees at equivalent rates, Black and Hispanic students are more underrepresented among STEM bachelor's degree recipients than they are among recipients of degrees in non-STEM fields (Figure 12.2). As a consequence, Black, Hispanic, and Native people are also significantly underrepresented in the adult STEM workforce (Figure 12.3).

Within STEM fields, non-White employees are further stymied as they try to climb the professional ladder of their chosen industries. Racially minoritized programmers are profoundly underrepresented in Silicon Valley's upper- and middle-management positions. Although 27% of Silicon Valley's employees are Asian American, less than 20% are managers and less than 14% are executives (Gee, Peck, & Wong, 2015). Similarly, in STEM, non-White academics are underrepresented among those receiving full

Figure 12.1. Distribution of STEM[1] degree recipients by race/ethnicity versus U.S. youth population.

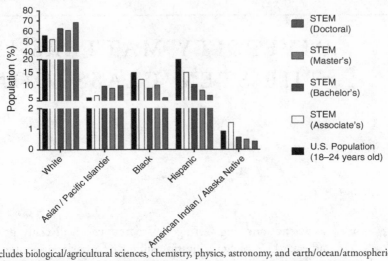

[1]Includes biological/agricultural sciences, chemistry, physics, astronomy, and earth/ocean/atmospheric sciences, computer sciences, mathematics/statistics, engineering, psychology, and social sciences.

Source: National Science Foundation, 2012.

Figure 12.2. STEM or non-STEM bachelor's degrees versus race/ethnicity of recipients.

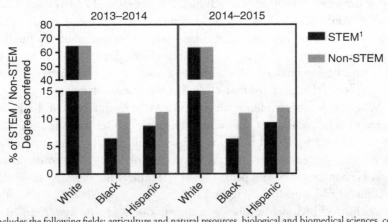

[1] Includes the following fields: agriculture and natural resources, biological and biomedical sciences, communications technologies, computer and information sciences, engineering, engineering technologies and engineering-related fields, mathematics and staticstics, mechanic and repair technologies, military technologies and repair technologies, military technologies and applied sciences, and physical sciences and science technologies.

Source: U.S. Department of Education, National Center for Education Statistics, Integrated Postsecondary Education Data System (IPEDS), Fall 2014 and Fall 2015, completions component.

Figure 12.3. Distribution by race/ethnicity of total population versus employees in STEM occupations.

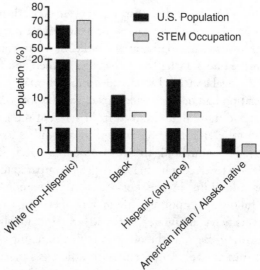

Source: U.S. Census Bureau, 2011 American Community Survey

professorships compared to their White peers (National Science Foundation, 2017). Furthermore, surveys of women of color scientists reveal that they frequently face sexual harassment, and that this workplace as harassment is often informed by racial stereotype (Williams, Phillips, & Hall, 2014). Given these facts, which appear to describe a STEM workplace as hostile to people of color, it might come as no surprise to find that minority STEM graduates are more likely than White STEM graduates to leave the STEM labor force altogether (Landivar, 2013). More alarmingly, this process appears to begin as early as in the postsecondary STEM classroom.

For STEM educators who recognize diversity as key to excellence in the field, this trend is distressing. It demands that we speak up as STEM educators within the broader higher education discourse; emphasize the evidence showing the positive teaching and learning benefits of a racially diverse STEM classroom; and take tangible steps as STEM educators to cultivate the STEM classroom as a racially and culturally engaging learning environment for minority and nonminority students. This chapter dismantles the public myth that diversity is irrelevant to the STEM classroom. It then demonstrates, through a summary of extensive empirical research, the value of diversity in STEM teaching and learning in developing the next generation of STEM professionals. Finally, I provide tangible teaching strategies to leverage and advance diversity in STEM classrooms.

Confronting the Myth That Diversity Doesn't Matter in the STEM Classroom

The overwhelming evidence demonstrating severe racial disparities in college access to STEM classrooms demands immediate and direct public policy intervention. However, affirmative action policies, which contributed toward cracking open the doors of the Ivory Tower to women and racial minorities, continue to face legal attacks. Two decades after affirmative action programs in higher education had become widespread, the number of Black bachelor's degree holders had more than doubled from 4.7% of the Black adult population in 1965 to 11.1% in 1985, according to studies issued by the U.S. Census (1999). The same holds true for women; in 1965, 7.1% of the adult female population received a bachelors' degree, compared to 16% in 1985.

These seismic shifts in the postsecondary classroom's demographics revealed the following important (if, in retrospect, unsurprising) insight: Classroom diversity has an innate, profound, and undeniably positive impact on student learning. Beyond the obvious and compelling moral imperative to address institutionalized American racism, there is a practical justification for affirmative action policies, too. Simply put: A diverse classroom is an educationally enriched classroom. In the 2003 *Grutter v. Bollinger* decision, the U.S. Supreme Court reaffirmed its recognition of the value of classroom diversity to U.S. higher education and society at large, substantiated by overwhelming amounts of research. "The substantial, important, and laudable educational benefits that diversity is designed to produce, including cross-racial understanding and the breaking down of racial stereotypes," wrote Justice Sandra Day O'Connor in the Court's majority opinion, establishes a "compelling interest" of colleges and universities to consider the racial diversity of incoming students (*Grutter v. Bollinger*, 2003, p. 308).

Yet, that "compelling interest" continues to face harsh criticism from opponents of affirmative action, who question the value of a racially diverse student body to higher learning. An oft-invoked rebuttal to affirmative action argues that some academic subjects—and specifically, the so-called hard STEM sciences—involve the teaching of generic facts that are not a priori affected by the racial diversity of their associated classrooms. For example, in the second round of oral arguments for *Fisher v. University of Texas* (2016)—a case heard by the U.S. Supreme Court in 2013, and again in 2016, wherein the constitutionality of affirmative action programs at the University of Texas was considered—Chief Justice Roberts challenged University of Texas lawyer Gregory Garre to outline the value of classroom diversity in a STEM setting. "What unique perspective does a minority student bring to a physics class?" (p. 55) asked Chief Justice Roberts during oral arguments, criticizing the court's overall ruling against plaintiff Abigail Fisher and upholding the University of Texas's admission practices.

Chief Justice Roberts's pernicious question vocalizes a popular sentiment among affirmative action's critics who dismiss the effect of student demographic homogeneity—or heterogeneity—on a STEM classroom. After all, argue these critics, Einstein's theory of relativity remains true regardless of the student who learns it. For opponents of affirmative action, the STEM classroom is—and should remain—a politically deracialized space wherein racial justice issues simply do not permeate. Also implicit in Chief Justice Roberts's reasoning is the subtly derogatory suggestion that conversations of classroom diversity are unseemly and subjective, and that STEM classrooms are focused on more objective, and therefore, presumably intellectually rigorous, pursuits than that of other classrooms.

Currently, this faulty and short-sighted argument goes largely unchallenged in part because of the reluctance of the STEM community to engage en masse the mainstream affirmative action debate. Yet, our general silence on this subject is deafening. Our failure to speak up on affirmative action and student diversity initiatives implies a concession to Chief Justice Roberts on the myth that student diversity doesn't matter in the STEM classroom.

In reality, there is ample evidence to show that Chief Justice Roberts is wrong. As educators who labor at the frontlines of STEM education, we know the value of student diversity on teaching and learning in higher education—including (and perhaps, in particular) in the context of a STEM education. We can see and measure those benefits in our own classrooms and among our own students. But, it is no longer sufficient to merely know diversity's value in the STEM classroom; as diversity's opponents encroach upon the programs that ensure equal opportunity in higher education, it falls to us as scientists and educators to relay our experiences to those outside of the Ivory Tower. It is incumbent upon us as progressive-minded and antiracist citizens of the STEM community to take action and break down the barriers that continue to block minority student access to our classrooms. We can do so first and foremost by openly confronting (and ultimately dismantling) the myth that student diversity doesn't matter to the STEM classroom and to training the next generation of scientists.

The Science of Active Teaching and Learning Paradigms and Diversity in the Classroom

In his comment, Chief Justice Roberts casually dismissed any possible benefit of racial diversity in the classroom. Other critics of affirmative action take their opposition a step further, and argue that a diverse student body is harmful to student learning. A popular theory among affirmative action's critics argues that initiatives to address student diversity engineer a "mismatch" between student learning capacity and their learning environment (Sander, 2004). According to this notion, Black students admitted to competitive law schools are disadvantaged by their enrollment in these classrooms, and progressively fall behind their more capable (White and Asian) peers. Sander (2004) concluded that Black law students would fare better if enrolled in less competitive and lower tiered law schools, where students' educational, as well as economic, racial, and presumably lower academic capacities would be more well-matched.

Both Sander's assertions about the harm of student diversity as well as Chief Justice Roberts' dismissal of its relevance are baseless. Numerous scholars (Alon & Tienda, 2005; Kurlaender & Grodsky, 2013) have debunked the quantitative and qualitative evidence that Sander used as the basis of mismatch theory. An entire 2005 issue of the *Stanford Law Review* featured publication of a vast array of counterevidence to Sander's work.

Moreover, Chief Justice Roberts's assertion that diversity is irrelevant in STEM teaching and learning is unsubstantiated by education sciences. His comments were couched in an outdated and dehumanizing *teacher-centered* model of teaching and learning, wherein students are expected to assume the passive role of "empty vessels" into which teachers are tasked with pouring education. (For further discussion on the limits of this outdated model and its promotion of a restrictive relationship between teacher and student, please see Freire, 1993.) In such a model, student perspectives seem immaterial; indeed, if students truly are nothing more than passive receptacles for new knowledge, we might conclude that the distinctions of individual students are irrelevant. However, modern learning science increasingly recognizes that student learning is much more complex than the passive process of Chief Justice Roberts's imagining (Crouch & Mazur, 2001; Watkins & Mazur, 2013). Furthermore, research now shows that new advances in teaching paradigms are augmented by diversity in the student body to improve classroom performance (Chang, Denson, Sáenz, & Misa, 2006; Denson & Zhang, 2010).

Passive teaching and learning models are based on the core dogma that all students begin at the same baseline of knowledge and that learning is limited only by each student's innate ability to absorb new facts. However, advances in learning science now suggest that passive teaching approaches are suboptimal and flawed in that they center the teacher over the learner. Contemporary American classrooms increasingly reject teacher-centered passive learning models in favor of *student-centered* active learning models, wherein students engage in and guide their own learning through "opportunities to . . . meaningfully talk and listen, write, read, and reflect on the content, ideas, issues, and concerns of an academic subject" (Meyers & Jones, 1993, p. 6).

Empirical studies repeatedly show that active learning environments are far superior to their traditionally passive counterparts, particularly in the context of STEM education. A meta-analysis of 225 independent learning science studies that compared active versus traditional (i.e., passive) learning styles, specifically in the STEM postsecondary classroom, reveals that active learning environments significantly enhances student performance in STEM subjects (Freeman et al., 2014). Across 158 separate studies considered in Freeman and colleague's meta-analysis, active learning, which included classrooms that emphasized more interstudent discussion and peer teaching, increased overall test scores by nearly 6%, and STEM students enrolled in active learning environments were more than 50% less likely to fail their courses compared to those enrolled in traditional lecture-style courses. These results were found to hold true regardless of class size or STEM discipline. Willingham (2010) argued that traditionally "teacher-centered" classroom models fail because they do not address essential principles that govern how student learning occurs.

Instead, active learning environments, which maximize peer-to-peer interactions through small group discussion and other approaches, draw strength from classroom diversity to optimize learning for all students, including those historically overlooked and underserved by conventionally passive STEM teaching practices. For example, one study found that undergraduate psychology students at a historically Black college and university who expressed an initial distaste for the biological sciences—describing its teaching as boring and unappealing—showed greater engagement and more rapid mastery of neurophysiological concepts when enrolled in a STEM course structured using active learning techniques (Talley & Scherer, 2013). Willingham (2010) speculated that students in diverse, active-learning classrooms demonstrated better learning because they are able to build relationships between new material and their own personal histories. Furthermore, Willingham reasoned that the variation in student mastery of a particular subject is due to the vast experiential diversity found in any cohort of students. Thus, when compared to a demographically homogenous classroom, a diverse classroom produces a broader range in student insights on any given subject, which best stimulates learning.

Consistent with the science showing diversity as foundational to optimal teaching and learning praxis, the U.S. Supreme Court observed in *Grutter v.*

Bollinger (2003) that "'classroom discussion is livelier, more spirited and simply more enlightening and interesting' when the students have 'the greatest possible variety of backgrounds'" (p. 18). Further, diversity in small groups also increases both perception, as well as quantifiable measures, of discursive complexity among the group's participants, suggesting that in a diverse, active STEM learning environment, students will be encouraged to engage course material in more critical and complex ways (Antonio et al., 2004). According to Chang and colleagues (2006):

> Because of the persistent power of race to shape life experiences, racial and ethnic compositional diversity can create a rich and complex social and learning environment that can subsequently be applied as an educational tool to promote students' learning and development. (p. 432)

Diverse student bodies encouraged to engage in small group discussion improve learning of new subjects by encouraging *lateral teaching* and *lateral learning*, wherein students with better mastery of new material teach their peers in a process that seems to mutually benefit both student-teachers and their student-learners. One reason for this is that students challenged to assume the role of teacher typically approach the task in a way that optimizes complex learning among their peers. For example, in a study by Avrahami and colleagues (1997), students were instructed to teach another student how to place examples in an unfamiliar category. They found that student-teachers chose to teach their student-learners using a highly stereotyped sequence that invokes several principles of active learning. Student-teachers presented their learners with correctly categorized examples followed by incorrectly categorized examples in order to emphasize the relationships among multiple parameters of the category; they then permitted students to practice on ambiguous examples to further engage analytical problem-solving skills while assessing learner proficiency of the new information. Students are efficient and intuitive teachers of their peers compared to conventional teachers. In another study specifically related to STEM education, active learning robustly increased overall performance for all students enrolled in an economically and educationally diverse college-level introductory biology class (Haak, HilleRisLambers, Pitre, & Freeman, 2011). In this example, a highly structured but lecture-free active learning approach—which relied primarily on periodic low-stakes assessments as well as extensive informal group work among members of the course's demographically diverse students—enabled the greatest student learning for the entire cohort.

The potent combination of (a) constructing demographically diverse classrooms, and (b) implementing student-centered active learning environments, holds the key to improving student outcomes in the teaching of many subjects, including STEM. STEM instructors, as well as other instructors, should therefore prioritize the pursuit of both goals in tandem if we seek to improve student learning in our classrooms.

The Science of Diversity, Student Learning, and STEM Career Preparation

Beyond the positive impact of student diversity on overall classroom performance, individual students derive personal benefit from immersion in a racially diverse classroom. Classroom diversity not only enhances the development of individual students but also prepares each student for a future career in the contemporary STEM workforce.

The primary mission of the STEM classroom is to cultivate the next generation of American scientists, engineers, and technicians. In the landmark 1978 *Regents of the University of California v. Bakke* majority opinion, Justice Lewis Powell established an early diversity rationale for affirmative action when he wrote the

> atmosphere of "speculation, experiment, and creation"—so essential to the quality of higher education—is widely believed to be promoted by a diverse student body. . . . It is not too much to say that the nation's future depends upon leaders trained through wide exposure to the ideas and mores of students as diverse as this Nation of many peoples. (p. 312)

Justice Powell could have been referring specifically to STEM education. As in most other industries, speculation, experimentation, and creation are crucial for success as a scientist.

Over the past several decades, an abundance of independent studies, including those reviewed in an amicus brief filed by the American Educational Research Association (2013) in *Fisher v. University of Texas*, have shown that routine interactions between diverse student peers not only increase academic performance in a specific field of study but also improve general cognitive skills. This includes enhancing self-reported cognitive development and self-confidence (Chang et al., 2006), analytical problem-solving and critical thinking skills (Hurtado, 2005), and other general academic skills (Denson & Chang, 2009; Luo & Jamieson-Drake, 2009). Further, a meta-analysis of 23 studies showed a robust relationship between college diversity and improvements in cognitive tendencies (inclination toward styles of thinking) or skills (critical thinking and problem-solving skills), with the specific cognitive outcome dependent on the types of diversity experiences available to students (Bowman, 2010).

Perhaps the most important benefit conferred onto the STEM classroom by student diversity is its demonstrated ability to improve the interpersonal skills of individual students. This is crucial because, regardless of STEM specialty, science is a group activity. In one recent (albeit extreme) example, thousands of authors were listed as contributing toward the publication of a single high-profile paper (as cited in Plume & van Weijen, 2014). Indeed, many industry leaders feel the global competitiveness of American STEM is due largely to its collaborative culture—the best scientists are those who work well with others. Indeed, Raymond Gilmartin, chief executive officer of one of the world's largest pharmaceutical companies, Merck & Co., Inc. (1999), wrote the following for *Harvard Business Review*:

> Whether it's in the lab or in the marketplace, competitive advantage in a business like ours rests on innovation. To succeed, we must bring together talented and committed people with diverse perspectives—people who can challenge one another's thinking, people who collectively approach problems from multiple points of view. (p. 144)

If the purpose of the STEM classroom is to train the next generation of young scientists, we must also instill in future scientists the full range of skills needed to succeed in the contemporary STEM workforce, through proven pedagogical approaches.

The U.S. Supreme Court has long recognized the role of the classroom and importance of diversity in preparing students for professional life; furthermore, that preparation is not merely academic. In *Sweatt v. Painter* (1950), the court sided with a Black applicant who sought admission to a prestigious, historically White law school. In striking down the school's segregationist policies, the court noted that

> the law school, the proving ground for legal learning and practice, cannot be effective in isolation from the individuals and institutions with which the law interacts. Few students and no one who has practiced law would choose to study in an academic vacuum, removed from the interplay of ideas and the exchange of views with which the law is concerned. (p. 399)

The U.S. Supreme Court's decision in *Sweatt v. Painter* was based in earlier precedence. In *McLaurin v. Oklahoma State* (1950), the court ruled that a Black student at the Oklahoma Graduate School who was forcibly segregated into specially designated "colored only" areas had been unconstitutionally denied the "ability to study, to engage in discussion and exchange views with other students, and, in general, to learn his profession" (p. 638). Four years later in the landmark *Brown v. Board of Education* (1954/1955) decision that abolished Jim Crow segregation in public schools, Chief Justice Earl Warren reasoned that a public school education is "a principal instrument in awakening the child to cultural values, in preparing him for later professional training, and in helping him to adjust normally to his environment" (p. 494).

The classroom must instill not only academic knowledge but also the cultural skills needed to navigate an increasingly diverse American workforce. Students who graduate from colleges and universities that place a premium on campus diversity typically feel more prepared for, and fare better in, future employment (Bowen & Bok, 1998; Bowen, Bok, & Burkhart, 1999). Classroom diversity improves student problem-solving and teamwork skills (Denson & Zhang, 2010), self-confidence (Hu & Kuh, 2003), leadership (Parker & Pascarella, 2013), and civic development (Astin, 1993).

In addition to gaining general collaborative skills, students in diverse STEM classrooms gain specific experience in navigating a racially diverse workforce with respect and understanding. In *Grutter v. Bollinger* (2003), the U.S. Supreme Court recognized that student diversity "promotes 'cross-racial understanding,' helps to break down racial stereotypes, and 'enables [students] to better understand persons of different races'" (pp. 17–18). Indeed, exposure to classroom diversity improves individual student attitude, outlook, empathy, and related social skills. Meta-analysis of 515 separate studies found statistical evidence that students exposed to demographically diverse peers are less prejudiced, and are more comfortable with intercultural and interracial interactions (Pettigrew & Tropp, 2006). Indeed, interactions between racially diverse students enhanced social development and reduced cross-racial prejudices (Chang et al., 2006). Further, Jayakumar (2008) found that contact among diverse students improved students' *pluralistic orientation*, a term used to describe a number of qualities, including tolerance, open-mindedness, and inclusivity. These positive outcomes can occur regardless of an individual student's choice to actively engage with students of other backgrounds; that is, mere immersion in a diverse learning environment can prepare students with skills necessary to succeed in an increasingly diverse STEM workforce (Denson & Chang, 2009).

Cultivating a Better STEM Classroom

Once a profession reserved primarily for White men, the STEM industry is slowly opening its doors to scientists of color. Black, Asian American, and Hispanic Americans now comprise approximately 27% of the STEM workforce and can only be predicted to expand further (Landivar, 2013). High school interest in science is at a 15-year high, particularly among Black, Hispanic, and American Indian students (Cook, Mason, Morse, & Neuhauser, 2015). The percentage of first-year Black, Hispanic, and Native American college students who declared an interest in a STEM major has nearly doubled since 1971 (Eagan, Hurtado, Figueroa, & Hughes, 2014), and the rate at which Black and Hispanic college graduates are pursuing advanced degrees in STEM is growing faster than for other demographic groups (Cook et al., 2015).

With these changing demographics, it is important to keep in mind that the quality of classroom interaction, leveraging increased classroom diversity, matters as well. At the same time, strong negative contact between diverse students can have the opposite effect in solidifying bias against peers of different backgrounds (Chang, 2011). In other words, educators and college campuses that take affirmative stepts to enhance the quality of interactions among diverse students—often addressing disparities in the educational experiences of underrepresented students—are rewarded with better student outcomes (Engberg, 2007) than campus environments that do not proactively address diversity. Thus, it is not enough for STEM educators to merely seek better access for minority students to our classrooms. We must also improve the quality of the educational experience within STEM classrooms to foster growth and development for all of our students, because STEM students of color tend to face numerous educational obstacles, including overarching stereotypes against their academic capabilities as well as traditional course curricula that privilege Whiteness. In a survey of more than 1,200 female and underrepresented minority members of the American Chemical Society, more than 40% of the respondents reported having been discouraged from pursuing STEM careers by college educators (Bayer, 2010). Taken together, these obstacles might help explain the high attrition rates of students of color from the STEM pipeline, particularly given that several studies, including many referenced earlier in this text, suggest that students of color routinely face a hostile climate in STEM academic spaces (Hurtado, Newman, Tran, & Chang, 2010).

Practical Suggestions for Improving STEM Classrooms

STEM educators must reform our classrooms to ensure that all students receive equal access to a high-quality educational experience within our classrooms—one in which we adapt our approaches to ensure that the development of all learners is prioritized. This has become especially apparent within a growing antiscience political climate. As the 2017 March for Science made clear, science plays an important role in discourses of justice in a troubled world (Achenbach, Guarino, & Kaplan, 2017), and STEM educators must respond through research, civic engagement, and in our classrooms. The following are a few guiding principles and practical suggestions, based on the reviewed literature, for putting into practice a better, more diverse STEM classroom.

1. Build a student-centered STEM learning environment. I have discussed throughout this chapter the value of refocusing college classrooms toward a student-centric learning and teaching model. To put such principles into practice, at the start of the semester, we should at the outset establish with students our intent to work with them in developing a classroom designed specifically to meet student needs. We could invite students to introduce themselves—either through in-class interaction or in an after-class written assignment—and share with us their expectations for the coming semester, as well as their specific learning goals and potential obstacles. We should further provide frequent opportunities for student feedback on classroom structure and teaching approaches, and we should be willing to adapt our teaching strategies as necessary. Above all, we must find ways to communicate to students that we would like to design our classrooms around their learning, and that we would like them to invest themselves in doing so as well. In centering our teaching strategies away from ourselves and toward the goal of maximizing students' individualized experiences (including the experiences of non-White students), we can cultivate a sense among diverse students that they truly belong in STEM alongside their White peers, and that the STEM classroom is their own, too.

2. Encourage frequent small group discussion. As discussed throughout this chapter, student mastery of STEM subjects is optimized when students are invited to collaborate with one another to solve a common problem. Thus, STEM teachers should revise their curricula to include frequent opportunities for small group discussion particularly focused on encouraging student collaboration and peer-to-peer learning. Such methods need not supplant traditional lecturing; instead, they augment student learning when paired alongside the traditional lecture format.

   One example of such an approach comes from my own classroom. I sought to teach an upper-level undergraduate class a unit on the electrical impulses that govern heart function. My students were pharmacology majors of diverse racial and economic backgrounds, and although most found physiology to be a dry subject, they shared a mutual interest in the effects of drugs on the human body. Many of my students also expressed broad interest in popular music and film. To teach these students about cardiac physiology, I opened my lesson with an excerpted scene from the 2006 James Bond film *Casino Royale*, wherein the protagonist is poisoned with digitalis, a toxin that disrupts the electrical conduction of the heart. After discovering he is poisoned, Bond uses a defibrillator to return his heart to normal sinus rhythm.

Following a traditional lecture on core cardiovascular principles, students were invited to treat the *Casino Royale* scene as a case study, and to consider how Bond's heart might function—from the molecular, to the cellular, to the whole organ level—normally and under the influence of digitalis toxin. Furthermore, students were invited to examine the (many) ways in which the film's creators took artistic liberties with digitalis's effects on the human body.

By couching my lesson plan around this film's scene, I capitalized on students' knowledge and preexisting familiarity with the James Bond mythos to offer the basis for a personal connection with cardiac physiology. Each additional lesson objective returned to a different detail in the movie scene to help students build on their growing knowledge on the subject, and to challenge students to view the same scene from multiple perspectives. Periodically throughout the class, students were encouraged to break into small group discussion to apply newly taught concepts to solve a common problem.

Afterward, I received feedback that students found the lesson memorable and engaging, and that it was among their favorite units of the semester. The James Bond reference proved to be a common cultural touchpoint among my students, and using it as a prompt helped students "break the ice" and work together on class problems, which they did with enthusiasm.

As illustrated by this example, STEM educators of all disciplines can and should revise our curricula to include more opportunities for student discussion—either in large group or small group formats. These opportunities should be designed to engage students across vast differences in demographic backgrounds, and encourage students to share their distinct perspectives on a common prompt with their classmates. Such small group discussions break the passive lecture format and foster a more engaged classroom culture wherein students become active participants in their own learning.

3. Develop prompts that situate course material within a diversifying world. Traditionally, non-White students of STEM have complained that in-class case studies and course assignments were boring, and lacked relevance to their specific identities and backgrounds. One way to address this problem might be to reexamine our curricula to include a more diverse and culturally relevant range of scenarios or examples in our lessons. Life science teachers might write new case studies that focus on patients of diverse backgrounds, including backgrounds that reflect the demographics of their students. Computer programming or engineering teachers might center homework assignments around creating projects related to a student's own identity or personal passions, such as to design apps for their specific local communities or for their personal daily life. Teachers of math might include narrative prompts for their in-class assignments that integrate stories from their students' own backgrounds. Alternatively, teachers might invite students—through in-class discussion or homework assignments—to share the ways that each student personally relates to course material.

Ideally, STEM educators would create lessons that inspire students of many diverse backgrounds to forge a unique connection with the subject matter of the class, and that might further allow fellow students to connect with one another over their shared engagement in the lesson. One compelling way we might stimulate student discussion is to use prompts that involve the intersection of STEM with the politics of race and personal identity: Such topics are and often individually engaging for students and often result in stimulating conversations. For example, a course on biomedical engineering or the biological sciences might invite students to debate the racial and ethical issues raised by the story of Henrietta Lacks, a Black woman whose cervical cancer cells were harvested and cultured in 1951 without her informed consent (Skloot, 2011). Lacks's cells were distributed by her doctors to research laboratories without her knowledge and have since facilitated countless biological discoveries—yet neither Lacks nor her family have been formally acknowledged or compensated for their part in enabling these scientific advances. Lacks died, unacknowledged and unknown, and without access to comprehensive medical care due to the laws and customs of racial segregation that characterized her life as a Black woman during Jim Crow segregation.

Another example for teachers of computer programming or engineering might be to center a homework assignment focused on voting machines in the United States. Students might be invited to discuss how technology has changed voting in the United States—whether by increasing voter turnout and/or by contributing to voter disenfranchisement along racial lines—while they are also asked to develop their own voting software and hardware that might address these questions.

These are just two of several possible strategies for incorporating contemporary questions around race and gender into the teaching of STEM subjects in the postsecondary classroom. Individual teachers should take time to reassess their curricula and to think creatively about ways to contextualize their course subject matter in the broader—and increasingly racially diverse—modern America.

4. Prioritize mentorship of students. We must not limit our reform efforts to our own curricula; we must also reform our behavior as STEM mentors. Mentorship is crucial for recruiting, retaining, and developing young scientists, and yet many students of color lack access to meaningful and engaged advising (Cole & Griffin, 2013). Moreover, existing mentorship opportunities may prove inadequate or even damaging. When female scientists of color are commonly counseled to exit the profession (Bayer, 2010), different mentors and approaches to mentoring are clearly needed.

As STEM educators, we must take the time to cultivate students of color and young scholars in their professional growth and development, through all aspects of our teaching responsibilities. We should make ourselves accessible with regular office hours, and encourage students to attend. When we can, we should offer ourselves as coaches to help aspiring young scientists or engineers of color toward success in STEM. We might incorporate lessons on career development into our existing STEM classes, and we might encourage students contemplating a career in STEM to reach out for professional development advice. Lastly, we might help connect our students to on-campus and off-campus opportunities to gain practical or professional experience in STEM fields. Above all, we must in all aspects of our teaching concern ourselves with the educational and professional growth of *all* the students under our care.

Diversity Matters in STEM

Opponents of diversity initiatives loudly dismiss the possibility that classroom diversity might confer any benefits to the teaching of STEM subjects. Yet, the scientific literature refutes such a claim. Studies repeatedly demonstrate that a diverse STEM classroom provides myriad benefits to minority and nonminority students alike, and that these effects help prepare our nation's future scientists for successful careers that advance the STEM profession. Nonetheless, as educators committed to breaking down racial barriers in STEM education, we can do more. We must not only champion the benefits of diversity in the STEM classroom but also reform our classrooms to better engage and support minority students enrolled in STEM majors so that we can reverse the attrition of these students from the STEM pipeline.

Frankly, I am tired of the question: "What value does a minority student bring to a physics class?" Instead, I find myself asking this question: "Why do some continue to presuppose—despite all evidence to the contrary—that a minority student is *not* valuable in a physics class?" After all, the facts are compelling: Diversity clearly matters in the STEM classroom.

References

Achenbach, J., Guarino, B., & Kaplan, S. (2017, April 21). Why scientists are marching on Washington and more than 600 other cities. *The Washington Post.* Retrieved from https://www.washingtonpost.com/news/speaking-of-science/wp/2017/04/20/why-scientists-are-marching-on-washington-and-more-than-400-other-cities/?utm_term=.1c9bf504f7bd

Alon, S., & Tienda, M. (2005). Assessing the "mismatch" hypothesis: Differences in college graduation rates by institutional selectivity. *Sociology of Education, 78*(4), 294–315.

American Educational Research Association, American Association for the Advancement of Science (AAAS), American Sociological Association (ASA), Association for the Study of Higher Education (ASHE), Law and Society Association (LSA), Linguistic Society of America (LSA), & National Academy of Engineering (NAE), as Amici Curiae in Support of Respondents, *Fisher v. University of Texas.* No. 11-345. (2013). Retrieved from http://www.scotusblog.com/wp-content/uploads/2016/08/11-345-respondent-amicus-AERA.pdf

Antonio, A. L., Chang, M. J., Hakuta, K., Kenny, D. A., Levin, S., & Milem, J. (2004). Effects of racial diversity on complex thinking in college students. *Psychological Science, 15*(8), 507–510.

Astin, A. W. (1993). Diversity and multiculturalism on the campus: How are students affected? *Change: The Magazine of Higher Learning, 25*(2), 44–49.

Avrahami, J., Kareev, Y., Bogot, Y., Caspi, R., Dunaevsky, S., & Lerner, S. (1997). Teaching by examples: Implications for the process of category acquisition. *The Quarterly Journal of Experimental Psychology, 50*(3), 586–606.

Bayer Corporation. (2010). *Bayer facts of science education XIV: Female and minority chemists and chemical engineers speak about diversity and underrepresentation in STEM.* Whippany, NJ: Bayer. Retrieved from http://bit.ly/2wKAGWQ

Bowen, W. G., & Bok, D. (1998). *The shape of the river: Long-term consequences of considering race in college and university admissions.* Princeton, NJ: Princeton University Press.

Bowen, W. G., Bok, D., & Burkhart, G. (1999). A report card on diversity: Lessons for business from higher education. *Harvard Business Review, 77,* 138–149.

Bowman, N. A. (2010). College diversity experiences and cognitive development: A meta-analysis. *Review of Educational Research, 80*(1), 4–33.

Brown v. Bd. of Ed. of Topeka, Shawnee Cty, Kan., 347 U.S. 486, 489-90 74S. Ct. 686, 689, 98 L. Ed. 873 (1954), supplemented sub nom. Brown v. Bd. of Educ. of Topeka, Kan., 349 U.S. 294, 75 S. Ct. 753, 99 L. Ed. 1083 (1955)

Chang, M. J. (2011). *Quality matters: Achieving benefits associated with racial diversity.* Columbus, OH: Kirwan Institute for the Study of Race and Ethnicity, The Ohio State University. Retrieved from http://bit.ly/2iu0v82

Chang, M. J., Denson, N., Sáenz, V., & Misa, K. (2006). The educational benefits of sustaining cross-racial interaction among undergraduates. *Journal of Higher Education, 77,* 430–432.

Cole, D., & Griffin, K. A. (2013). Advancing the study of student–faculty interaction: A focus on diverse students and faculty. In M. B. Paulsen (Ed.), *Higher education: Handbook of theory and research* (pp. 561–611). New York, NY: Springer.

Cook, L., Mason, M., Morse, R., & Neuhauser, A. (2015, June 29). The 2015 U.S. News/Raytheon STEM index. *US News and World Reports.* Retrieved from https://www.usnews.com/news/stem-index/articles/2015/06/29/the-2015-us-news-raytheon-stem-index

Crouch, C. H., & Mazur, E. (2001). Peer instruction: Ten years of experience and results. *American Journal of Physics, 69,* 970–977.

Denson, N., & Chang, M. J. (2009). Racial diversity matters: The impact of diversity-related student engagement and institutional context. *American Educational Research Journal, 46*(2), 322–353.

Denson, N., & Zhang, S. (2010). The impact of student experiences with diversity on developing graduate attributes. *Studies in Higher Education, 35*(5), 529–543.

Eagan, K., Hurtado, S., Figueroa, T., & Hughes, B. (2014). *Examining STEM pathways among students who begin college at four year institutions.* Commissioned paper for the Committee on Barriers and Opportunities in Completing 2- and 4-Year Stem Degrees, National Academy of Sciences, Washington, DC. Retrieved from http://bit.ly/2vbhQsb

Engberg, M. (2007). Educating the workforce for the 21st century: A cross-disciplinary analysis of the impact of the undergraduate experience on students' development of a pluralistic orientation. *Research in Higher Education, 48*(3), 283–317.

Fisher v. University of Texas at Austin, 136 S. Ct3 2198, 2203, 195 L. Ed. 2d 511 (2016).

Freeman, S., Eddy, S. L., McDonough, M., Smith, M. K., Okoroafor, N., Jordt, H., & Wenderoth, M. P. (2014). Active learning increases student performance in science, engineering, and mathematics. *Proceedings of the National Academy of Sciences of the United States of America, 111*(23), 8410–8415.

Freire, P. (1993). *Pedagogy of the oppressed.* New York, NY: Continuum.

Gee, B., Peck, D., & Wong, J. (2015). *Hidden in plain sight: Asian American leaders in Silicon Valley.* Report for Ascend Foundation. Retrieved from https://c.ymcdn .com/sites/ascendleadership.site-ym.com/resource/resmgr/Research/Hidden InPlainSight_Paper_042.pdf

Gilmartin, R.V. (1999). *Diversity and competitive advantage at Merck.* Published as part of Bowen, W. G., Bok, D., and Burkhart, G. (Eds.), A report card on diversity: Lessons for business from higher education. *Harvard Business Review, 77*(1), 138–149.

Grutter v. Bollinger, et al. 539 U.S. 306, 306, 123 S. Ct. 2325, 2327-28, 156 L. Ed. 2d 304 (2003).

Haak, D. C., HilleRisLambers, J., Pitre, E., & Freeman, S. (2011). Increased structure and active learning reduce the achievement gap in introductory biology. *Science, 332*(6034), 1213–1216.

Hu, S., & Kuh, G. D. (2003). Diversity experiences and college student learning and personal development. *Journal of College Student Development, 44*(3), 320–334.

Hurtado, S. (2005). The next generation of diversity and intergroup relations research. *Journal of Social Issues, 61*(3), 595–610.

Hurtado, S., Newman, C. B., Tran, M. C., & Chang, M. J. (2010). Improving the rate of success for underrepresented racial minorities in STEM fields: Insights from a national project. *New Directions in Institutional Research, 148,* 177–190.

Jayakumar, U. M. (2008). Can higher education meet the needs of an increasingly diverse and global society? *Harvard Education Review, 78*(4), 615–651.

Kurlaender, M., & Grodsky, E. (2013). Mismatch and paternalistic justification for selective college admissions. *Sociology of Education, 86*(4), 294–310.

Landivar, L. C. (2013). *Disparities in STEM employment by sex, race, and Hispanic origin.* Report for American Community Survey Reports. Retrieved from https:// www.census.gov/prod/2013pubs/acs-24.pdf

Luo, J., & Jamieson-Drake, D. (2009). A retrospective assessment of the educational benefits of interaction across racial boundaries. *Journal of College Student Development, 50,* 67–86.

McLaurin v. Oklahoma State Regents for Higher Ed., 339 U.S. 637, 638, 70 S. Ct. 851, 852, 94 L. E. 1149 (1950).

Meyers, C., & Jones, T. B. (1993). *Promoting active learning: Strategies for the college classroom.* San Francisco, CA: Jossey-Bass.

National Science Foundation, National Center for Science and Engineering Statistics. (2017). *Women, minorities, and persons with disabilities in science and engineering: 2017.* Special Report NSF 17-310. Retrieved from www.nsf.gov/ statistics/wmpd/

Parker, E. T., III, & Pascarella, E. T. (2013). Effects of diversity experiences on socially responsible leadership over four years of college. *Journal of Diversity in Higher Education, 6*(4), 219–230.

Pettigrew, T. F., & Tropp, L. R. (2006). A meta-analytic test of intergroup contact theory. *Journal of Personality & Social Psychology, 90*(5), 751–753.

Plume, A., & van Weijen, D. (2014). Publish or perish? The rise of the fractional author. *Trends Journal of Sciences Research, 38.* Retrieved from https://www .researchtrends.com/issue-38-september-2014/publish-or-perish-the-rise-of-the-fractional-author/

Regents of Univ. of California v. Bakke, 438 U.S. 265, 98 S. Ct. 2733, 57 L. Ed. 2d 750 (1978).

Sander, R. H. (2004). A systemic analysis of affirmative action in American law schools. *Stanford Law Review, 57,* 367–483.

Stanford Law Review. Vol. 57, No. 6, May, 2005. Retrieved from https://www.jstor .org/stable/i40002101

Skloot, R. (2011). *The immortal life of Henrietta Lacks.* New York, NY: Broadway Books.

Sweatt v. Painter, 339 U.S. 629, 631-32, 70 S. Ct. 848, 849, 94 L. Ed. 1114 (1950).

U.S. Census Bureau (2011). *American Community Survey.* Retrieved from https:// www2.census.gov/acs2011_1yr/summaryfile/

U.S. Census Bureau (1999, December 09). Statistical Abstract of the United States: 1999. Retrieved from https://www.census.gov/library/publications/1999/compendia/statab/119ed.html

U.S. Department of Education (2017). *Integrated Postsecondary Education Data System (IPEDS).* Retrieved from https://nces.ed.gov/ipeds/

Talley, C. P., & Scherer, S. (2013). The enhanced flipped classroom: Increasing academic performance with student-recorded lectures and practice testing in a "flipped" STEM course. *Journal of Negro Education, 82*(3), 339–347.

Watkins, J., & Mazur, E. (2013). Retaining students in science, technology, engineering, and mathematics (STEM) majors. *Journal of College Science Teaching, 42*(5), 36–41.

Williams, J. C., Phillips, K. W., & Hall, E. V. (2014). *Double jeopardy? Gender bias against women of color in science.* Report for Tools for Change. Retrieved from http://www.uchastings.edu/news/articles/2015/01/double-jeopardy-report.pdf

Willingham, D. T. (2010). *Why don't students like school?: A cognitive scientist answers questions about how the mind works and what it means for the classroom.* San Francisco, CA: Jossey-Bass.

13

BETWEEN CRITIQUE AND PROFESSIONAL AMBITION

Akhila L. Ananth

Nearly every quarter, I teach a course called Multiculturalism in the Criminal Justice System, in which I walk students through the centuries of slavery, Indigenous genocide, class repression, mass incarceration, civil uprising, and violence against women and queer communities that manifested the criminal justice system as it is today. My students are all earning undergraduate degrees in criminal justice in a majority-Latinx and working-class teaching institution, and at the end of the term, I take a minute to ask each student what their plans are after graduation. Sometimes, I hear the stories of students who, after taking in everything we work through in the course, have come to the conclusion that they cannot participate in the criminal justice system and are looking for opportunities to build community resilience against the punitive forces built into public programs. The vast majority of responses, though, go something like this:

"LAPD."
"Sheriffs. I'm taking the test this week!"
"FBI."
"I used to think LAPD, but now I want to be in Probation."

Alone in my office, I sometimes snicker thinking about the impact of my teaching on students. Which response to this course is better, I wonder? Should I celebrate turning students away from stable government jobs in the criminal justice system, not having prepared them for the diminished earning potential and other perils awaiting them in the nonprofit industrial complex? Or, should I accept my students' earnest promises that taking my course has broken open their worlds and will change the way they perform their duties as government agents of public safety? Underlying these musings is a fundamental dilemma, common for critical educators in service-oriented fields. Are the perspectives we offer chipping away at the hegemonic power of state institutions, as we desperately hope they do, or do we buttress the state's power by building our critique into its workforce?

In this chapter, I offer a glimpse into the alternative pedagogical universe I find each quarter with this course, where my students bring their experiences from various marginalized communities to begin imagining what they want for those whose voices they represent and for those whose material and psychic realities they cannot fathom. I admit that it is an imperfect universe, in which I regularly fail in my attempts to ethically engage with histories that not all of us have lived. But, I check my privilege at the door with the rest of the class, and I find myself as engaged in the mysterious pedagogies of my students as they are with my relatively simple classroom tricks. What follows is the story of a strange classroom space, where discussions on radical politics are enabled, rather than stifled, by the professional ambitions of criminal justice students. I begin with a contextualization of the institution and student body, continue with a discussion of the course structure and goals, and end with a list of classroom exercises that I have found to be helpful in accomplishing my pedagogical goals.

The State Teaching Institution and Its Discontents

Like other state institutions, our funding is shifting from predominantly public to increasingly private sources, and we have seen a concomitant rise in funding for administrative personnel to secure external funding. This is a survival tactic and a marketing strategy, and most of us recognize that the burden of these structural changes falls on faculty, even if we gain some benefits. Expectations of faculty in teaching institutions are different today than they were in decades past. We are asked to secure more research grants, publish more papers, gain more scholarly accolades, and partner more with private and public agencies. We are told that we must do this in addition to teaching four classes per semester of increasingly large classrooms. And we are encouraged to think critically about how to support our unique student body, many of whom are the first in their families to attend college; who have incarcerated siblings or parents; who grew up in foster care; who juggle one or two full-time jobs in addition to a full course load; who support elderly parents and young children in their families; who experience post-traumatic symptoms from military service; who only recently acquired temporary authorization to be in the United States; who save for months to pay for one class; who are or were homeless; who are coming out to their families; who give birth during finals week. These are only the stories I have personally heard from my students in my few years of instruction at this institution; in another 20 years, I will be able to fill an encyclopedia. We teach students who have never experienced adversity and students who defy many of the aforementioned challenges at once. We grapple with complex theoretical concepts, and we provide basic instruction on how to apply for a job.

In our public teaching institution, difference in the classroom is the only constant, and most faculty members (whether lecturers, tenured, or tenure-track) must demonstrate at least a willingness to engage diversity in order to be hired. I won't romanticize this; not all actually do it, and even fewer do it well. But, in this context, the creative pedagogies that my colleagues and I bring to the classroom are valued, both in terms of what we offer to students and in regard to our progress toward tenure or job security. Regardless of our pedagogical training, and in many cases the lack thereof, we aren't usually punished by our superiors or in student evaluations for addressing diversity, no matter the course topic. In fact, even as one of the two women of color in my department, I have found the contrary to be true. The more I connect with students and expose them to critical paradigms outside my colleagues' reach, the greater my perceived value. If even as a release valve for radical critique in the neoliberalizing institution that employs me, I have been made to feel that I fill an important role.

My students are also uniquely situated in our institution. Due to massive interest in the criminal justice major, our department received "impacted" status some years before I joined the faculty, meaning that students must finish their general requirements first (either at our institution or at a community college) and then apply to be a criminal justice major before taking any of our classes. Practically, this means that my classes comprise only criminal justice majors and minors and that the students before me have already met a series of benchmarks, including a minimum GPA requirement. Our students are competent if not compelling writers. Although many still struggle with the skills related to academic success, most are readily capable of overcoming those struggles. Despite all the assumptions about youth graduating from underfunded high schools in underserved neighborhoods, these are the students who received the support—any support—to thrive in a professionally oriented major at the 24th-ranked university based on accessibility, affordability, and completion by *TIME* magazine's standards in 2014 (California State University–Los Angeles, n.d.).

As I see it, students elect to major or minor in criminal justice for a variety of reasons. Some students want to be seen as more employable for the stable positions with government benefits afforded by a growing criminal justice system. Others believe they can make a difference through criminal justice and change their communities for the better. Yet others selected it as a conduit into law school or public administration, finding the topic of criminal justice to be of greater interest to them than other majors on campus. At play in these responses are students' personal experiences with the criminal justice system, the intrigue of crime scene investigation sold by mainstream media stories and movie plotlines, and the financial ambitions of an upwardly mobile student body.

I include this information to situate the relationships between students and myself in the classroom. We share the experience of walking through the world in bodies of color, but my relative class privilege has afforded me the ability to imagine a future for myself beyond modest boundaries. On the first day of class, I ask students to take one of the implicit association tests on Harvard University's Project Implicit website (https://implicit.harvard.edu/implicit/takeatest.html) and share their personal experiences with racial bias. More than a few in the room attest to being subjected to street harassment in predominantly White spaces, for example having had objects thrown at them while walking on the street (myself included). But, only a few of my students each term are Black, and not all have had the intergenerational experience of being the target of law enforcement and criminal justice. Later, when I ask students to talk about the professions that combat existing inequality in the world, almost none imagine themselves at the helm of systemic political and social change in this country.

Perhaps this is the most important work in our teaching institution: We help students name the social phenomena they have survived, situate those phenomena in their respective political contexts, and reorient students in formulating their futures. Having come to academia from the nonprofit world, I don't make the assumption that working outside the criminal justice system is any less toxic, exploitative, or complicit than working inside it. But I have developed a deep resentment for the classist educational systems that enabled my furious efforts to imagine a world without the prison industrial complex while clipping it in my students. At the end of the course, if I have walked them through one new way of thinking about social change, I will have served as a marker in my students' trajectories, like my grandfather, the first socialist I knew, who saved newspaper articles about global politics to discuss with me after coming home from school. Or like my seventh-grade English teacher, who gave us the assignment of writing then-President Bill Clinton a persuasive letter critiquing any public policy of our choice. Again, not all of my students lack access to these forms of support. But for those who do, our classroom offers an important space—at a critical moment—for reflection, critique, and ultimately, a reformulation of their hopes for the world they inherit.

The Goals and the Texts

Multiculturalism in the Criminal Justice System was established as an elective in our department prior to my faculty appointment and is now a lower-division requirement. The main objectives of the course were to expose students to the experiences of marginalized communities and overview the problems and promises of cultural diversity in the criminal justice system. When I first picked up the course, a colleague suggested a textbook that began with an overview of race, ethnicity, prejudice, and discrimination. It continued with chapters for each minority group under the section heading Cultural Specifics in the Criminal Justice System and ended with two poignant subheadings: "The Future of Multiculturalism: Strategies for Success," and finally, "Progress?" (Burns & McNamara, 2008).

This had been one of my first interactions with criminal justice, a practitioner-oriented field entirely insulated from the radical critiques (and even the social scientific empiricism) I had been trained to teach. It was the summer of 2014, and as the streets of Ferguson, Missouri, lit on fire, I held in my hands a veritable weapon of the police state. In bold-faced print, public servants were being served "cultural sensitivity" in corporate diversity frameworks that treated identity as singular, fixed, knowable, and *conquerable*—with the primary objective of fatally disarming marginalized communities' well-earned distrust. I felt ashamed for not having known better. And, I felt a great grief come over me, as my mind turned to the countless Black, immigrant, Muslim, and Native people assassinated by overseers, lynch mobs, police officers, prison guards, and vigilantes acting as agents of a White supremacist nation state. Young, Black girls and boys; community elders; and everyone in between who dared to exist, publicly or privately, in a society structured by anti-Blackness, settler colonialism, and global imperialism.

I owed my students more than this. I resolved to find the most accessible critiques of criminal justice and cobbled together 10 weeks of the most pressing controversies in the American legal system. It would be a sort of top-10, introductory course on radical critique of the institution of criminal justice with three central goals. My first goal was to incite shock and, if I was lucky, a good dose of rage. Having been immersed in reformist conversations about "what works," I wanted students to grasp the murderous functions of criminal justice. My intention was not to shame students for their chosen professions but to draw on their experiences and suspicions to acknowledge exactly what these institutions are capable of. My second goal was to recognize our relative privilege and orient class conversations away from unethical analogies between axes of marginalization, common in non-Black, non-Indigenous, and non-abject spaces of color. My third goal was to get students to consider the alternative to endless reform. I wanted to collectively engage with the destruction of criminal justice and all its ancillary institutions to imagine a dramatic restructuring of society on more ethical, humane, and (yes, even) multicultural terms. My course description read:

> This course explores the historical and contemporary dynamics between race, class, gender, and other identifications that undergird the daily operations of the criminal justice system. With the recent uprisings in Ferguson, New York, Oakland, and across the nation for Black lives simply to matter, it has become more important than ever to understand the intricate ways race and class power dynamics and criminal social control in the Unites States are interwoven. We will look first at a history of social control and then turn to the patterns of law enforcement, decision-making in courts, and uses of incarceration that shape the American experience with criminal justice. In this course, emphasis will also be placed on students' personal reflections and experiences related to course materials.

In its first iteration, we covered the following topics: slavery, Jim Crow and civil rights; race and class privilege; the war on drugs; Latinos and the law; women and gender-based violence; prisons; civil uprising; American Indians and criminal justice; and the criminalization of queer youth of color. Later, I added: welfare and social control; immigration and federal detention; and race, place, and space (inspired by a colleague in Chicano studies). We read: Manning Marable, George Lipsitz, Kaaryn Gustaafson, Joy James, Doris Provine, Kenyon Farrow, Victor Rios, Natalie Sokoloff, Nikki Jones, Mariame Kaba, Jelani Cobb, Ta-Nehisi Coates, Michelle Alexander, Christina Hanhardt, and Laura Barraclough. We watched videos published by *The Atlantic* and *Race Forward*; TED Talks given by Jose Antonio Vargas and Bryan Stevenson; and screened documentaries on the Los Angeles civil uprising and South Central farms. We read the narratives of women in prison (Waldman & Levi, 2011), the statements of youth-led organizations like GenderJUST, and a broad range of online think pieces collected by a colleague who found herself inspired by my task.[1] Polling friends and scouring the Facebook pages of politically trustworthy activists, the syllabus became a living document, a powerful testament of the academic and political community I had built, and a great labor of love. In the end, the very exercise of reconstructing Multiculturalism in Criminal Justice felt like a revolutionary act. For myself and the 30 to 40 students enrolled in the class each term, my classroom offered the space to dismantle our faith in progressive reform.

The Exercises

In addition to the active learning exercises used throughout lectures and class sessions, there are a handful of classroom exercises that had profound impacts on students each term. Explained next in further detail, I use these exercises every term I teach this course with moving outcomes. Notably, these are the exercises that students identify at the end of the course as memorable and transformative. Some exercises have stayed exactly the same each quarter, and others I adjust slightly from term to term. Regardless, they are tried and true, and I have memories of the conversations that ensued each time I offered the course.

Weekly Reflections

The evidence is clear: To get students to relate emotionally to academic material (see Estill's chapter in this book for more on emotion as a pathway to knowing), they must reflect in writing regularly. In this course, students were required to write at least 400 words each week on the assigned readings and classroom discussion on our online forum, Moodle. Importantly, students were mandated to respond to a classmate in addition to writing their own response to receive credit, and I found this requirement resulted in a number of productive conversations online. I used weekly reflections to force students to research current events for related stories to our week's topic, to explore web-based resources, including interactive art projects and the Implicit Bias tests, and to write letters to elected officials or incarcerated people in California prisons. During election cycles, students wrote analyses of campaign debates; after field trips to the county jail, students narrated the most jarring moments of their visit. Anchored in the course materials and in relation to current events, reflections forums allowed a safe space for students to locate their political and social commitments and monitor personal change through the course.

Debate

During the week we discuss violence and political change, I run a class-wide debate. Prior to the class, I have students write about what they know and believe relating to the civil uprisings in Ferguson, Oakland, Los Angeles, and New York, ideally *before* beginning the week's readings. Students then finish the readings, listen to my 30-minute lecture on the social and political history of violent protest, and are split into two groups of 15 to 20 students each. One side will argue that violence is necessary for political change, and the other side argues that violence is unnecessary for political change. I allow 10 minutes for discussion in the groups, then 5 minutes each for opening statements; 8 minutes for further discussion, and 3 minutes each for each group's responses to the previous round; and finally, 5 minutes to discuss, and 2 minutes for closing statements. After hearing the arguments, I make a decision about which side won, based purely on the argument (admittedly, I always declare a "tie"). Finally, and most importantly, I assign reflections for the next week, asking students to reflect on their experience in the debate, what they learned, and what surprised them. Every quarter, students report emerging from the debate suspicious of their strongest convictions and acutely aware that all ethical debates have important "gray" areas. One student wrote, "I could not believe how much my perspective changed with this activity. I was no longer close-minded about this issue and was able to understand the other side." Another student responded to a classmate's reflections, noting, "I agree with you [that] I would love to see a protest performed effectively through nonviolence, but the reality is that the way the world is structured, ... the violence approach has been proven to be the most effective." Students' conversations on this exercise spill out of the classroom and change the class dynamic for the remainder of the quarter.

"Taking Sides"

On the week we discuss immigration and federal detention, I end the class with a 30-minute exercise in which I display hypothetical situations and tell students to move to one side of the classroom if they think the scenario presents a deportable offense and to the other side if they think the person should be able to stay in the country. This exercise is inspired by an exercise developed by StreetLaw.org. Examples of scenarios include the following:

- A person who was addicted to illegal drugs while living in the United States but who is now sober
- A person convicted of two cases of food stamp fraud on two separate days
- A person who voted in a local election who was not a registered voter

Although the vast majority of the students in my class come from immigrant households, students encounter their internalized assumptions and "bottom lines" quite quickly. A benefit of this exercise is that quieter students can make a statement without saying anything at all. By moving to one side of the classroom or the other, they are responding to the question. Many times, I have found that this exercise encourages quieter students to speak up, having felt emboldened by the crowd surrounding them, or lack thereof.

Mapping Concepts

After we have encountered a number of "industrial complexes" in their readings, I have students select one and draw a diagram of it. Then, I ask student volunteers to project their diagram onto the screen and explain their thought process in putting it together. Apart from the benefit of visually representing complex concepts, students also gain from seeing others' drawings. Typically, students are also talking in low voices with one another as they are drawing as well.

Mapping Places

In a guest lecture, a colleague[2] asked a couple of students to draw a map of downtown Los Angeles on the white board, with the help of the rest of the class. The point was to draw attention to the ways the class recognized and categorized spatial boundaries. This exercise resulted in a lively group discussion about students' relations to downtown Los Angeles, sitting in classroom only seven miles east. One student interjected, "What about the *callejones*?" to which another responded, "Yeah, that's the fashion district right here," noting language differences in students' relationships to space.

Personal Manifestos

The morning after the 2016 presidential election, students poured into my classes in various states, from numbness to shock to genuine fear. That particular week, I had unknowingly scheduled a class field trip to Men's Central Jail in downtown Los Angeles, where we saw men pacing in chain-link cages to fulfill required "outside" time, presumably exactly as they had the week before. Reflecting on this experience amidst the sobering state of national politics, I spent 15 minutes of the next class having students draft and share personal manifestos in response to the following questions: What are your core values? What communities do you want to create or be surrounded by? What do you want your impact to be in the world? Recommended by a colleague in Chicano/a Studies,[3] this exercise had the impact of centering students on what changes and what stays the same through election cycles. It gave students physical evidence of their dreams to hold on to as they moved forward in their degrees, careers, and lives. And, it reminded me that no matter our shock reading the daily news, absolutely nothing changes for those inside a county jail. The work we have to do is always there waiting.

Course Summary Exercise

On the last day of class, I affix 10 large pieces of paper (poster board-size Post-its) on the walls around the classroom. At the top of the boards, I write the topics from each of the 10 weeks, and directly underneath I include two columns labeled Issues and Solutions. I ask groups of three to four students to walk up to each board, and in the way speed-dating works, to spend about three minutes writing at each board before moving to the next one in a clockwise fashion. In the first round, students write the issues we covered in each week's topics, and in the second round, they write the solutions we have covered in class or that they thought up on their own. The exercise takes almost an hour and offers students the opportunity to reflect on their trajectory through the course. After students leave, I take pictures and send the class a PDF of the exercise, so they can use it to review for the final exam as well.

The Outcomes

As I write these words, a bomb has destroyed Baghdad, queer and trans folks of color have been massacred, and two more Black men were slain by police. I am no valiant community organizer, and I haven't learned how to process these daily assaults through social media. What I do have is the soft space this course has provided to grieve and dialogue about the weights of this world. Term after term, my students and I work through the internalized assumptions about right and wrong as they map onto raced, classed, gendered, *identified* bodies. I'd like to believe that I have planted seeds that will root as my students navigate their personal and professional lives. What I can say with certainty is that walking through this process every week of every term, and in conversation with my trusted community of scholars and organizers of color, I find myself growing in all the ways I dream for those in my courses. More than the impact of mentors, former or current, the horizontal relationships I have built with colleagues and in my quarterly offering of Multiculturalism in Criminal Justice have been both transformative and healing.

In supportive community and looking out at the profound thinkers sitting in lined desks of the classroom, I feel the solace I need to continue my work: to continue incisive critiques of the criminal justice; to continue supporting radical Black action against a White supremacist police state; to continue fighting for those dispossessed and dehumanized by global imperialism and settler colonialism; to continue activating the potential of young women, queer and trans people of color (QPOTC), and undocumented students; to continue all of this work together in all the ways disparate axes of inequality, although never analogous, produce and are produced by one other. I feel myself growing more patient and more generous, and I see similar progressions in my students. A young Black student, "R.," just e-mailed me to say she will be applying to law school with the hopes of working with youth in the juvenile justice system, instead of the FBI. And, "A.," a

Latino Los Angeles native, is now facilitating restorative justice circles for Long Beach high school students being diverted out of juvenile justice. An undocumented student, "M.," graduated magna cum laude and provides Spanish language assistance to an immigration attorney in federal detention centers. All came into my life through the discussions in this course, and all march steadily ahead of me.

To the educators reading this: I wish you a similar space as often as you can manage it. When you find it, take my grandmother's advice to me, and write everything down. Keep track of your movement, and return to your words in times of deep mourning. Be dialogical in your pedagogy, and model the fierce convictions you want to send forward in your students. And to all the fallen souls on whose graves this work is built, my only hope is that we are doing you right. May you rest in power.

Notes

1. Jasmine Montgomery, doctoral candidate in criminology, law, and society (University of California–Irvine).
2. Jih-Fei Cheng, assistant professor of feminist and gender studies (Scripps College).
3. Priscilla Leiva, assistant professor of Chicano studies (California State University–Los Angeles).

References

Burns, R., & McNamara, R. (2008). *Multiculturalism in the criminal justice system.* New York, NY: McGraw-Hill.

California State University–Los Angeles. (n.d.). Cal State LA proud to be among *Time* magazine's best colleges. Office of Communications and Public Affairs. Retrieved from http://www.calstatela.edu/univ/ppa/publicat/cal-state-la-proud-be-among-time-magazine%E2%80%99s-best-colleges

Waldman, A., & Levi, R. (2011). *Inside this place, not of it.* Oakland, CA: McSweeney's Books.

14

UNCOMFORTABLE LEARNING

Teaching Race Through Discomfort in Higher Education

Jasmine L. Harris

Today, new images and examples of institutional racism are available every minute, yet conversations which include them are met with tense, careful response, if any at all, as frank discussions about race, and structural inequalities that encourage racism and discrimination in the United States are thought to be difficult, uncomfortable, and unproductive. In higher education, increasing student of color enrollment outpaces the racial diversification of faculty and administration, perpetuating social distance between student and teacher, and limiting the availability of participants willing to join the discussion. Likewise, knowledge on stratification, social hierarchies, and their resulting inequities is disproportionately concentrated in social sciences and humanities departments with faculty who engage in empirical research on and teach courses devoted to these topics. The desire to avoid, rather than confront, issues of racial inequality in the classroom impacts campus interactions, culture, and learning outcomes. College campuses, especially liberal arts campuses with their small class sizes and close living quarters, are a microcosm of the tense race-based interaction plaguing broader U.S. society, but many students are left without either support structures to help deal with issues of racial inequities, or the opportunity to engage in productive discussion on these topics.

In the classroom, teachers have traditionally relied on pedagogies that emphasize the safety of institutional spaces and subsequent freedom to voice opinions, as well as the bravery necessary to access and utilize that voice (Arao & Clemens, 2013). In many cases, a revolving door of trial-and-error techniques serve as placeholders for discussions of inclusion. These models are insufficient for tackling issues of race and racial inequality in the classroom because they position engagement as a neutral-sum game, ignoring the pervasiveness of racist ideologies in American society, the associated feelings of shame, guilt, anger, and fear that discourage open and honest discourse, and create risk imbalance in said discourse. Both students and faculty are grappling with these issues, unarmed with the skills necessary for productive discussion, stunting learning growth on the topic of racial inequality, and impeding social change on the issue. This chapter introduces an alternative instrument to address issues of racial inequality in the classroom, designed to confront painful emotions and use them to encourage personal, social, and academic deep learning.

It is important to cognitive learning objectives that students consistently engage in discourse about racial inequality via a diverse set of disciplines throughout their academic careers. Various pedagogical approaches to teaching race and racial inequality must encourage students to engage in consistent meaning-making, while acknowledging the differing social cost of such engagement. In this way, collective synthesis of racial inequality can help breach the emotional, social, and physical walls many build around these issues. Such engagement can help students understand, learn, and create new knowledge in an effort to broaden perceptions of racial and institutional discrimination, and to encourage social change.

This chapter presents uncomfortable learning as an alternative pedagogical theory for generating productive classroom discourse on race, racism, and racial inequality. It seeks to address roadblocks to productive discussions on race in classroom settings, acknowledge disproportionate risk associated with discourse participation on these issues, and improve perceived learning outcomes of students on predominantly White college campuses. Although safe space and brave space pedagogies have been used for this purpose, I argue that both are missing discomfort and its connection to risk imbalance in racial discourse, important elements of fruitful discussion about racism.

Although it is relatively easy to generate discomfort, few have willingly embraced and employed this emotion. This is especially true in an environment like the classroom, where students feel vulnerable. As a pedagogical tool, discomfort allows for complex analysis of emotional responses to issues of race, and acknowledges risk imbalance in the confrontation of racism and racial inequality. Using real-world examples, student-focused group data, and existing theoretical frameworks, this case study uses uncomfortable learning as a pedagogical tool to answer the following questions: (a) How can faculty handle emotional roadblocks to facilitate deep learning on issues of race in the classroom?; and (b) What are the benefits of making intellectual spaces simultaneously therapeutic ones?

Critical Race Theory

The uncomfortable learning pedagogical approach derives from the critical race theory (CRT) framework, prioritizing a critique of color-blindness (Solórzano, 1997), storytelling as a valid methodological approach (Bernal & Villalpando, 2002; Solórzano & Bernal, 2001; Solórzano & Yosso, 2002; Villalpando, 2003), legal and social ramifications of racism (Alexander, 2010; Coates, 2015), intersectionality (Crenshaw, 1989), White privilege (Bernal, 1998; Delgado, 1998; Ladson-Billings, 2000), and the use of microaggressions and their damaging impacts in the classroom (Delgado & Stefancic, 2011). These themes collectively represent a challenge to the traditional social science pedagogy because of the use of race, racism, and privilege as the centralizing force. The use of CRT to frame the pedagogical theory of uncomfortable learning implies the intent to break down existing institutional structures that prioritize and privilege White supremacy, and thus White fragility, in the academy (Matias & DiAngelo, 2013). CRT in higher education classrooms is an important theoretical and analytical framework that challenges the ways race and racism impact educational structures, practices, and discourses within an institution founded on notions of privilege, race, gender, and class-based inequities.

For example, sociologist Jennifer Mueller (2011) used critical race pedagogy to teach millennial students the connections between racial and economic inequality by asking them to collect oral histories from their families. In doing so, Mueller taps into the power of emotional connections to cognition. In Mueller's example it is impossible for students to avoid emotional responses to the data when the data comes from a personal place. Instead, it requires a confrontation of emotions, and asks students to process them thoroughly. However, higher education often prioritizes objectivity in on-campus discourse production (Collins, 1998), with high valuation given to student participation devoid of negative emotional responses, implicitly ignoring the inequity of such participation. What measure of privilege or sacrifice is required by students and faculty to maintain objectivity on the topics that personally affect them? The institutional perpetuation of emotionality as a sign of some educational deficit limits the ability of both students and faculty to engage with emotional responses in the classroom, as well as the desire to do so and perpetuates inequity in this regard.

Safe Space and Brave Spaces

Traditionally, attempts to counteract students' avoidance of uncomfortable topics in both the classroom and the broader campus community have centered on the concept of *safe space*. Originally conceptualized during the women's movement and the gay rights movement, the notion of safe space represents the freedom to speak and act as a form of resistance to existing gendered hierarchies (Kenney, 2001). Over the years this term has been reappropriated to describe classrooms in which students can express their opinions without fear of being criticized, attacked, or socially sanctioned.

Initially, safe spaces were meant to ensure actual physical safety for groups so "othered" by American society that the threat of physical harm for simply being was imminent (Raeburn, 2004). Today, however, some have suggested that "safe space" denotes campus environments designed to shield students from the realities of the outside world, rather than expose them to its harshness (Green, 2015; Shulevitz, 2015). This "protection" effectively stunts the ability of faculty and students to generate engaging discussions on difficult topics. The "safety" implied in this pedagogy is White safety, it is male safety (Arao & Clemmons, 2013); and like so many pedagogical predecessors, safe space is a reflection of those original exclusionary practices.

More recently, beginning with social justice activists, the focus has shifted from the creation of safe space to *brave space* (Arao & Clemens, 2013). The emergence of brave space pedagogy came in response to the important and disconcerting side effect of safe spaces—the eagerness of students to equate safety with comfort. The conflation of terms creates environments in which student participation in provocative discussion is a direct result of how comfortable they are with the topic (Arao & Clemmons, 2013). It is counterintuitive for faculty to attempt to ensure students' high comfort levels from the outset of discussion. Just as there would be no guarantee to a student in their first statistics course that they will feel an immediate sense of comfort with statistical analysis, why guarantee comfort around issues of racial inequality, when a student is probably relatively uneducated on the topic? Instead, brave space pedagogy encourages students to confront and challenge each other on sensitive topics. It focuses on active learning in the classroom where students are responsible for listening to each other, holding each other accountable for misguided opinions, having the courage to be vulnerable and open to critique, and working together to create calls for change (Arao & Clemens, 2013).

Conceptually, brave space falls short in its mission to teach productive conversation skills in the classroom. Connotations of braveness provide students the option to lean on individual privilege as an excuse to make stereotypical statements, often a result of students' shared awareness of racial difference, but lack of understanding of how injustice is reproduced by social structures (Trujillo-Pagan, 2013). This shifts the flow of discussion from an educational and perhaps transformative one to catering to the lowest common denominator of prejudicial ideologies under the guise of "bravery," a willingness to say those things you would never say publicly. Additionally, the brave space pedagogy positions discussion in brave spaces as consistently positive experiences, the implication being that participation in brave space automatically assumes students will walk away feeling good about the discussion. This expectation of "good" feelings is borne out of connotations of bravery. Being brave is something to be proud of, it is heroic, daring, and courageous, something to be applauded. At its conclusion, bravery should leave one feeling positive. How many students simply choose to ignore those ideas, theories, or data that can't leave them feeling "good"?

There is also a built-in assumption that all students experience and express bravery in the same way. What feels brave to students who come from privileged backgrounds, or the ways in which bravery is expressed (via class participation, critical analysis papers, participation in campus movements), among those (mostly White) students is not necessarily similar to that of racially minoritized students who often find themselves as alone and isolated in specific classrooms as they do within the larger institution. If these students of color refuse to be "brave" in classroom discussions on inequalities they've personally experienced, and allow themselves and their experiences to be placed on display for others, then are they cowardly? Here, as with safe spaces, brave spaces are raced and gendered.

Some have misinterpreted or misappropriated the notion of brave spaces in ways that encourage students to embrace their comments, however misguided and hurtful, to defend them vehemently, and often to disregard any contrarian information. This allows students to stop engagement with difficult subjects at the individual level, thus limiting their ability to unpack emotions like guilt, anger, and fear as they pertain to issues of racial inequality, and subsequently blocking the process of deep learning for all students by discouraging engaged discussion. Many faculty either stop here or engage in lengthy trial-and-error processes as they attempt to uncover an answer for best practices, with little mind paid to the symbolic violence[1] many students endure as part of that process (Watson & Widin, 2014).

Finally, brave space pedagogy ignores the importance of discomfort in the learning process beyond basic self-reflection to include broader institutional and structural racism. Being brave assumes a shedding of discomfort and a willingness to push forward at all costs and in every way. This assumes that same willingness is present in a majority of students, can be easily tapped into by a facilitator, and extends beyond analysis of and engagement with the individual. Because brave space pedagogy is focused on the bravery of self-reflection, individual students can simultaneously acknowledge their own behavior and experiences without extrapolation to the broader social world. Safe space and brave space pedagogies have in common their attempts to create anti-oppressive classroom environments by depersonalizing discussions of racial inequality. Instead of asking students to confront the emotions that accompany a critical analysis of racial inequality, these pedagogies focus on discussions, activities, and assignments about the structural and cultural mechanisms that perpetuate inequities and ignore socialization processes that encourage the individual internalization of subsequent racist ideologies. One common example is the *absolution of guilt* approach. When students claim exhaustion with discussions of race, faculty may make blanket statements about the unnecessary nature of personal guilt about racism. In his work on dismantling racism in White America, Barndt (1991) laments the mistake of racial guilt absolution. Absolving students of implicit racism without an unpacking of socialization, structural racism, and the imbalance in benefits and disadvantages that result acknowledges surface discomfort, but does not require a deeper reading of the source of negative emotions related to racism. This approach often gives the illusion of a more equitable environment, while leaving intact existing power dynamics between both teacher and students (as students search for the right answer). Black students with limited power and little privilege must then acquiesce to White students whose privilege imbues power in their on-campus interactions and whose behavior steadfastly maintains their "right" to opt-out of classroom discussions on topics that make them uncomfortable. Encouraging students to acknowledge and embrace that discomfort is important to their learning and maturation process, and most importantly, to developing a set of communication skills that will prepare them for productive contributions to public discourse on topics of inequality in the future.

Taxonomy of Uncomfortable Learning Approach

I built the uncomfortable learning pedagogy using a revised version of Bloom's Taxonomy (Anderson et al., 2001), a set of hierarchical models that classify learning objectives. Each of the five learning objectives that make up the cognitive-domain model[2] have been considered with respect to guiding principles within the pedagogy and applied to all aspects of the course case study, including syllabus creation, required reading, active learning exercises, group work, writing assignments and exams, and assessment of learning objectives.

The following case study illustrates the use of uncomfortable learning as a pedagogical tool to teach race within each of the components of Bloom's Taxonomy in a real-world classroom. Using examples observed and analyzed via ethnographic and focus group data over two years at a liberal arts college in the northeast, I taught the 15-week Race and Ethnic Relations course in the Department of Anthropology and Sociology as an empirical test of the pedagogical strategy. Students from this case described their desire to enroll in the course as a reflection of the lack of discussions of race in other disciplines on campus. Junior biology major Jamie, a woman of color, explains "I was hoping to get a more complete picture of race and racial difference in the world because that's a perspective we don't get in my major. We don't talk about race at all, so I would have never gotten this experience if it weren't for this class."

In an attempt to bridge the gap between need and availability of courses on race that stress engagement, the basic tenets of the uncomfortable learning pedagogy were used to facilitate the course. Following Bloom's taxonomy and six learning objectives, these tenets are as follows: *remembering; understanding; applying, analyzing, and evaluating;* and *synthesizing.* Volunteer students from the course participated in focus groups at its conclusion to gauge the success and usefulness of the pedagogy to students' perceived learning outcomes.[3]

Remembering

Although often referred to as *surface learning,* a function of student recall ability, remembering is integral to facilitating deep learning on difficult topics. Pedagogically, it is important to set the boundaries for uncomfortable learning from the very first day of class in a way that provides for a broadening of understandings and a challenging of preconceptions of all students. Uncomfortable learning emphasizes this skill in a nontraditional way, asking students' help in constructing the boundaries of course discussions.

Setting boundaries is integral to successful implementation of uncomfortable learning pedagogy in the classroom. The following activity addresses remembering as a principle of knowledge-based taxonomy via definitions of *respect* in course discussions. Students are asked to answer one question in an open forum: How do you define *respect* in the context of course discussion? In this activity students openly discuss individual definitions of respect, which allows students to create a (mostly) unilaterally agreed upon definition of *respect* with which to work.

The objective of this activity is to develop a collective consciousness within the group, borne out of the framing of respect from the outset.

Students collaborating on definitions of *respect* within their class space are more likely to adhere to the guidelines that they've laid out together. Moreover, it includes students in the work of maintaining classroom boundaries, where recall of this jointly created definition is used daily in class discussion. Sophomore sociology major Heidi, a White woman, discusses the problems she anticipated in class discussions on race, stating, "I'm always scared to discuss race in class because people say the wrong things and I've seen stuff really blow up. I don't want to get involved."

This activity helps mitigate some of the trepidation students feel discussing race without absolving them of the negative emotions that create the dread Heidi describes. A sense of autonomy both in the shape and in the flow of conversation may encourage more genuine honesty than in classrooms where faculty members create and enforce these definitions. Such micromanagement is discouraged within this uncomfortable learning paradigm. The approach instead creates a space for questions, rather than agreements, allowing openness around students' hidden "isms" (racism, sexism, classism, etc.) and encouraging them to grow, rather than to change. Art and science double major and first-generation immigrant woman Zoe, highlights the importance of this activity to the course's forward movement. She explained: "A few times [a class member] reminded people about our definition of respect which I really liked. Things were already tense but that seemed to calm everybody down. I thought it was good because sometimes we get emotional about race and say stupid things."

As a catalyst for such transformative change, embracing uncomfortable learning removes traditional scaffolding from potentially tense classroom discussions, as such professors refrain from shielding students who make controversial statements from potentially volatile responses. This initial activity asks students to be responsible for one another, as well as for the tone of course discussions. Asking them to rely on each other to remember and apply definitions of *respect* in real time helps facilitate deep knowledge-based learning.

Understanding

Many students and faculty across racial identities face a basic lack of awareness of the prevalence of structural inequality based on race (Harper & Davis, 2016; Stevenson, 2014), often using willful ignorance to shield themselves and subsequent classroom environments from these topics all together. At a recent faculty meeting to discuss broad issues of inclusion in the classroom, a White female natural science professor stated, "We don't discuss race in my classroom because it's about science, not social issues." These comments are typical of faculty unaware or unwilling to recognize all the ways race plays a role in their classroom (i.e., racial identity of assigned reading authors, racial make-up of the class, race-based science research), and highlights the *liability model of responsibility* (LMR). Using the LMR model, students and faculty divert personal responsibility for social problems from themselves to avoid negative, often uncomfortable, emotions associated with guilt, shame, blame, and fault (Applebaum, 2007).

Understanding as a knowledge-based learning objective encourages students to extrapolate out from traditional positivist data and rhetoric to demonstrate a complex interpretation of existing data and theories. The uncomfortable learning pedagogy uses tangible experiences as a facilitation tool to that end. It does not rely solely on the instructors' knowledge to relay information that encourages understanding. Instead, it asks teachers to introduce marginalized voices to course discussions. This can happen in a variety of ways, including field trips, guest speakers, and empirical research projects, which can all provide experiential knowledge from which students can draw to aid their understanding of racial inequality.

Drawing from critical race theory, the use of guest speakers in this pedagogical approach highlights storytelling as a valid and useful methodological approach. Guest speakers also break down the wall between the guest's anecdotal evidence of racial inequality and the attitudes of many of the White and/or upper-class students who often have difficulty empathizing with issues of racial inequality. The course in this example included talks from local urban educators and community leaders to discuss personal experiences with structural and institutional racism.

Field trips are long-documented to help achieve a variety of learning goals including improving recall ability (Falk & Dierking, 1997; Salmi, 2003), connecting physical experience to affective response (Nadelson & Jordan, 2012), and increasing engagement on a topic (Bonderup Dohn, 2011; Kisiel, 2005). The case study example used a walking tour of Germantown Avenue in Philadelphia, Pennsylvania, where class and race-based inequality are clearly delineated and observable. The repercussions for such stratification are also on display at this field trip site. Walking tours are a useful tool for this pedagogical approach because it removes barriers between students and real life. It forces students to confront the realities of racial inequality. Zoe describes the impact of this experiential learning activity, explaining, "In my other sociology courses we touch on the fact that racism is an institutionalized system, but I think this course really delved into that and confronted us with examples we couldn't ignore, and gave us the tools to go out and talk to other people about it, and point things out."

Junior biology major Jamie, a woman of color, adds, "I'd never taken a trip like that before. For anything. It was hard taking that walk, looking and talking to people. I would never have done anything like that on my own."

Lastly, the use of empirical research projects amalgamates student experiences via walking tours and the introduction of marginalized voices using guest speakers. Asking students to develop a small research project where they will collect and analyze raw empirical data encourages the kind of understanding vital to knowledge-based learning. For faculty of color the combination of guest speakers, field trips, and empirical research projects also works to jettison student rhetoric on potential faculty bias by adding additional voices, experiences, and empirical methodologies to the conversation, expanding the definition of *expert* beyond just the faculty. Brave and safe space, in comparison, by generally relying on the professor to create discussion parameters and define course goals via bravery and safety, puts minority faculty at a disadvantage among students who assume bias based on said faculty's racial identity. For example, senior art student Sarah, a White woman, describes the difficulty in generating understanding among White students by a Black female professor in the class. Sarah describes a group of White male students "felt a little bit threatened because you [the professor] were pointing out that they have the most privilege which made them very uncomfortable, but they do talk about the course outside of class and notice issues of institutional racism they hadn't seen before, which I thought was very cool." She believes that changing the race and gender of the professor might have made them more comfortable, but they probably would not have learned as much, adding, "I do think things would have been different if you were a White male professor because they would have definitely felt less threatened and have more to relate to."

The sense of threat is another negative emotion with which students are unable to grapple. White students, especially male, very often feel threatened by the presence of faculty of color, especially in courses where race is a topic of discussion, thus impeding their ability to understand as a learning objective. Uncomfortable learning, by widening the definition of *expert*, and simultaneously confronting students with real-world experiences, removes much of the hesitation and suspicion levied at faculty of color by White students in higher education classrooms. This pedagogical approach asks students to work to identify the source of these emotional responses as a way of minimizing them.

Applying, Analyzing, and Evaluating

Bloom's taxonomy separates these learning objectives into three distinct categories; however, for the uncomfortable learning approach these objectives are too interconnected to parse individually. Taken together, applying, analyzing, and evaluating asks students to solve problems and build arguments using knowledge acquired throughout the course and via empirical evidence, thus eliminating the prescriptive element from class participation by encouraging students to conceive class discussion as a series of arguments. This teaches students the difference between personal opinion and theoretical or empirical claims, and eliminates the tendency for students to rely solely on personal experience, which can be limited, in discussions of structural inequities. The catalyst to this kind of complex thinking is the faculty member's ability to frame courses using uncomfortable learning pedagogy as argument-driven.

Students are advised and reminded throughout the course that only clearly formed arguments are welcome contributions to class discussion. Using this approach, an *argument* is defined in the course syllabus as a series of statements built using theoretical or empirical evidence leading from a premise to a conclusion. Opinions are welcome, but they are not validated as constructive contributions to class discourse without the inclusion of empirical knowledge to develop the line of reasoning. Uncomfortable learning encourages skill building in this manner via writing, podcasting, and empirical data collection. Many students come to college with very little experience building complex arguments via critical thinking skills, instead depending on individual experiences, limited by race, class, and gender boundaries. This approach to course participation stifles the wall-building prevalent among students thrust into racial discourse and encourages cognitive-based learning by devaluing opinions and encouraging the application and analysis of newly acquired knowledge as a tool for argument formation and evaluation.

As the faculty member, it is important to acknowledge student motivations for contributing to classroom conversations. Students often participate in class discussion because they want to please the teacher; they are attempting to find the "right" answer. This issue is magnified when faculty of color ask students to engage with materials addressing racial inequality. Heidi, a White female student, reminds us, "If you [the faculty member of color] pose a question it is automatically assumed to be racial, whereas if Dr. [redacted—White male faculty member] asks the same question it doesn't necessarily feel racial to us. It's more theoretical and I think that definitely does influence it, which might make people defensive and feel guilty."

Heidi speaks to a major problem for racially minoritized instructors teaching race. The uncomfortable emotions which accompany these topics encourages students, especially White students, to put up their guard. By contrast, framing the course as one centered on the development of arguments does not eliminate emotion from discourse, but instead allows students a device to productively focus those emotions into a legitimate and coherent argument.

Synthesizing

In any course, regardless of topic, information synthesis is often the most difficult type of cognitive-based knowledge for students to achieve, as it asks students to compile evidence into new patterns and encourages the formation of alternate solutions to the same problem. The ability to communicate across social boundaries is imperative to successfully synthesizing a diverse set of course materials, as proposed by the uncomfortable learning pedagogy. The significant generational and technological gap between faculty and students means the two communicate differently. Both groups want information in drastically different forms, and from very different places. Millennials, who represent a large segment of traditional-aged students currently, receive and communicate information rapidly, diversely, and informally, unlike their faculty counterparts; as a result, the traditional classroom inherently limits student engagement (Gibson, 2009). As a way to bridge this communication gap in the classroom, the uncomfortable learning approach uses student-created podcasts to reinforce class lessons via a communication style students prefer, and a method that encourages engagement.

In the course example, each student leads topical discussions on a predetermined class day by provoking the readings and posing questions to fellow students. The weekly podcasts, each conceived and executed by the week's "provocateur," provide an opportunity for students to discuss issues of race and racism in a more informal environment and without the pressure of speaking in front of fellow students. The result is a much deeper, more critical discourse on issues of race and racism from a diverse set of viewpoints. Students reference social media, current events, celebrity happenings, and on-campus experiences in their synthesis of these issues on the podcasts. The discussion continues among the remaining students via blog posts on the course website. Sophomore biracial sociology major Amaya points to the course podcast as one way the course successfully addresses engagement issues in the classroom, sharing: "I liked the podcasts and the blogs because it was a way to speak up and state your opinions without having to worry about the professors saying, 'you're wrong.' It took the spotlight off you."

Successful information synthesis is often thwarted in courses on race thanks to the loaded emotions that accompany these topics. Podcasts act as public discourse without the pressure of being live, the preparation for which requires students to synthesize course material before joining the discussion, rather than in the classroom in real time. This added layer of perceived privacy encourages students to let down their guards and express emotions in a way they have been socialized against in traditional classrooms.

Discussion

Higher education has reached a turning point, where 24-hour news cycles and ever-expanding social media options consistently intersect with continued examples of institutional discrimination and privilege. Uncomfortable learning pedagogy acknowledges the complex emotional responses to institutional racism in the United States. As a pedagogical tool, it acts as a kind of educational therapy, using intense emotional responses to facilitate learning. For students participating in a course on racial inequality, using the uncomfortable learning pedagogy leads to deep learning and emotional breakthroughs from students used to ignoring the experiences of emotions in the classroom. Jamie, a student from the course, explains how transformative taking this class and engaging with those emotions was for her, stating, "I felt uncomfortable throughout the class just because I didn't know a majority of these facts, but I almost cried at certain points. . . . I just got so emotional because I couldn't understand how or why this keeps happening." She goes on to describe how taking this course has changed her willingness to engage in discussions of race and encouraged her friends to do the same, explaining,

> With me and my friends we didn't talk about it [race] at all, but coming after this course, after each class I would be so infuriated and mad that I would go back to my friends and say, "can you believe this!" I also went home and talked to my parents about it and they don't understand, but I would be so angry that I would just need to get my voice out there.

Fellow classmate and sophomore science major Kerri, a Black woman, added,

> It [institutional racism] was the first thing I talked to my parents about when I went home for Thanksgiving break, and I was like, "can you believe this is happening?" I was just so frustrated about it and they couldn't really understand, but I spent so much time getting them to understand what is going on and what they can do about it. That was important to me.

Faculty in the academy must move away from teaching as a form of coercion or persuasion (Bizzell, 1991), seeking to move students from their points of view to those of the faculty member. This method is devoid of the engagement necessary for deep student learning. Students of this generation are generally leery of the persuasive approach, raised to embrace their individuality and independence from traditional dichotomies like race, gender, class, and religion (Broido, 2004). Perceptions of coercion or persuasion in the classroom are likely to cause students to shut down and disengage from class discussions. Uncomfortable learning pedagogy asks students to tap into that individuality and explore what are sure to be complex feelings on difficult subjects as a road to the kind of deep learning that encourages long-term recall.

All students in the course example discussed learning to harness these emotions into positive discussion. Senior humanities major Daniela, a White woman, described herself as willing to engage in discussions of race before taking the course, but being unable to continue in the face of silencing rhetoric. She explains that this course provided her with the tools for handling emotional conversations. According to Daniela, "There were just so many ways you gave us to continue conversation even when other people wanted to end it as quickly as possible. I've taken other courses on race, but I feel like this class gave me the tools to be confident in talks about race." Fellow senior Zoe elaborates:

> I would talk to people about White privilege and it would be sort of a "blamey" [*sic*] conversation whereas now I think this class has really provided me with an understanding of how we should go about talking about this [race]. And we obviously aren't going to get anywhere if we blame people. Like we blame people for being White and White guilt is a thing and there are so many different layers that we need to address. It's not just Black or White.

Sophomore business student Cherry, a White woman, adds, "I think this course should be required because I felt like I learned a lot of things that I've been feeling but wasn't able to back up when I talked to other people." Heidi, who had recently participated in public discussions on institutional curricula and diversity, echoed Cherry's sentiment, adding, "Other classes that fulfill the diversity requirement only talk about the positive side of it, but this class really unveiled the ugly side of race which I think is important for students to understand. And I think it would be really cool if this class were more of the requirement than the others."

On the whole, this uncomfortable learning pedagogy, unlike its safe space and brave space peers, rejects the idea that conceptions of safety or bravery are homogenous across student and faculty populations, and cannot, therefore, be used to generate productive discourse on sensitive topics, or provide students with the communication skillset necessary to contribute to public discourse on these issues. The uncomfortable learning pedagogy demands students really feel the discomfort—revel in it almost—and then encourages them to use it, understand social frameworks that create these feelings, and leave them behind as a part of their growth.

Conclusion

Previous research on the impact of racial diversity in the classroom suggests that Black students engage with course material differently than their White counterparts, with Black students more likely to use complex connections between race and class identity often as a result of personal experiences (Packard, 2011). It is hard for many White students to develop a deep understanding of issues with which they have little firsthand knowledge. The resulting fear and reservations can prevent White students from successfully engaging with issues of racial inequality and White privilege, creating a barrier to their learning that most do not even know is there. Uncomfortable learning helps all students work past these negative emotions. It acknowledges risk differentials in the process of classroom-based emotion work, provides a door to a more complex way of thinking, and helps students through that door even as it probably is not the perfect size for easy pass through. Uncomfortable learning dissects the visceral experience of discomfort, what it feels like and is triggered by, then explores the unique connection to each student's personal experiences, simultaneously building a diversity of ideas into course expectations about participation in discussion and acceptable behavior in the classroom.

Notes

1. *Symbolic violence* is a form of violence, mostly perpetrated against poor minorities in the United States, which limits their access to practical knowledge and experiences necessary for upward social mobility (Bourdieu & Passeron, 1977). The process of symbolic violence simultaneously perpetuates the disproportionate presence of minorities in the lower and working classes while legitimizing the reason for this social position in their minds via this limited access (Richardson, 2011).

2. The five learning objectives in the cognitive domain are *remembering, understanding, applying, analyzing, synthesizing,* and *evaluating* (Bloom, Engelhart, Furst, Hill, & Krathwohl, 1956).

3. The course was taught as a 200-level special topics course and met two afternoons per week for 75 minutes during the 15-week semester. Twenty-five students registered for the course at the beginning of the semester. Two students dropped the course before the drop deadline, citing that the course "wasn't for them."

References

Alexander, M. (2010). *The new Jim Crow: Mass incarceration in the age of colorblindness*. New York, NY: The New Press.

Anderson, L. W., Krathwohl, D. R., Airasian, P. W., Cruikshank, K. A., Mayer, R. E., Pintrich, P. R., Raths, J., Wittrock, M. C. (2001). *A taxonomy for learning, teaching, and assessing: A revision of Bloom's Taxonomy of educational objectives*. New York, NY: Pearson, Allyn & Bacon.

Applebaum, B. (2007). White complicity and social justice education: Can one be culpable without being liable? *Educational Theory, 57*, 453–467.

Arao, B., & Clemens, K. (2013). From safe spaces to brave spaces: A new way to frame dialogue around diversity and social justice. In L. M. Landreman (Ed.), *The art of effective facilitation* (pp. 135–150). Sterling, VA: Stylus.

Barndt, J. R. (1991). *Dismantling racism: The continuing challenge to White America*. Minneapolis, MN: Augsburg Books.

Bernal, D. D. (1998). Chicana/o education from the civil rights era to the present. *The Elusive Quest for Equality, 150*, 77–108.

Bernal, D. D., & Villalpando, O. (2002). An apartheid of knowledge in academia: The struggle over the "legitimate" knowledge of faculty of color. *Equity and Excellence in Education, 35*, 169–180.

Bizzell, P. (1991). Power, authority, and critical pedagogy. *Journal of Basic Writing, 10*, 54–70.

Bloom, B., Engelhart, M., Furst, E., Hill, W., & Krathwohl, D. (1956). *Taxonomy of educational objectives: The classification of educational goals. Handbook I: Cognitive domain*. New York, NY: David McKay.

Bonderup Dohn, N. (2011). Situational interest of high school students who visit an aquarium. *Science Education, 95*(5), 337–357.

Bourdieu, P., & Jean-Claude Passeron. (1977). *Reproduction in education, society, and culture*. London, UK: Sage Publications.

Broido, E. M. (2004). Understanding diversity in millennial students. In M. D. Coomes & R. DeBard (Eds.), *Serving the millennial generation: New directions for student services* (pp. 73–85). Hoboken, NJ: Wiley.

Coates, T. (2015). *Between the world and me*. New York, NY: Spiegel & Grau.

Collins, Patricia H. (1998). *Fighting words: Black women and the search for justice*. Minneapolis, MN: University of Minnesota Press.

Crenshaw, K. (1989). Demarginalizing the intersection of race and sex: A Black feminist critique of antidiscrimination doctrine, feminist theory, and antiracist politics. *University of Chicago Legal Forum, 1*, 139–167.

Delgado, R. (1998). Using a Chicana feminist epistemology in educational research. *Educational Review, 68*(4), 555–582.

Delgado, R., & Stefancic, J. (2011). *Critical race theory: An introduction*. New York, NY: New York University Press.

Falk, J. H., & Dierking, L. (1997). School field trips: Assessing their long-term impact. *Curator: The Museum Journal, 40*(3), 211–218.

Gibson, S. E. (2009). Intergenerational communication in the classroom: Recommendations for successful teacher–student relationships. *Nursing Education Perspectives, 30*(1), 37–39.

Green, A. (2015). Do historically Black colleges provide the safe spaces students are after? *The Atlantic.* Retrieved from http://www.theatlantic.com/education/archive/2015/11/are-hbcus-necessary-racial-sanctuaries/416694/

Harper, S. R., & Davis, C. H. F., III. (2016). Eight actions to reduce racism in college classrooms. *Academe, 102*(6), 30–34.

Kenney, M. R. (2001). *Mapping gay L.A.: The intersection of place and politics.* Philadelphia, PA: Temple University Press.

Kisiel, J. F. (2005). Understanding elementary teacher motivations for science fieldtrips. *Science Education, 89*(6), 936–955.

Ladson-Billings, G. (2000). Fighting for our lives: Preparing teachers to teach African American students. *Journal of Teacher Education, 51*, 206–214.

Matias, C. E., & DiAngelo, R. (2013). Beyond the face of race: Emo-cognitive explorations of White neurosis and racial cray-cray. *Educational Foundations, 27*, 3–20.

Mueller, J. C. (2011). Tracing family, teaching race: Critical race pedagogy in the millennial sociology classroom. *Teaching Sociology, 41*, 172–187.

Nadelson, L., & Jordan, R. (2012). Student attitudes toward and recall of outside day: An environmental science field trip. *The Journal of Educational Research, 105*(3), 220–231.

Packard, J. (2011). The impact of racial diversity in the classroom: Activating the sociological imagination. *Teaching Sociology, 41*, 144–158.

Raeburn, N. C. (2004). *Changing corporate America for inside out: Lesbian and gay workplace rights.* Minneapolis, MN: University of Minnesota Press.

Richardson, C. (2011). "Can't tell me nothing": Symbolic violence, education, and Kanye West. *Popular Music and Society, 34*(1), 97–112.

Salmi, H. (2003). Science centres as learning laboratories: Experiences of Heureka, the Finnish science centre. *International Journal of Technology Management, 25*(5), 460–476.

Shulevitz, J. (2015, March 22). In college and hiding from scary ideas. *The New York Times.* Retrieved from http://www.nytimes.com/2015/03/22/opinion/sunday/judith-shulevitz-hiding-from-scary-ideas.html?_r=0

Solórzano, D. G. (1997). Images and words that wound: Critical race theory, racial stereotyping, and teacher education. *Teacher Education Quarterly, 24*, 5–19.

Solórzano, D. G., & Bernal, D. D. (2001). Examining transformational resistance through a critical race and Latcrit theory framework: Chicana and Chicano students in an urban context. *Urban Education, 36*, 308–342.

Solórzano, D. G., & Yosso, T. J. (2002). Critical race methodology: Counter-storytelling as an analytical framework for education research. *Qualitative Inquiry, 8*, 23–44.

Stevenson, Howard C., Jr. (2014). *Promoting racial literacy in schools: Differences that make a difference.* New York, NY: Teachers College Press.

Trujillo-Pagan, Nicole. (2013). *Modern colonization by medical Intervention: U.S. medicine in Puerto Rico.* Leiden, Netherlands: Brill.

Watson, J., & Widin, J. (2014). Maintaining the status quo: Symbolic violence in higher education. *Higher Education Research and Development, 34,* 658–670.

Villalpando, O. (2003). Self-segregation or self-preservation? A critical race theory and Latina/o critical theory analysis of a study of Chicana/o college students. *International Journal of Qualitative Studies in Education, 16,* 619–646.

Difficult Subjects for Difficult Times

Badia Ahad-Legardy and OiYan A. Poon

This volume was in progress well before the election of Donald Trump to the U.S. presidency. It was produced in light of significant social moments, the emergence of #BlackLivesMatter, Justice for Palestine, and protests against sexual assault on college campuses across the nation, to name a few. This collection felt urgent then, and it feels even more urgent now. The chapters in this collection reflect the multivalent ways that faculty from varying disciplines and institutions have worked to make their universities, in general, and classrooms, in particular, socially just spaces. Our purpose as intellectuals and pedagogues has never been clearer, especially as we work to attune students to the historical and social contexts that brought us to this new era.

Certainly, the authors of this volume count ourselves among many faculty who recognize the import of a collective pedagogy in the face of tumultuous social moments. The Lemonade (Benbow, 2016), Ferguson (Sociologists for Justice, n.d.) and Trump (Connolly & Blaine, 2016) syllabi are clear evidence of a generative move on the part of faculty to become "undisciplined" in our research and teaching praxis and form essential networks that will inspire and inform the knowledge that we produce as scholars and share in the classroom as teachers. In the same week as the election of Donald Trump, the Facebook group Teaching in the Aftermath was created, and as of January 24, 2017, had 1,492 members. The name of the group parallels the ominous sentiments of most of the nation but, as scholars who value not only academic freedom but also education more generally as a public good, the fear of repression under the new administration is a portentous foreshadowing of increased efforts to hijack higher education from so-called leftists. Recently, lawmakers in both Missouri and Iowa have proposed bills to either discontinue the practice of tenure for new faculty hires or end tenure for faculty who already have it. In Wisconsin, Assemblyman David Murphy has led the charge to pressure the University of Wisconsin to cancel a course titled The Problem of Whiteness. Claiming that "taxpayers" should not have to pay for a course that labels Whites as "racists," Murphy and his supporters have effectively doubled down on existing efforts by lawmakers and conservative social and political groups to treat students as consumers and faculty as service providers (Wootson, 2016). The corporatization of the university enables such backlash against professors who trouble the standard of American exceptionalism, and who assert the notion that education must go beyond simply being a narrow tool for vocational or marketplace advancement.

Our students are also at risk. Recent gag orders placed on governmental offices not to release information to the press or the public regarding climate change foreshadows a future of limited funding and resources for scholars to perform critical research. The research we perform as scholars informs the work we share with students in the classroom. In turn, the pursuit of knowledge and democratic exchanges of ideas rely on free exchange of information.

Yet, as Homi Bhabha has written, "the state of emergency is also always a state of emergence" (Bhabha, 1994, p. 59). This volume offers insights and strategies that individual university faculty have employed to not just teach the difficult subjects of race, sexuality, and gender, but to do so in institutional and classroom environments that work directly against their efforts. Although each chapter represents a unique experience and set of strategies, the collection of experiences and strategies reflect a shared narrative of resistance to the neoliberal practices of the university.

In this age of spectacle and chaos threatening the exchange of ideas, development of research, and the questioning of prevailing systems of oppression, the responsibility of college educators to challenge and teach students how to critically engage in difficult public discourses and critical thinking about social problems is greater than ever. At the same time, college educators who wish to invite their students into conversations about difficult subjects must be aware of and attend to the risks and challenges associated with such efforts. Therefore, this volume is intended to embolden our colleagues to engage in collective acts of pedagogical resistance against systemic oppression, and to open new possibilities for justice and hope.

References

Benbow, C. (2016). *The lemonade syllabus*. Retrieved from http://www.candicebenbow .com/lemonadesyllabus/

Bhabha, H. (1994). *The location of culture*. New York, NY: Routledge.

Connolly, N. D. B., & Blaine, K. N. (2016, June 28). Trump syllabus 2.0. *Public Books*. Retrieved from http://www.publicbooks.org/trump-syllabus-2-0/

Sociologists for Justice. (n.d.). *Statement on Ferguson*. Retrieved from https://sociologists forjustice.org/ferguson-syllabus/

Wootson, Jr., C. R. (2016, December 28). A professor wants to teach "The Problem of Whiteness." A lawmaker calls the class "garbage." The Washington Post. Retrieved from: https://www.washingtonpost.com/news/grade-point/wp/2016/12/28/a-professor-wants-to-teach-the-problems-of-whiteness-a-lawmaker-calls-the-class-garbage/?utm_term=.2dbaff62e862

EDITORS AND CONTRIBUTORS

Editors

Badia Ahad-Legardy is associate professor of English at Loyola University–Chicago. Ahad-Legardy teaches courses in contemporary African American literature, American studies, and cultural studies, and was recently named Master Teacher by the College of Arts and Sciences. Her research interests include twentieth and twenty-first century African American literary, social and cultural history, psychoanalytic culture, and visual and memory studies. In addition to her scholarly pursuits, Ahad-Legardy is the director of training and master coach for the National Center for Faculty Development and Diversity (NCFDD). Since 2011, she has organized monthly guest expert webinars and multiweek courses for the professional development university administrators, faculty members, and advanced graduate students. She is the author of *Freud Upside Down: African American Literature and Psychoanalytic Culture* (University of Illinois Press, 2010), and her work has been published in *American Studies*, *Journal of Popular Culture*, and *CR: The New Centennial Review*, among other publications.

OiYan A. Poon is an assistant professor of higher education leadership at Colorado State University. A nationally recognized scholar on the racial politics of college access, affirmative action, and Asian Americans, Poon received a 2014 Emerging Scholar award from the American College Personnel Association and was a featured keynote speaker at the National Conference on Race and Ethnicity in Higher Education in 2013. Poon currently serves on the editorial board for the *Journal of College Student Development* and the *Journal Committed to Social Change on Race and Ethnicity* and as a reviewer for the *Journal of Diversity in Higher Education*, *Amerasia Journal* and the *Journal of Asian American Studies*. Poon has been involved in advocacy, research, institutional development, and organizational change efforts in higher education for more than a decade. She earned her PhD in race and ethnic studies in education with a certificate in Asian American studies from UCLA.

Contributors

Rucha Ambikar holds a PhD in social and cultural anthropology and is currently assistant professor of sociology and anthropology at Bemidji State University. She was born and raised in India, and her current scholarly interests revolve around pedagogy, nationalism, and right-wing politics in India and the United States.

Akhila L. Ananth is an assistant professor in the School of Criminal Justice and Criminalistics at California State University–Los Angeles. She received her doctorate from the University of California–Irvine in the Department of Criminology, Law, and Society. Her research examines constructions of race, class, and gender in the architecture and design of juvenile law, including children's courthouses, group homes, and juvenile detention centers. Her most recent research used ethnographic and archival research to draw an analogy between the racialization of foster care and the architecture of the children's courthouse in Los Angeles, published in *Studies in Law, Politics, and Society*. Ananth's other research interests include juvenile justice in the global context (specifically, in India) and the legal construction of childhood and family.

Brandon Arnold is a current senior undergraduate student at the University of Denver (DU) studying philosophy and political science. Arnold is a member of the university honor's program, and is currently working on a thesis between both departments. Arnold also serves as the vice-president for the DU men's rugby team. Arnold hopes to attend law school in the fall of 2018 and pursue a legal career.

Azura Booth is from Harlem, New York. She is currently a junior at Pitzer College, majoring in Africana studies. At present, she is interested in looking at the effect of gentrification on Black urban populations, and recently had an article published in the *Amsterdam News*. In the future, she hopes to be involved in activism for underrepresented communities.

Erica Chu is a visiting faculty member in the gender and women's studies program at the University of Illinois–Chicago. Chu is also a PhD candidate at Loyola University–Chicago in English with a concentration in women studies and gender studies. Chu's dissertation, *Identity Positivity,* explores theoretical frameworks that affirm all kinds of identities including those emerging and those not yet imagined. One of Chu's chapters appears in *Asexualities: Feminist and Queer Perspectives* (Routledge, 2014).

Sherry L. Deckman is an assistant professor of education at Lehman College, the City University of New York. Her current research explores how undergraduate students from diverse backgrounds negotiate race, class, and gender while participating in culturally focused performing arts groups. She is also interested in how educators are formally prepared to work with students from diverse race and class backgrounds and how educators address issues of race, class, and gender inequity in schools. Deckman's selected publications include "Leaving the Space Better Than You Found It Through Song: Music, Diversity, and Mission in One Black Student Organization" (*Harvard Educational Review*, 2013), the forthcoming book chapter "Dangerous Black Professor: Challenging the Ghettoization of Race in Higher Education Through Life Texts Pedagogy," (*RIP Jim Crow: Fighting Racism Through Higher Education Policy, Curriculum, and Cultural Interventions* (coauthor; Peter Lang, 2016).

Adriana Estill teaches American studies and English at Carleton College, a historically White small liberal arts college in Minnesota. Her scholarly interests focus on Latinx Studies with emphases in questions of genre, place-making, embodiment, and the production of raced, gendered, and classed identity. Her work ranges from discussions of the library in *Buffy the Vampire Slayer* to the historical and social development of ideals of beauty for Mexican and Latinx communities. Her most recent work addresses the rise of the telenovela on U.S. primetime and considers the way in which the genre mediates White American anxieties around Latinidad.

Breanne Fahs is an associate professor of women and gender studies at Arizona State University, where she specializes in studying women's sexuality, critical embodiment studies, radical feminism, and political activism. She has a BA in women's studies/gender studies and psychology from Occidental College and a PhD in women's studies and clinical psychology from the University of Michigan. She has published widely in feminist, social science, and humanities journals and has authored four books: *Performing Sex* (SUNY Press, 2011), an analysis of the paradoxes of women's "sexual liberation", *The Moral Panics of Sexuality* (Palgrave, 2013), an edited collection that examines cultural anxieties of "scary sex," *Valerie Solanas* (Feminist Press, 2014), a biography of author/would-be assassin Valerie Solanas; and *Out for Blood* (SUNY Press, 2016), a book of essays on menstrual activism and resistance. She is the director of the rambunctious Feminist Research on Gender and Sexuality Group at Arizona State University, and she also works as a clinical psychologist in private practice where she specializes in sexuality, couples work, and trauma recovery.

Jennifer S. Fang is founder, editor, and primary blogger of Reappropriate (www.reappropriate.co). Created in 2001, Reappropriate is one of the web's oldest and most popular Asian American and Pacific Islander (AAPI) race advocacy and feminism blogs. The blog's writing focuses on race, gender, identity, and Asian American history, and recent topics include affirmative action, mental health, and criminal justice. A vascular biologist with an undergraduate degree in biology from Cornell University (where she also minored in Asian American studies), Fang received her doctoral degree in physiology from the University of Arizona, where she established a dual interest in research and STEM teaching and mentoring. Currently, she is a postdoctoral research associate at Yale University, and is helping launch the Minority Inclusion Project, a start-up nonprofit organization dedicated to improving the representation of people of color in the leadership of the nonprofit sector in Connecticut and throughout the United States. Outside of Reappropriate, Jenn's writing has also been featured in Quartz, BlogHer, Good Men Project, Asian Pacific Americans for Progress, Asian Americans for Obama, Angry Asian Man, Northwest Asian Weekly, Change.org, Blog for Arizona, and The Nerds of Color.

Paula Groves Price is the associate dean for diversity and international programs in the College of Education and associate professor of cultural studies and social thought in education at Washington State University. She is the editor in chief of the *Western Journal of Black Studies*, and her research agenda is focused on issues of race, culturally responsive pedagogy, and Black feminist epistemology. She received a PhD from the University of North Carolina–Chapel Hill in social foundations of education, and BA degrees from the University of California–Berkeley in social welfare and interdisciplinary field studies. She teaches undergraduate multicultural education courses for preservice teachers as well as graduate-level courses in the areas of critical ethnography, qualitative research methods, multicultural education, race theory, and educational philosophy.

Daniel Guentchev holds a PhD in philosophy and is currently assistant professor of philosophy at Bemidji State University. He was born and raised in Bulgaria. His main areas of interest are aesthetics, phenomenology, and classical American pragmatism.

Jasmine L. Harris is assistant professor of sociology at Ursinus College where she teaches courses on race, Black culture, gender, and research methods. Her research focuses on the experiences of the marginalized in predominantly White spaces.

David J. Leonard is professor and chair in the Department of Critical Culture, Gender, and Race Studies at Washington State University–Pullman. He regularly writes about issues of race, gender, inequality, and the criminal justice system. He is the author of *After Artest: The NBA and the Assault on Blackness* (SUNY Press, 2012). He is also author of *Screens Fade to Black: Contemporary African American Cinema* (Praeger, 2006); and coeditor of *Visual Economies of/in Motion: Sport and Film* (Peter Lang, 2006) and *Commodified and Criminalized: New Racism and African Americans in Contemporary Sports* (Rowman and Littlefield, 2011). His work has appeared in both academic and popular venues.

Dennis Lunt holds a PhD in philosophy and is currently assistant professor of philosophy at Bemidji State University. He was raised in rural Ohio and presently researches American traditions of conscience, civil disobedience, and religious violence.

Cheryl E. Matias is an assistant professor in the School of Education and Human Development (SEHD) at the University of Colorado–Denver, and affiliate faculty for the University of Colorado–Denver's social science master's program and freshmen year seminar program. She is faculty founder of Research Advocacy in Critical Education (RACE), a collaborative think tank that brings together local community activists, educators, students, and community members in the pursuit for racial and social justice in education. A former K–12 teacher in both Los Angeles and New York City, she earned her bachelor's in cultural communication from University of California–San Diego, a master's in social and multicultural foundations at California State University–Long Beach, and a doctorate in education with an emphasis in race and ethnic studies at UCLA. She recently was awarded the 2014 American Educational Research Association's Division K (teacher education) Innovations in Research on Diversity in Teacher Education Award and the 2014 Colorado Rosa Parks Diversity Award. Some of her publications can be found in *Race, Ethnicity, and Education*; *Teacher Education Quarterly*; *Journal of Critical Thought and Praxis*; *Equity and Excellence*; and *Multicultural Perspectives*. Recently, she finished her first solo-authored book titled *Feeling White: Whiteness, Emotionality, and Education* (Sense Publishers, 2016).

Esther O. Ohito is a doctoral candidate, research fellow, and teacher educator at Teachers College, Columbia University's Department of Curriculum and Teaching. She is especially attentive to issues of embodiment in her scholarly areas of concentration, which are curriculum studies and teacher education. Ohito employs feminist frameworks to research or question how knowledges about social identities—particularly *race* and *gender*—are (re)produced through curriculum, broadly defined, and how these knowledges circulate among bodies in pedagogical spaces. Her dissertation focuses on this inquiry in the context of social justice-oriented teacher education, with an emphasis on university-based teacher educators' antiracist pedagogies.

Lori Patton Davis is a professor in the higher education and student affairs program at the Indiana University School of Education. Her scholarship broadly examines race and racism in college environments through a critical race lens, Black women in higher education, and college access and success for racially-minoritized populations. Patton Davis is editor of the book, *Campus Culture Centers in Higher Education* (Stylus Publishing, 2012), which highlights various types of racial/ethnic-specific culture centers in higher education, their continued relevance, and implications for their existence in relation to student retention and success, and is lead the author of the third edition of *Student Development in College: Theory, Research, and Practice* (Jossey-Bass, 2016), the most widely read text in student affairs graduate programs. Collectively, Patton Davis has over 70 publications, which have appeared in highly regarded venues such as *Teachers College Record; International Journal of Qualitative Studies in Education, Race, Ethnicity, and Education; Journal of Higher Education; and Journal of College Student Development*. She has presented over 140 research papers, workshops, symposia and keynote addresses nationally. She has also been featured in various media outlets including NPR, *Huffington Post*, and *The Chronicle of Higher Education*.

Chavella Pittman is the owner of Effective & Efficient Faculty (effective faculty.org), a faculty development company that works with faculty and campuses across the country to help them develop strategies for inclusive college classrooms, efficient teaching, and documenting teaching effectiveness for tenure and promotion reviews. She is also an associate professor of sociology at Dominican University. Her research interests and expertise include higher education, interpersonal interactions, and marginalized statuses. Pittman completed both a PhD in sociology and a MA in higher education at the University of Michigan. She was also a UC Presidential Postdoctoral Fellow in the sociology department at the University of California, Los Angeles.

Thomas Poon, PhD, is executive vice president and provost at Loyola Marymount University. Poon is a professor of chemistry who served in many senior leadership positions at Pitzer College, including interim president, acting president, and senior associate dean of faculty. He has written numerous peer-reviewed articles, and has received multiple National Science Foundation grants to investigate topics ranging from his S-STEM work in the molecular sciences and other projects aimed at integrating the sciences into curricula. His research and analyses on the American sweetgum tree have been referenced in academic publications and extensively reported by news media.

Lisa Silverstein has been in education, working with urban youth and adults, for more than 15 years, most recently serving as a faculty member and director at the Community College of Denver for 8 years. Her expertise is in developmental /remedial education, acceleration, learning communities, and faculty and curriculum development. She worked closely with the Hispanic Association for Colleges and Universities, collaborating with other institutions on a national Minority Serving Institution grant, advocating for underrepresented populations' access to higher education. She has a bachelor's in public health from San Diego State University and received her master's in education in curriculum and instruction from the University of Colorado–Denver. Currently, she is a doctoral student in the School of Education at the University of Colorado–Denver, and teaches the community field-based experience course for undergraduate preservice teachers. She is also a teaching assistant for Problematizing Whiteness, the first course of its kind on critical Whiteness studies at the university, and a research assistant for a teacher education program. She serves on the Rise Up community school board in Denver, a community-based school for former high school dropouts.

Dian D. Squire is a postdoctoral fellow in the University of Denver's Interdisciplinary Research Incubator for the Study on (In)Equality (IRISE). Squire's research focuses on issues of diversity, equity, and justice in higher education. He has published multiple peer-reviewed manuscripts, book chapters, and periodical pieces. He was the cofounder and first editor in chief of the *Journal of Critical Scholarship on Higher Education and Student Affairs* housed at Loyola University–Chicago. Prior to pursuing his doctorate, Dian was the assistant director of orientation and new student programs at the University of Maryland–College Park. During that time, he created a national award-winning first-year experience program for LGBTQA students called The One Project. He has served on the board of directors for NODA, the association for orientation, retention, and transition in higher education; and the governing board of ACPA, College Student Educators International. Squire received his PhD in higher education from Loyola University–Chicago. He received his MA in educational leadership and policy studies in higher education from the University of Maryland–College Park and his BS in secondary English education from Florida State University.

Nicole Truesdell is interested in radical pedagogy, academic hustling, and social justice. Her research focuses on the intersections of race, racism, gender, class, citizenship and belonging, nationalism, community organizing and activism, higher education, and radical Black thought in the United States and the United Kingdom. As a trained socio-cultural anthropologist, Truesdell examines larger systems of oppression and focuses on local means of resistance within marginalized communities. She received her PhD in socio-cultural anthropology from Michigan State University in 2011.

diversity and, 79–80, 94, 132, 257
engagement by, 258
feminism for, 66
FIRE and, 81
incivility for, 57–59, 65–68
marginalization of, 61–65, 68–70, 258–59
microaggression against, 81–82
in neoliberalism, 190, 260–61
pedagogical challenges for, 9–12
politics for, 2–3, 8–9
privilege in, 106, 238, 250
problematic behavior by, 55–56
for racial justice, 100–101
racism in, 27–28
on social media, 5
for STEM education, 200–202
tolerance in, 141
Fat Pedagogy Manifesto, 148
fat studies, 145–55
Fat Studies Reader, 147–48
feedback. See evaluations
feminism
    for African Americans, 99
    on campuses, 94
    for faculty, 66
    praxis for, 145–46
Ferguson, Missouri, 241–43
field trips, 256–57
FIRE. See Foundation for Individual
    Rights in Education
fishbowls, 120–23, 184, 187
Fisher, Abigail, 220
Fisher v. University of Texas, 193, 220–21, 225
Foundation for Individual Rights in
    Education (FIRE), 81
FOX News, 82–85
freaks. See bodies
free speech
    political correctness and, 81–82, 86
    in politics, 83
    vulnerability and, 73
Freire, Paulo, 2

Garbology (Humes), 151
Garner, Eric, 1, 100
Garre, Gregory, 220
Garza, Alicia, 92–93, 103
"Gay Basics: Some Questions, Facts,
    and Values" (Mohr), 22
geeks. See bodies
Geertz, Clifford, 96
gender
    for administration, 174–75
    gender attribution, 161
    in identity politics, 161–64
    lesson planning for, 173–76
    misgenderism, 161–63
    as pedagogical challenges, 158–61
    stereotypes about, 171
    strategies for, 164–73
    in syllabi, 166
Gender Outlaws (Bornstein), 149–50
Gilmartin, Raymond, 226
Giroux, Henry, 74–75, 80, 118
global capitalism
    higher education and, 74, 83
    United States in, 178
goal setting, 151–53, 206–7. See also
    taxonomy
Gray, Freddie, 1
group work, 229, 254–55
Grutter v. Bollinger, 220, 223–24, 227
guilt absolution, 253

health, 147–48
heart mapping, 142n9
    in classrooms, 139–40
    emotionality in, 141
    memory in, 137, 142n8
    for racial justice, 137–40
    strategies for, 138–39
hegemony, 48–49, 130
heterosexism. See gender
higher education. See also American
    studies
    ableism in, 40–41, 150–51

Beginning with an analysis of the impacts on mental and physical health and cognitive capacity, of poverty, racism, and other forms of social marginalization, Cia Verschelden presents strategies for promoting a growth mind-set and self-efficacy, for developing supports that build upon students' values and prior knowledge and for creating learning environments both in and out of the classroom so students can feel a sense of belonging and community.

22883 Quicksilver Drive
Sterling, VA 20166-2102   Subscribe to our e-mail alerts: www.Styluspub.com

Also available from Stylus

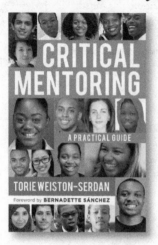

Critical Mentoring
A Practical Guide

Torie Weiston-Serdan

Foreword by Bernadette Sánchez

"*Critical Mentoring* is a savory blend of theories, thoughtful concepts, and evidence. Perhaps its practical utility is the book's most praiseworthy feature. Readers learn not only what this unique brand of mentoring is but also how to more effectively develop and support youth, particularly those who are often pushed to the margins." —*Shaun R. Harper, Professor and Executive Director, University of Pennsylvania Center for the Study of Race & Equity in Education*

Torie Weiston-Serdan outlines the underlying foundations of critical race theory, cultural competence and intersectionality, describes how collaborative mentoring works in practice in terms of dispositions and structures, and addresses the implications of rethinking about the purposes and delivery of mentoring services, both for mentors themselves and the organizations for which they work.

This book offers strategies that are immediately applicable and will create a process that is participatory, emancipatory and transformative.

Bandwidth Recovery
Helping Students Reclaim Cognitive Resources Lost to Poverty, Racism, and Social Marginalization

Cia Verschelden M.S.W., Ed.D.

Foreword by Lynn Pasquerella

"Verschelden convincingly makes the case that many lower income and minority students struggle in college not because of lower ability or poor preparation, but because they deal with life situations that deplete cognitive resources that are needed for learning. Offering us a distinctly different lens through which to view these students, she describes concrete strategies we can implement to replenish their cognitive resources so that they don't just survive, but thrive in the college environment with recovered 'bandwidth'." —*Saundra McGuire, (Ret.) Assistant Vice Chancellor & Professor of Chemistry; Director Emerita, Center for Academic Success, Louisiana State University; Author of Teach Students How to Learn*

(Continues on preceding page)